The Gardener's
Guide to Growing
HOSTAS

The Gardener's
Guide to Growing
HOSTAS

Diana Grenfell

TIMBER PRESS
Portland, Oregon

FOR MY MOTHER, MURIEL

PICTURE ACKNOWLEDGEMENTS

Derek St Romaine pages 2, 6, 10, 29, 32, 38, 48, 52, 55, 66, 87, 90, 94, 140; Neil Campbell-Sharp 1, 3, 12, 16, 18, 21, 22, 35, 41, 42, 44, 60, 62, 64, 65, 70, 76, 77, 95, 98, 101, 102, 105, 107, 112, 113, 116, 117, 119, 126, 130, 132, 136, 138, 139, 142, 148, 149, 150; Diana Grenfell 9, 14, 15, 125; Ali Pollock 34, 85, 110, 118; James Wilkins 59; Simon Fraser 68, 69; Richard Ford 73; Y. Hirose 81; Gordon Collier 93, 96; Gert Fortgens 78, 79, 109; Payne Jenkins 121

Illustrations by Jenny Brasier

Page 1: *H.* 'Sea Dream': the chartreuse colouring quickly turns to bright yellow.
Page 2: The bold foliage of *H.* 'Fortunei Aureomarginata' adds substance to a border at Sun House, Long Melford, Suffolk. Corydalis, euphorbia, variegated iris and *H.* 'Fortunei Albopicta' all contribute to a charming composition.
Page 3: The small, elegant leaves of *H.* 'Lemon Lime' can add a dash of sharp yellow to a shaded garden.

Typeset by ACE
and printed in Italy by Lego SpA
for David & Charles
Brunel House Newton Abbot Devon

First published in North America in 1996 by
Timber Press, Inc.
The Haseltine Building
133 S.W. Second Avenue, Suite 450
Portland, Oregon 97204, U.S.A.
1-800-327-5680 (U.S.A. & Canada only)

ISBN 0-88192-355-9

CONTENTS

FOREWORD

by Graham Stuart Thomas, OBE, VMH

The genus *Hosta* is a comparative newcomer to the annals of horticulture. When I was learning the art, craft and science of gardening in the 1920s there was not a single specimen to be seen in the University Botanic Garden at Cambridge. Hostas – or funkias, as they were then called – were not mentioned by William Robinson in his *English Flower Garden* until the fifth edition in 1896. Nor was one to be found in E. A. Bowles' trilogy about his gardens in 1914, and A. T. Johnson did not include the genus until after the Second World War, despite his predilection for ground-covering plants. On the other hand, we find several species in Bailey's *Cyclopedia of Horticulture*, the 'new' edition of which was published in the USA in 1927. My first sight of them was in Gertrude Jekyll's garden, where she grew them in pots to decorate the terraces.

Today, with other favourites of the times like hellebores, euphorbias and hemerocallises, they are much to the fore on both sides of the Atlantic and in the Southern Hemisphere. I think it may be said that much of their popularity today stems from their use at flower shows, particularly at Chelsea. In the 1950s they proved to be just the thing to hide the rootballs of rhododendrons on our Sunningdale Nursery exhibits, besides providing a lovely foil to other plants.

In our gardens today – which are sometimes overcrowded with widely disparate plants – the great tumps of smooth foliage exert a calming effect in cool positions, a role that is echoed in sunny places by bergenias. They are also eminently good garden plants, thriving in all soils apart from pure chalk and boggy ground as long as their few needs are studied, and they usually get bigger and better every year. They do not seem to suffer from any significant diseases and their only enemies are the molluscs – both slugs and snails. The rounded clumps act as a podium for the airy flights of the cool lilac-tinted lily-flowers which the selectors and breeders have so far left in an unalloyed state, concentrating their attention chiefly upon the wide range of size, poise and variegation of the handsome foliage.

With breeding and selection at fever pitch all over the gardening world, I have long felt the need of a compact and straightforward book which would tell us all we want to know about hostas. Now, thanks to Diana Grenfell's enterprise and the skills and knowledge which she and the band of experts under her wing have brought to bear on the subject, I believe we have the right volume, and I heartily commend it.

Diana has been growing and studying hostas for 30 years and surely knows the answers to all the queries that are put by beginners and experienced growers alike. From the newer tinies up to giants of 1.2m (4ft) or so, from the dense clump-formers to the slow-spreaders, she has their uses all thought out. Besides being an enthusiast of long standing, she is also a good and tasteful gardener and has kept abreast of the flood of new varieties coming to the fore. I doubt whether a better guide to hostas could be found than this well-illustrated book.

Hosta 'Happiness' surrounding the base of a lionhead fountain at Sun House in Long Melford, Suffolk.

INTRODUCTION

I became interested in hostas quite by chance. When I was expecting my daughter Claudia nearly 30 years ago I used to listen to *Woman's Hour*, and a series on famous women and their favourite plants caught my imagination. The late but still lovingly remembered Lady Isobel Barnett, of *What's My Line* fame – someone who, to my mind, had exceedingly good taste – extolled the virtues of hostas; in her opinion, they were the perfect plants for gardening in the shade. I had never heard of them, but immediately set off to the local garden centre and bought the very few which were available at that time. But that was enough. From then on I was hooked and I became utterly fascinated by them.

When I first started collecting hostas we were grateful for any and every new one that came our way. We tolerated faults such as leaves that scorched at the slightest bit of sun, thin, limp leaves that were scarcely a credit to the genus, yellow leaves which faded to dull green before the season had really got under way. Now we are much more discriminating. We want the leaves to be well-shaped and beautifully coloured and to form a pleasing symmetrical mound; the scape height to be in proportion with the leaf mound; the flowers to open well, be well presented, a good colour and preferably scented too; and, as a final bonus, we want the leaves to die off gracefully in the autumn, giving an extra season of leaf colour. Flowers arrangers probably need to be even greater perfectionists than gardeners. They are keen judges of variegation and the poise of a leaf, and they need leaves which remain turgid for long spells in water.

The amazing thing is that breeders have not only come up with hostas that meet all these demanding criteria but more besides, and we are

spoiled for choice. The purpose of this book is to guide not only the general gardener but also the keen collector through this wealth of delectable hostas, to help them make choices of which to grow, and to give such cultural advice as will help growers to get the best from their hostas.

The excitement of first seeing the firm new shoots in shades of claret, violet, white and deep brown piercing the bare earth in late spring bearing a promise of summer glories ahead is enough to make the spirits rise. The complex detail in the seersuckering of *H.* 'Aspen Gold'; the soft, grape-like bloom clothing the leaves of *H.* 'Blue Seer'; the furrowed leaves of *H.* 'Green Acres', looking like sand left by the receding tide; the shine and leatheriness of *H.* 'Invincible', reminiscent of highly polished shoes; the sheer bulk and *gravitas* of *H.* 'Blue Mammoth' and its contrast with the filigree foliage of ferns – these are the things that give me a *frisson* of delight. The lily-like fragrance of *H. plantaginea* wafting into the evening air is an added bonus, and the sere spikes and seedheads that are left behind in the winter border are ghostly reminders of what we have so recently enjoyed.

With such a wealth of wonderful hostas available it is difficult to see how one could make a garden without them. Indeed, it is my opinion that a garden without hostas would not be a garden at all.

H. 'Blue Seer', one the bluest and most puckered of the Elegans Group.

1

HISTORY, HABITAT AND CLASSIFICATION

Hostas are natives of the East and of Japan in particular, and when they were first discovered by Westerners their correct placing in the plant kingdom was not at all clear. Englebert Kaempfer (1651–1715), a doctor/botanist with the Dutch East India Company, was, as far as the written record goes, the first Westerner ever to see a hosta and certainly the first to draw and describe one. He gave them names in the discursive, pre-Linnaean style. One he called *Joksan, vulgo gibbooshi Gladiolus Plantagenis folio* (meaning 'the common hosta with the plantain-like leaves'); the other he named simply *Gibbooshi altera* (meaning 'the other hosta'). The next doctor/botanist to work at the Dutch East India Company's trading post in Japan, Carl Thunberg (1743–1828), renamed them in the then new Linnaean binomial style, calling one of them *Aletris japonica*, transferring it to the genus *Hemerocallis* in 1784.

The generic name *Hosta* was first proposed by the Austrian botanist Leopold Trattinick (1761–1848) in 1812. It honours an Austrian, Nicholas Thomas Host (1761–1834), who was not only a botanist, the author of *Flora Austriaca* and a work on grasses, but also physician to the Emperor Frances II. A further generic name, *Funkia*, was then proposed by Kurt Sprengel in 1817, but this name was eventually to be rejected as illegitimate. However, it passed into many European languages as the common name for hostas.

Meanwhile, the plants themselves had started reaching the West. The first species to arrive was *H. plantaginea*, seed of which was sent by the French consul in Macao to the Jardin des Plantes in Paris somewhere between 1784 and 1789. Originally called *Hemerocallis plantaginea*, it was soon grown by the thousand in public gardens in France. Another Chinese species, *H. ventricosa*, followed soon after.

The main influx of hostas to the West was started about 40 years later by Philipp von Siebold (1791–1866), another of the several doctor/botanists who worked in Japan, his first shipment of Japanese hostas reaching Europe in 1829. He was subsequently followed by other famous plant collectors such as Robert Fortune (1813–80) and the American Thomas Hogg Jr (1819–92).

The practice of introducing hostas from their native countries to the West still continues to this day. In 1985 an expedition mounted by the US National Arboretum and led by Barry Yinger under the auspices of the Friends of the US National Arboretum brought back two new species of hosta from Korea, *H. yingeri* and *H. jonesii*, while members of the American Hosta Society visited Japan in 1995 and returned with some examples of rare hostas, including a white-margined form of *H.* 'Tortifrons'. They also reported that they had been able to see many rare forms that had only recently been collected in the wild.

H. plantaginea and its forms and hybrids. Top row, left to right: *H. plantaginea* 'Grandiflora', *H.* 'Fragrant Bouquet', *H.* 'Sweet Standard', *H.* 'Honeybells'. Bottom row, left to right: *H.* 'Chelsea Ore', *H.* 'Sugar and Cream', *H. plantaginea*, *H. p.* 'Aphrodite'.

HABITAT AND CLASSIFICATION

12 Hostas are liliaceous plants – that is, they have flowers roughly resembling those of lilies – and until recently they were placed in *Liliaceae*, one of the largest of all plant families. Within the *Liliaceae* they were placed in the Tribe *Hemerocallidaceae* along with *Hemerocallis*, *Leucocrinum* and *Hesperocallis*. In 1985 R. M. T. Dahlgren, H. T. Clifford and P. F. Yeo proposed a new classification for the monocots, which includes the *Liliaceae*, and this scheme was accepted by the Royal Botanic Gardens, Kew, in 1987. Under this scheme *Hosta* was placed in the family *Funkiaceae*, which it shared with *Leucocrinum* and *Hesperocallis*. The genus *Hemerocallis*, to which *Hosta* originally belonged, was placed in its own family, *Hemerocallidaceae*. In a subsequent revision by B. Matthew, *Hosta* was placed in a family of its own, *Hostaceae*.

The genus *Hosta* is now considered to consist of about 40 species and well over 1000 cultivars. Species are the basic units of classification. A species may be defined as a plant which arose and can sustain itself in the wild, whereas a cultivar is a plant which may have arisen either in cultivation or in the wild but which cannot sustain itself in the wild though it may flourish in gardens, as is the case with many variegated forms and, often, those with double flowers.

Over the years many fine minds have been brought to bear on the hosta species. The Swedish taxonomist Dr Nils Hylander concentrated on hostas cultivated in Swedish gardens and his Dutch counterpart Dr Karel Hensen on hostas introduced by von Siebold, while in the USA Liberty Hyde Bailey took a broader view, as did Professor W. T. Stearn in England.

The first attempt at a comprehensive treatment of the species was that of Dr Fumio Maekawa, who spent five years studying hostas in the wild in Japan and a lifetime trying to classify them. Unfortunately his monograph was published in 1939, the timing of its publication

The exotically fragrant *H. plantaginea*, showing the extraordinarily long tube and the floral bracts.

militating against its acceptance in the West, and it is only recently that its importance has been fully appreciated. Another major contribution to our understanding of hostas was made by Dr Noboru Fujita, who spent 20 years studying hostas in the wild, paying particular attention to their ecology.

The most recent major work on hostas is W. George Schmid's monumental monograph *The Genus Hosta*. In it he confronts a fundamental problem in hosta classification, namely that many of the hostas that have always been considered species are without doubt cultivars, and he reclassifies them accordingly.

Cultivars present problems of their own. In the past, descriptions were too vague. To say of a hosta that it has large grey leaves and lilac flowers is not sufficient to identify it, but this is what tended to happen. In 1966 the University of Minnesota Landscape Arboretum became the International Registration Authority (IRA) for *Hosta*. In association with the American Hosta Society, the IRA has drawn up strict guidelines for the description of hostas being registered and insists that every registration is accompanied by photographs. Meanwhile, in Britain, the National Council for the Conservation of Plants and Gardens (NCCPG) has established a system of Standard Specimens for cultivars. A Standard Specimen is to a cultivar what a lectotype is to a species. Herbarium material of every Standard Specimen, accompanied by photographs of the living plant, will be kept at the Royal Horticultural Society's Laboratory at Wisley, where they will be available for inspection.

The classification and habitat of hostas are inseparable subjects, because although the classification is based on their physical characteristics, these in turn are largely determined by where the hosta comes from, both in terms of general geographic distribution and of more specific ecological niches.

The genus *Hosta* has been classified into three subgenera and these reflect geographical distribution. The Subgenera are themselves further divided into Sections, each of which contains but a few species, those few being very closely related. The classification of hostas is fluid, and is likely to change as and when new knowledge becomes available.

SUBGENUS *HOSTA*

This subgenus is not subdivided, containing only *H. plantaginea* from south-eastern China, the conspicuous characteristics of which are its extraordinarily long, narrow flower tube, the tube being round in section, the flowers night-opening, fragrant, white and funnel-shaped. In its geographical distribution it is the most southerly of all the species cultivated in the West, which explains its liking for warmth.

SUBGENUS *BRYOCLES*

Section *Eubryocles* Contains a single species, *H. ventricosa*, from China and northern Korea. It is essentially a mountain species, characterized by its widely bell-shaped purple flowers, round scapes, narrow, grooved floral tube and narrow bracts.

Section *Lamellatae* Contains mainly small species, the majority of them from mainland Korea and all of them having lamellar ridges along the scape which can be felt quite easily if the scape is held between finger and thumb. It is divided into two subsections:
a) *Capitatae* This contains two species, *H. capitata* and *H. nakaiana*, characterized by solid scapes and ball-shaped buds. They are natives of southern and central Korea.
b) *Spicatae* This contains two species, *H. venusta* and *H. minor*, which are characterized by hollow scapes and spike-shaped buds. *H. minor* is thought to have evolved along the southern and eastern coasts of Korea, and *H. venusta* is thought to have evolved from it on the island of Cheju, off the southern coast of Korea. Both are therefore natives of coastal mountains, regions of much mist and high rainfall.

Section *Arachnanthae* Contains two recently collected species, *H. yingeri* and *H. laevigata*,

which are characterized by small flowers with narrow lobes or petals of a somewhat spider-like appearance, and by the thick, succulent leaves that look almost as if they have been polished, the latter having evolved in order to help them cope with their rather impoverished habitats. They come from remote islands off the coast of Korea, where they grow on rocks on shaded, north-west facing slopes and in pine forests, the floor of which they share with ferns and grasses.

Section *Stoloniferae* Contains a single species, *H. clausa*, which has a wide range and much

H. ventricosa growing with *Liriope spicata* in deep shade at Dumbarton Oaks, Washington DC.

variation. It is closely related to *H. yingeri*, and is characterized by its narrowly bell-shaped flowers and by the floral tube, which is grooved. Typically, it does not open its flowers and this seems to be an adaptation to its habitat. It is native to central and northern Korea, where it grows along river banks and is subject to inter-mittent flooding as a result of typhoons. Such flooding destroys the normal sexual modes of reproduction, and *H. clausa* has largely abandoned this method in favour of a stoloniferous root system which enables single plants to spread into extensive colonies. In extreme forms it does not even develop flower stems. In cultivation it makes excellent ground cover.

SUBGENUS *GIBOSHI*

This contains all the Japanese species and is subdivided into the following three groups, with their sections.

Group I Characterized by having white or nearly white flowers with a narrow tube that is round or hexagonal. The flowers are funnel-shaped or narrowly bell-shaped.

H. hypoleuca, pictured here growing in the wild on Mount Chiiwa, Japan.

Section *Helipteroides* Contains five species from central and northern Japan, *H. crassifolia*, *H. fluctuans*, *H. montana*, *H. nigrescens* and *H. sieboldiana*, distinguished by their nearly white flowers and their dense flowerheads with spreading, overlapping bracts. They are mostly large or very large hostas, coming not only from rich, fertile soils in mountain valleys and forest margins but also growing along the sunny, rocky coasts of north-western Honshu.

Section *Rynchophorae* Contains *H. kikutii* and *H. shikokiana*, two species from central and south Japan, extending to the south-west tip of the Japanese archipelago. They have leaning scapes and flower buds resembling the long necks and heads of Kutari cranes, and overlapping, boat-shaped bracts which are leafy and whitish. These are high mountain species from wet rock outcrops and ridges above 3000ft (900m).

16

Section *Intermediae* Contains three seldom-grown species from central Japan, *H. densa*, *H. kiyosumiensis* and *H. pachyscapa*. They are similar to the species in Section *Rynchophorae* but are distinct in having green, not whitish, leafy bracts. They are natives of rich soils in mountain valleys and forest margins.

Group II This group has bell-shaped lavender flowers, again with a narrow tube that is round or hexagonal.

Section *Picnolepis* Contains eight species from central Japan, *H. aequinoctiiantha*, *H. hypoleuca*, *H. longipes*, *H. okamotoi*, *H. pulchella*, *H. pycnophylla*, *H. rupifraga and H. takiensis*, distinguished by their densely packed, white or purple, boat-shaped bracts, and by the lateness of their flowering (though not so late as the species in Section *Tardanthae*). They are mainly rock-dwelling species often found growing in crevices in rocks, or occasionally epiphytic, growing on mossy tree-trunks and in similar situations. Such habitats imply almost permanent mist and a high rainfall, together with perfect drainage.

Group III The flowers in this group are striped and narrowly bell-shaped, the tube being narrow and grooved. All the plants in the three sections of *Nipponosta* are natives of wet soils.

Section *Nipponosta A* Contains six closely related species from Japan, *H. atropurpurea*, *H. calliantha*, *H. clavata*, *H. ibukiensis*, *H. rohdeifolia* and *H. sieboldii*, which are distinct in having elliptical leaves and large, green, leaf-like bracts which clasp the flower stem. They are natives of a variety of moist habitats from woodlands to forest margins, moorlands to open meadows and high mountain grasslands.

Section *Nipponosta B* Contains two species from central and northern Japan, *H. alismifolia* and *H. rectifolia*, both of which are quite distinct in that their leaves are held stiffly erect rather in the manner of an aspidistra or of *Alisma*, the water plantain. *H. alismifolia* inhabits wet sphagnum

---

H. nigrescens, one of the most elegant of all hosta species, growing at Apple Court.

bogs and marshy ground, while *H. rectifolia* comes from damp, lake-side moorlands.

Section Nipponosta C Contains a single species from central Japan, *H. longissima*, which is distinct in having linear rather than lance-shaped leaves, held erect. It is a native of swampy ground and wet places where it gets sun in the spring and until the surrounding vegetation (mostly grasses), grows up to shade it.

Section Tardanthae Contains seven species from Japan, Tsushima Island, southern insular Korea and north-eastern China, *H. cathayana*, *H. gracillima*, *H. jonesii*, *H. takahashii*, *H. tardiva*, *H. tibae* and *H. tsushimensis*, distinct on account of the lateness of their flowering. All have narrowly oval to heart-shaped leaves. As compared with other hostas, they come from relatively dry, open areas.

THE GENUS HOSTA
Subgenera, Sections and Species

SUBGENUS *HOSTA*		SUBGENUS *GIBOSHI* GROUP II	
	H. plantaginea	Section *Picnolepis*	*H. aequinoctiiantha*
SUBGENUS *BRYOCLES*			*H. hypoleuca*
			H. longipes
Section *Eubryocles*	*H. ventricosa*		*H. okamotoi*
			H. pulchella
Section *Lamellatae* I	*H. capitata*		*H. pycnophylla*
	H. nakaiana		*H. rupifraga*
			H. takiensis
Section *Lamellatae* II	*H. minor*		
	H. venusta	**SUBGENUS *GIBOSHI* GROUP III**	
Section *Arachnanthae*	*H. laevigata*	Section *Nipponosta* A	*H. atropurpurea*
	H. yingeri		*H. calliantha*
			H. clavata
Section *Stoloniferae*	*H. clausa*		*H. ibukiensis*
			H. rohdeifolia
SUBGENUS *GIBOSHI* GROUP I			*H. sieboldii*
Section *Helipteroides*	*H. crassifolia*		
	H. fluctuans	Section *Nipponosta* B	*H. alismifolia*
	H. montana		*H. rectifolia*
	H. nigrescens		
	H. sieboldiana	Section *Nipponosta* C	*H. longissima*
Section *Rynchophorae*	*H. kikutii*	Section *Tardanthae*	*H. cathayana*
	H. shikokiana		*H. gracillima*
			H. jonesii
Section *Intermediae*	*H. densa*		*H. takahashii*
	H. kiyosumiensis		*H. tardiva*
	H. pachyscapa		*H. tibae*
			H. tsushimensis

2

THE BOTANY OF HOSTAS

Hostas are hardy clump-forming herbaceous perennials springing from short, sometimes stoloniferous rhizomes with fleshy white roots. The leaves are mostly basal, stalked, large and simple, forming a mound. The flowers are large, tubular, funnel- or bell-shaped with usually six spreading lobes, white to dark purple, the stamens bent, resting on the tube, presented in a raceme at the top of a usually unbranched scape.

PLANT SHAPE

Most hostas develop into dome-shaped mounds as typified by *H. sieboldiana* 'Elegans'. Some hostas, however, make low, rather flattened mounds, as with *H.* 'Resonance', while others are decidedly upright in habit, the petioles being clearly visible as one looks at the hosta, as with *H. nigrescens* or *H.* 'Krossa Regal'. In the descriptions that follow the assumption is made for the sake of brevity that all hostas are dome-shaped unless otherwise mentioned.

Stoloniferous hostas (those with creeping roots) generally form colonies of interlocking individuals. The colony as a whole may appear flat but the individuals within it will still be dome-shaped,

The archetypal hosta, *H. sieboldiana* 'Elegans', still one of the most sumptuous hostas to be seen.

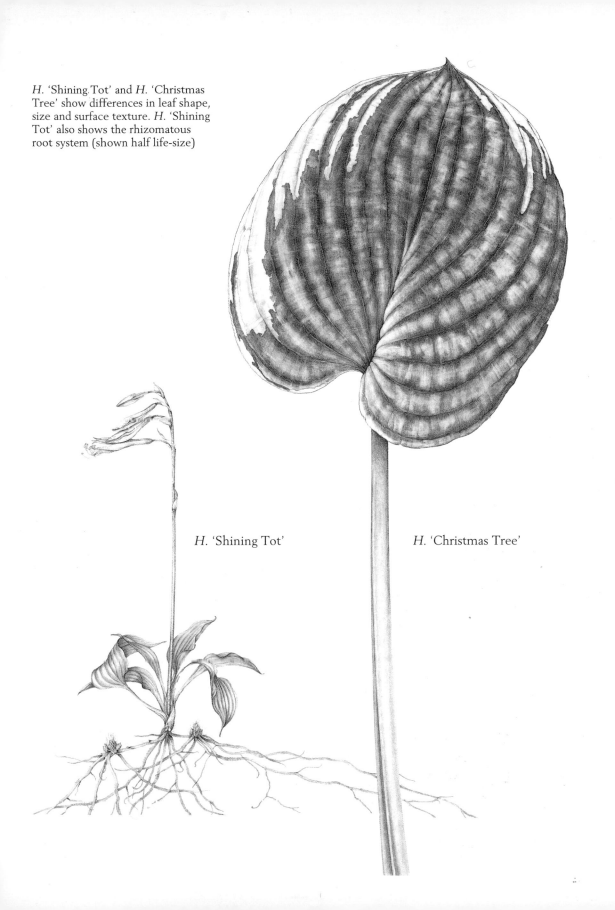

H. 'Shining Tot' and *H.* 'Christmas Tree' show differences in leaf shape, size and surface texture. *H.* 'Shining Tot' also shows the rhizomatous root system (shown half life-size)

H. 'Shining Tot'

H. 'Christmas Tree'

H. 'Undulata
Univittata' H. 'Lancifolia' H. rupifraga H. kikutii
'Polyneuron'

H. 'Big Daddy' H. plantaginea H. plantaginea
'Grandiflora' H. 'Francee'

H. 'Tokudama' H. 'Tokudama
Aureonebulosa' H. montana H. 'Birchwood
Parky's Gold'

H. 'Love Pat' H. hypoleuca H. venusta H. 'Elata'

H. 'Undulata
Erromena' H. 'Crispula' H. 'Blue Wedgwood' H. 'Pacific Blue
Edger'

H. sieboldiana
'Elegans' H. sieboldii H. 'Fortunei
Hyacinthina' H. 'Fortunei
Aureomarginata'

Cross-section of 24 different petioles (leaf stalks) taken at a representative point nearer the ground than the leaf blade. This shows the variability which is often a means of identification. They can also vary even in the same plant.

flattened or erect and it is these characteristics to which the descriptions refer.

CLUMP AND LEAF SIZE

Hostas vary in size from minuscule to majestic and are classified on page 97.

LEAF SHAPE

Hosta leaves can vary as to their overall shape, the shape of the leaf base and the shape of the tip. The overall leaf shape is defined in terms of its length to breadth ratio. The ratio of an oval leaf will be 2:1 or 3:2. A broadly oval leaf will have a ratio of 6:5, but if it gets any wider the ratio becomes 1:1 and the leaf is then defined as round. At the other extreme the leaf may be narrowly oval, with a ratio of 3:1, but if it gets any narrower it becomes elliptical or lance-shaped (6:1).

Four different types of leaf base are found in hostas: heart-shaped (with two equal, rounded lobes on each side of the stalk or petiole at the point where it enters the leaf blade); truncate (as if cut straight across the base); wedge-shaped (with the sides straight but converging); or attenuate (the sides curved and converging). These categories are not hard and fast but drift gradually from one into the next, so that in practice one finds bases of hosta leaves that are neither heart-shaped nor truncate but somewhere in between.

The tip may be either mucronate (coming abruptly to a sharp point), cuspidate (tapering gradually to a sharp point), acute (coming to a point) or obtuse (rounded).

White-edged *H.* 'Francee' with *H.* 'Blue Boy' in the foreground and *H.* 'August Moon' to the right, *H.* 'Hyacinthina Variegata' back left and *H.* 'Tall Boy'.

JUVENILE AND ADULT LEAVES

Many hostas have juvenile and adult phases, the leaves produced in the former phase normally being narrower than those in the latter. This is particularly noticeable in tissue-cultured plants. In many hostas the spring leaves also differ from the summer leaves, the more recently produced leaves at the centre of the clump. A few hostas put on a distinct late flush of leaves, those of *H.* 'August Moon', for example, being longer and smooth, whereas the main leaves are rough and puckered. The second leaf flush of *H.* 'Undulata' produces leaves which are mottled green rather than crisply variegated.

LEAF SUBSTANCE

The substance, or thickness, of hosta leaves can vary considerably and this is a major factor in

The deeply cupped and puckered leaves of *H.* 'Brim Cup', an *H.* 'Wide Brim' derivative.

determining the extent to which leaves may be eaten by slugs and snails. The thickness or thinness of leaves is mentioned only where they depart substantially from the norm.

LEAF MARGINS

The margins of hosta leaves are always entire, which is to say they are never toothed, cut, serrated or lobed. They may, however, vary from flat, as in *H.* 'Devon Green', to slightly rippled as in *H.* 'Daybreak' or acutely crimped, goffered or piecrust as in *H. pycnophylla*.

LEAF PLANE

The blade may be wavy or twisted, variations which tend to accompany rippling of the margin. It may also be cupped, as in *H.* 'Tokudama', convex as in *H.* 'Brim Cup', or slightly arched as in *H.* 'Silver Lance'.

LEAF SURFACE

Hosta leaves may be smooth or puckered (dimpled) and the puckering may be slight or deep, often occurring on the leaves of mature plants but not on the leaves of young plants.

VEINING

Hosta leaves exhibit a typical veining pattern called campylodrome, which means that the veins entering the leaf at its base curve outwards as the leaf widens and then curve inwards as the leaf narrows towards the tip. The veins appear impressed when seen from above, but prominent when viewed from beneath. Where the veins are deeply impressed they give a furrowed or corrugated appearance, as in *H.* 'Green Acres'.

LEAF FINISH

Hosta leaves are always smooth – that is, without hairs – but may be conspicuous in other ways. They may be matt, or shining as in *H. yingeri*, but are most often satiny. They may also be covered

Contrasting leaf undersides of the rare and
beautiful white-backed species *H. hypoleuca*
and the projecting-veined *H.* 'Green Acres'
(shown half life-size)

H. 'Green Acres'

H. hypoleuca

in a waxy coating and this is invariably the case with blue hostas, their blueness being due to this coating. They may also be frosted or pruinose, having the appearance of being covered in frost or chalk. These effects are usually most pronounced on young leaves, fading as the season advances, or if grown in too much sun.

LEAF COLOUR

The reason that the leaves of plants are coloured is that they contain pigments carried in bodies called plastids. The dominant plastids throughout the plant kingdom are green ones called chloroplasts, and it is these structures which are mainly responsible for taking the energy from sunlight and converting it into the chemical energy which drives the plants' metabolism. Other colours in plant leaves are caused by other pigments, carried in other plastids. Significantly for hostas, all of these plastids are very, very similar, it taking a change in only a very few atoms to slip from one colour to another, and such changes can and do take place, if only occasionally, when cells copy themselves.

The plastids are not part of the cell nucleus but are contained in the area surrounding it. This means that they have no part in determining the shape of the organism, only its colour. They are, moreover, independent of the nucleus insofar that they have their own DNA, the essential programming code that tells them how to replicate themselves. However, the replication of cells is not like a modern factory line, at the end of which every item is identical. Errors creep in, and it is a simple fact of life throughout the natural world that the more copies that are made the greater the likelihood of error: and the probability of error also increases with the passage of time. Thus the older a plant gets, the more likely it is that such an error will occur. Whether such an error results in a significant new colour combination depends on where it occurs in the developing plant or shoot.

The growing tip of a plant is always essentially the same, whether it is an embryo or a new shoot, but different parts of the plant develop from different parts of the growing tip. Three different layers known as L1, L2 and L3 are involved here.

The outer layer is the part from which the epidermis or surface of the leaf arises, and this plays a particular part in determining the leaf margin. If coloured plastids occur in L1 this can result in a coloured margin. It is from the middle layer, L2, that the greater part of the leaf arises, and if coloured plastids are in this layer the result may be a coloured centre to the leaf. However, plastids can also move from layer to layer, plastids originating in L2, for example, moving to L1, which is what happens when the streaking in a streaked hosta migrates to the margin. Plastids can also lose their colour, for just as the laws of chance allow plastids to change colour, so there are mechanisms to correct the error, and when this occurs the plant or leaf is said to revert. All variegation and colouring other than green is essentially unstable, though marginal variegations are usually more stable than central variegations.

FLOWERS

The flowers of hostas are borne on elongated stems or scapes which arise directly from the leaf mound at ground level and terminate in a more or less crowded raceme. The scapes are usually round in section, but are sometimes ridged as in the Section *Lamellatae*. They are usually solid, but occasionally hollow, and usually simple, but occasionally branched, as with *H. tibae*. The scape may be upright or leaning, and straight or bent. In the descriptions that follow the measurements given for the scapes is the length, not the height.

The flowers are held away from the scape on short pedicels (little stems) which hold the flower in a drooping or horizontal attitude. Each pedicel emerges from a small bract (known as a flower bract) which clasps the stem. These may be so tiny they can scarcely be seen with the naked eye, as in *H. sieboldii*, or large enough to be quite noticeable, as in *H.* 'Summer Fragrance'. Often the flower bracts wither after blooming. In a few species and cultivars these flower bracts become so large that they look like leaves, sometimes wrapped around the flower bud as in *H. kikutii*.

Scapes may however bear a second type of bract called a leafy or foliaceous bract, which is

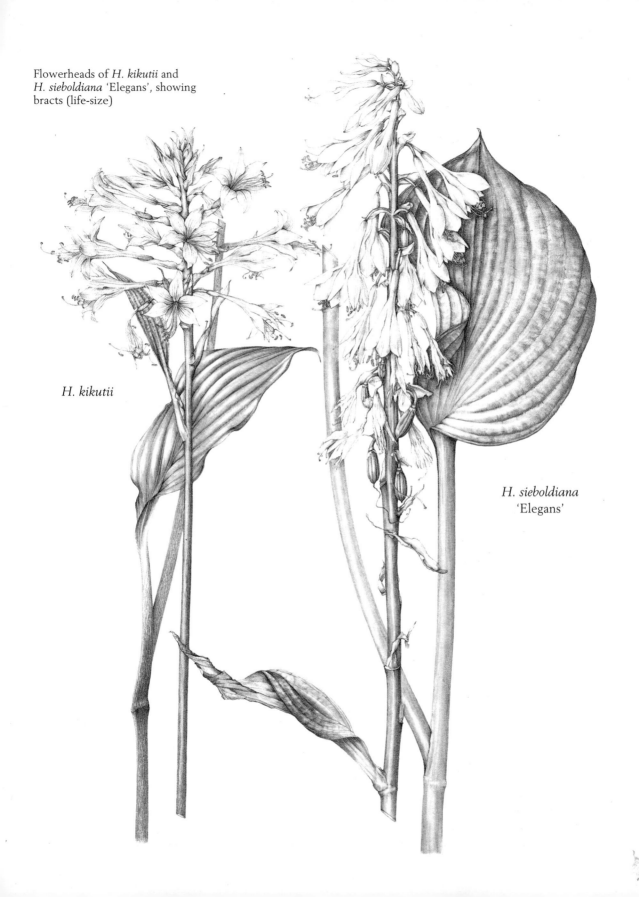

Flowerheads of *H. kikutii* and
H. sieboldiana 'Elegans', showing
bracts (life-size)

H. kikutii

H. sieboldiana
'Elegans'

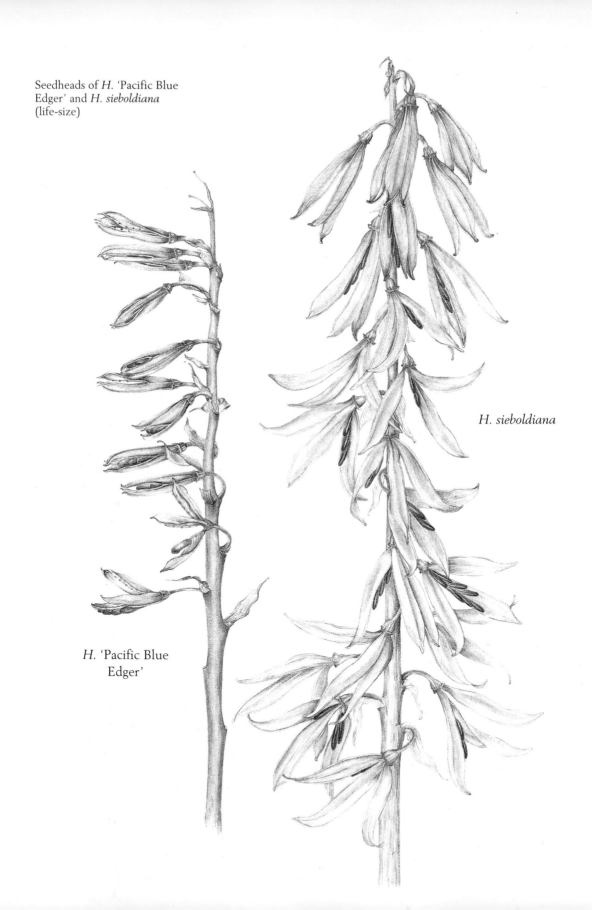

Seedheads of *H.* 'Pacific Blue
Edger' and *H. sieboldiana*
(life-size)

H. sieboldiana

H. 'Pacific Blue
Edger'

not always easily distinguished from a flower bract. Leafy bracts occur below the flowering part of the scape, and are usually largest nearest the ground. They are mostly outward-facing but some are small and clasp the scape, as in *H*. 'Opipara'. In several species and hybrids these bracts are conspicuous, as in *H*. 'Undulata'. If the leaves are variegated, they are usually variegated also.

In the descriptions that follow, a scape is described as bare if it has only flower bracts. If it has leafy bracts it is described as leafy.

FLOWER FORMS

The flowers of hostas are usually bell-shaped or funnel-shaped with six more or less spreading lobes and six stamens situated below the base of the ovary or attached to the tube, usually longer than the perianth and therefore protruding. The ovary is stalkless, three-celled, and the stigma usually protrudes beyond the stamens.

From a descriptive point of view the part of the flower that matters most is the middle section, between the tube and the lobes, for it is this that determines whether the flower is funnel-shaped or bell-shaped. If it is funnel-shaped the tube expands gradually so that in outline the tube and the lobes form a single continuous curve. If the flower is bell-shaped it expands abruptly just past the tube. In the descriptions that follow flowers are described as either funnel-shaped or bell-shaped, with very few exceptions. The flowers of some hostas are double, and in a few cases there are flowers which never open, as in *H. clausa*. *H. laevigata* and *H. yingeri* have flowers with very narrow lobes, described as spider-shaped.

The anthers are important diagnostically. In true species they are either yellow or purple: in hybrids they are usually bi-coloured. The colour can only be identified before the pollen is shed.

The flowers range from quite a deep purple to what appears to be pure white, though in fact even in *H. plantaginea* the lobes still retain a hint of violet. The majority of hostas have flowers that are more or less lavender. In this book, the flower colour described is as in British gardens; it will fade in hotter climates and deepen in cooler ones.

FRAGRANCE

Originally it was thought that only *H. plantaginea* was fragrant, and indeed all the fragrant hybrids that have been raised in the West owe their fragrance to *H. plantaginea*. However, it has recently been discovered that the Japanese grow a small number of fragrant cultivars which possibly owe nothing to *H. plantaginea*.

FLOWERING SEASON

Flowering seasons are denoted thus (southern hemisphere shown in brackets):

Early:	before 1 June (1 December)
Mid season:	1 June to 15 July
	(1December to 15 January)
Mid to late:	15 July to 1 September
	(15 January to 1 March)
Late:	after 1 September
	(after 1 March)

The majority of hostas flower mid-season. A few species and hybrids that flower late do not set seed because their growth is terminated by frost. This does not mean that they are sterile and if seed is needed they can be grown under glass.

SEED

After flowering, the ovary will swell into an elongated, many-chambered capsule. The colour of the capsules generally follows that of the leaves, being green with green-leaved varieties and glaucous with glaucous varieties. Occasionally they are purple as in *H*. 'Grand Master', and in variegated varieties they may be variegated.

The capsules open about six weeks after flowering. The seeds are ovoid and nearly flat. If they are fertile they will be black, if sterile they will be of a pale colour or nearly white. The production of capsules does not mean that they contain fertile seeds. Many cultivars do not form capsules at all, the scapes withering after flowering.

Hostas differ greatly as to their degree of fertility. Where sterility is known this is noted, otherwise the presumption is that they are fertile.

3

NOMENCLATURE

Piers Trehane

It is often thought that nomenclature and classification are one and the same thing. In fact, the differences are significant. Classification is the placing of items in groups; nomenclature is applying the correct name to those groups – two quite separate operations.

Every so often, a taxonomist will take all the information available about a group of plants, decide just how many good species there are in that group and then apply the correct name to each species. At the same time, all the names given to those plants previously thought to be species in their own right and now discovered to be only part of a species will be listed under the correct name. The procedure for establishing the correct name of a species is laid down in the International Code of Botanical Nomenclature (ICBN). This important book contains the rules which botanists follow to ensure that the same correct names are used the world over.

What makes an accepted species is very much up to the taxonomist working with a particular group of plants. If others agree with his or her species concept, the names will become fixed by general consensus.

The current opinion is that there are about 40 species of *Hosta* occurring in nature, although many more species have been described in the past. One of the most interesting aspects of *Hosta* is that many of the latter are in fact cultivated plants, and these have been exposed of late and removed from the general inventory of species. The first taxonomist to analyse this problem systematically was Noboru Fujita in his controversial revision of the genus in 1976. More recently, W. George Schmid's important book *The Genus Hosta*, published in 1991, has resolved many of the nomenclatural problems by formally reclassifying these man-made 'species' (specioids, as he calls them) as cultivars.

A cultivated plant may be defined as 'one whose origin or selection is primarily due to the intentional activities of mankind. Such a plant may arise either by deliberate or, in cultivation, accidental hybridization, or by selection from existing cultivated stock, or may be a selection from minor variants within a wild population and maintained as a recognizable entity solely by deliberate and continuous propagation'. A cultivar is defined as a 'taxonomic group of cultivated plants that is clearly distinct, uniform and stable in its characteristics and which, when propagated by appropriate means, retains those characteristics'.

The above definitions are taken from the 1995 edition of the *International Code of Nomenclature for Cultivated Plants* (ICNCP) which governs the names of cultivated plants in the same way as the ICBN provides for names of wild plants.

The discovery that what was thought to be a species is really a cultivated plant does not result in a change of name but in a different presentation of the original name – for example,

---

Hosta flower scapes. From left to right: top row, *H.* 'Opipara', *H.* 'Summer Fragrance', *H.* 'Birchwood Parky's Gold', *H.* 'Fragrant Gold', *H. ventricosa*; middle row, *H.* 'Ginko Craig', *H.* 'Tall Boy', *H.* 'Fortunei Aureomarginata'; bottom row, *H.* 'Phyllis Campbell', *H. longipes*, *H.* 'Invincible', *H. kikutii* 'Albo-stricta', *H.* 'Spritzer', *H.* 'Fragrant Bouquet', *H.* 'Grand Master', *H.* 'Wide Brim'.

30

rendering *Hosta opipara* as *Hosta* 'Opipara' demonstrates that the taxonomic group (taxon for short) is not found in the wild but is a product of cultivation.

The ICNCP deals with the rules for forming three categories of taxa of cultivated plants: the cultivar, the cultivar-group and the graft-chimaera (though the latter does not occur in *Hosta*). Cultivars are the main unit of classification in the ICNCP and the part of the name that denotes a particular cultivar is called the cultivar epithet. This is always written within single quotation marks in order to distinguish it from the genus name and other words in the text.

Cultivar epithets are fixed by act of proper publication in dated works. These works may include nursery catalogues, scientific papers or books, but not transient works such as newspapers or any other publications which are not designed to last. Since 1959, new epithets which are merely listed alphabetically do not count as being established unless they are accompanied by a description.

The rules for forming new cultivar epithets permit any epithet to be made up, provided it has never been used before in the genus and that it is not likely to be confusing or ambiguous. Epithets such as 'Red', 'Golden', 'Ogon', 'Kifukurin' (the last two are Japanese words) or 'Variegated' are not permitted to be used alone because of their generally adjectival nature.

The cultivar-group is a relatively recent concept developed as a means of assembling into a group named cultivars that have certain attributes in common. The attributes do not have to be strictly botanical, and may be horticultural. It is therefore quite possible that one cultivar-group might be based on, say, leaf shape or flower colour, while another cultivar-group might be based on season of harvest – especially useful in food crops. The main point is that cultivar-groups are only promoted when they have a useful purpose and it is not necessary to allocate all cultivars into one group or another.

There are a small number of obvious cultivar-groups in *Hosta*, the most common one being the *Hosta* Fortunei Group. This was based on *Hosta*

fortunei, a 'species' described (as *Funkia fortunei*) by J. G. Baker in 1876 but now known not to be represented in the wild. The history of this plant is not known, but it seems likely that the plant Baker described was descended from von Siebold's importations from Japan of around 1844. Nonetheless, the plant and its variations are well-known in gardens and are generally increased by vegetative means such as division.

The hostas 'Carol', 'Francee', 'North Hills' and 'Zager's White Edge' are all cultivars which share the general 'fortunei' characteristics and in the past these have been listed under *H. fortunei*. Under the provisions of the ICNCP, these may be listed directly under *Hosta* without reference to *fortunei* and are therefore written in the style *Hosta* 'Carol' or *Hosta* 'Carol' (Fortunei Group). Inclusion of the cultivar-group designation is not actually part of the name as required by the ICNCP, but its addition provides extra information about the cultivar.

In this book the author has in fact allocated all the above named cultivars to the Fortunei Albomarginata Group, conceived by W. George Schmid to cover all the white-edged *H. fortunei* cultivars, since she shares the view that it is far more useful to collect together cultivars with that attribute. She has also allocated to the *Hosta* Tardiana Group a number of cultivars which appear to share characteristics derived from a common parentage. It would not normally be allowable to raise this name since *Hosta* × *tardiana*, upon which the cultivar-group epithet is based, was never properly published and is therefore an invalid name. However, the name has been so widely used that a special application has been made to the Commission dealing with the names of cultivated plants to conserve the epithet to avoid confusion.

The rendering of what was previously *Hosta fortunei* as *Hosta* 'Fortunei' appears to present problems with the names of cultivars that were previously written as taxa below the rank of species. The ICNCP provides for this by allowing the old species name and the secondary epithet to be run together. *H. fortunei* var. *albopicta* and *H. fortunei* var. *albomarginata* may thus be written as *H.* 'Fortunei Albopicta' and *H.* 'Fortunei Albomarginata' respectively.

Many languages are written in characters other than the Roman alphabet used by Western cultures and have to be transliterated. The Japanese do not employ our Linnaean system of binomial names for plants, but have their own traditions that do not use cultivar epithets as such. In the past it has been Western custom to coin Western names for Japanese plants, but recent practice is far more sensitive about slaughtering Japanese names in favour of Western preferences and this is no longer allowed. Instead, the original characters (kanji) used in Japan are transliterated into the Roman alphabet, using the international standard called Hepburn. For example, the Japanese name for a golden-leaved *Hosta pycnophylla* is Ogon Setouchi Giboshi, the word 'ogon' meaning golden, 'setouchi' being the Japanese name of the species and 'giboshi' equating to hosta. Since cultivar epithets cannot be sole common descriptive words (such as ogon), nor may they contain the vernacular name of the genus (giboshi), the cultivar is rendered as *Hosta* 'Ogon Setouchi'.

International Registration Authorities (IRAs) are appointed by the International Society for Horticultural Science (ISHS). IRAs appoint a registrar who is charged to record all published cultivar and cultivar-group epithets and to issue checklists and a register of correct names. IRAs are obliged to operate within the rules of the codes of nomenclature and their work provides long-term stability of names. For *Hosta*, the IRA is the American Hosta Society and the Registrar is Dr David H. Stevenson, University of Minnesota Landscape Arboretum, P.O. Box 39, 3675 Arboretum Drive, Chanhassen, Minnesota 55317, USA. All new cultivar epithets should be registered with Mr Stevenson on a form which is obtainable from him and he will also advise any registrant on the acceptability of proposed names. In Great Britain, these forms may be obtained from the Hon. Registrar of the British Hosta and Hemerocallis Society, Mrs Ann Bowden, Cleave House, Sticklepath, Nr Okehampton, Devon, EX20 2NN.

Piers Trehane is a member of the Editorial Committee for the International Code of Botanical Nomenclature (ICBN), Chief Editor and *Rapporteur* for the International Code of Nomenclature for Cultivated Plants (ICNCP) and a member of the International Commission for Bionomenclature. He is also a member of the Horticultural Taxonomy Group (HORTAX) and edits Hortax News. He is vice-chairman of the Nomenclature Committee of the British Hosta and Hemerocallis Society. A member of the Nomenclature Advisory Panel for the Royal Horticultural Society, his main interest remains as compiler and editor of the Index Hortensis Project.

4

PEOPLE AND THEIR PLANTS

PAUL ADEN

Paul Aden is the world's most prolific hosta hybridizer and has had more influence on the hostas grown today than any other breeder. He was the first to raise and introduce a line of hostas with yellow leaves that keep their colour until they die down in autumn. *H.* 'Sun Power', introduced in the 1970s but not registered until 1986, is one of the most popular hostas grown today. He also raised and introduced many large blue leaved seedlings and selections from *H. sieboldiana* 'Elegans', including *H.* 'Big Daddy', *H.* 'Blue Angel' and *H.* 'Blue Mammoth'. He wrote the first book on hostas published outside Japan – *The Hosta Book*, published by Timber Press, Portland, Oregon in 1988.

SANDRA BOND

In 1988 Sandra Bond's Goldbrook Nursery was the first nursery in Britain to mount an exhibit of hostas at the Chelsea Flower Show. She was awarded a gold medal by the Royal Horticultural Society and has won gold medals every year since. Her exhibits feature hostas in woodland settings, usually with a pool as the centrepiece. Each year her exhibit has included hostas new to British gardeners and in 1994 she launched the British-raised *H.* 'Green With Envy'. She is the author of *Hostas*, published by Ward Lock, London, in 1992.

The George Smith Group. Left to right: top row, *H.* 'Great Expectations', *H.* 'George Smith', *H.* 'Color Glory'; middle row, *H.* 'Northern Lights', *H.* 'Borwick Beauty'; bottom row, *H.* 'DuPage Delight', *H.* 'Paul's Glory', *H.* 'Paul's Glory' (pot-grown), *H.* 'Northern Mist'.

CHRIS BRICKELL, CBE, VMH

Chris Brickell, who recently retired as Director General of the Royal Horticultural Society, is President of the British Hosta and Hemerocallis Society and Chairman of its Nomenclature Committee, two roles which reflect his lifelong interest both in hostas and taxonomy. He is chairman of the International Code of Nomenclature for Cultivated Plants (ICNCP) and of the ISHS Commission for Nomenclature and Registration.

At the Chelsea Flower Show in 1968 he was responsible for mounting a Scientific Exhibit on behalf of the Botany Department of the Royal Horticultural Society's Garden, Wisley. This exhibit displayed, in a Japanese garden setting, all the hostas the RHS could assemble, most of them at that time unknown to British gardeners. Many had been sent to Wisley by Dr Tsuneshige Rokujo of Tokyo, whose hobby was collecting hostas and other variegated plants. Others came from the Swedish collection of Nils Hylander and were 'originals' that related to his taxonomic analysis and papers on the genus. This Chelsea exhibit was pivotal; prior to it most gardeners in Britain had thought that there were only about half-a-dozen hostas in all. The exhibit opened their eyes to a whole new range of hostas and engendered a real interest in the genus in Britain.

DR WARREN POLLOCK

Ever since the formation of the British Hosta and Hemerocallis Society in the early 1980s Warren Pollock has provided a link between British and American hosta collectors, crossing the Atlantic regularly to keep up to date with British hosta people and plants. Each year he writes a comprehensive 'Letter From America' for the *British Hosta and Hemerocallis Society's Bulletin* in which he describes new hostas as they become available and gives information on American specialist hosta nurseries and hosta people in general. He was editor of the journal of the American Hosta Society from 1982 to 1988, during which time he raised the status of the journal, now internationally acclaimed, by issuing it biannually, introducing colour photographs and commissioning articles from hosta collectors worldwide. He is a prolific writer on hostas and a keen observer of the current hosta scene. In 1985 he received the Alex J. Summers Distinguished Merit Award.

PETER RUH

Peter Ruh of Homestead Division of Sunnybrook Farm, Chesterland, Ohio, has been growing and selling hostas for over 25 years. He is amassing a collection of historic hybrids and documenting the work of their raisers so that valuable records of those who laid the foundations for hosta-

growing as we know it today are not lost forever. He has named and registered many of the late David Stone's introductions which had formerly been known only under number.

In 1984 he received the Alex J. Summers Distinguished Merit Award for his valuable services to the *Hosta* genus.

W. GEORGE SCHMID

W. George Schmid has gathered together almost everything known about hostas in one massive reference book, *The Genus Hosta*, published by Timber Press in 1991. The book is the result of 25 years' research; in order to write it he studied Japanese and made visits to Japan to see hostas in the wild, and to Europe and Great Britain to meet other hosta collectors and see hosta gardens. His own garden, Hosta Hill, in Tucker, Georgia,

View of the hosta planting in Warren and Ali Pollock's back garden in Wilmington, Delaware.

The Hosta Walk at Hadspen House, Castle Cary, Somerset, where Eric Smith first grew many of his now-famous hostas.

houses probably the most comprehensive collection of hosta species in the world. Schmid is Hon. Historian of the American Hosta Society.

ERIC SMITH

Eric Smith always had a keen eye for a good cross. His most important contribution to hostas is his range of blue-leaved hybrids known as the Tardiana Group which he developed in the 1960s and 1970s when a partner at the Plantsman Nursery, near Sherborne, Dorset. These small to medium-sized hostas have inherited the intense glaucous-blue leaf colouring from *H. sieboldiana* 'Elegans' and the smaller leaf of the Tardiana parent. His well-known hosta collection, including what he called the GL (gold-leaved) series which he hoped would be improvements on *H.* 'Fortunei Aurea', was planted at Hadspen House, Dorset (where he was head gardener for Penelope Hobhouse) in what were originally his seedbeds, later known by hosta collectors everywhere as the Hosta Walk. Sandra and Nori Pope, who now run the garden, intend to retain the Hosta Walk in memory of a great hosta man.

GEORGE SMITH

George Smith, the internationally renowned flower arranger, admits to having had a life-long love affair with hostas. In his 1.2ha (3 acre) garden in Yorkshire, a mecca for flower-arrangers from all over the world, he grows hostas primarily for their leaves for use in arrangements and is continually testing new hosta varieties for their suitability for the purpose. The leaf qualities he looks for are turgidity, symmetry of shape, good clear colour, interesting surface texture and striking variegation. He regards *H.* 'Fortunei Albomarginata' as indispensable in the flower arrangers' repertoire of foliage plants.

Many of George's most treasured hostas date back to the time when Eric Smith (no relation) was introducing his famous hybrids. Whenever in Dorset George would call on Eric, thus acquiring many of Eric's newest hostas long before most other gardeners. One he particularly treasures was dug up for him by Eric from his own garden, Granary Cottage. This is *H.* 'Granary Gold', one of the best of Eric's GL series. It often features in George's much-photographed arrangements.

A founder-member of the British Hosta and Hemerocallis Society, George states that hostas are one of the essential plants for flower arrangement in the course of all his demonstrations to flower arrangement clubs worldwide. In 1989 he received the British Hosta and Hemerocallis Society's Eric Smith Award, a silver rose bowl awarded annually to the member who, in the opinion of the adjudicating committee, has done most to publicize hostas in the previous year.

ALEX SUMMERS

Alex Summers has been a nurseryman for some 60 years and has been growing and studying hostas for at least 35 years. He was a founder of the American Hosta Society and its first president, and the editor of its journal. To honour his outstanding contribution to the genus *Hosta* the American Hosta Society established the coveted Alex Summers Distinguished Merit Award in 1982. His present garden, Honeysong Farm, in Bridgeville, southern Delaware, to which he moved in 1981 from Roslyn, Long Island, New York, is a mecca for all hosta collectors. He has an unerring eye for a good hosta but has no qualms about dismissing those he considers worthless.

He corresponded and exchanged hostas with Eric Smith, and on his visit to England in 1979 he visited Eric at Hadspen House. There he chose what he considered the best 12 of the Tardiana Group and took them back to the United States; some of these he actually named, for example *H.* 'Blue Dimples' and *H.* 'Blue Wedgwood'. The beautiful green-margined sport of *H.* 'Gold Regal', has been named *H.* 'Alex Summers' in his honour.

KENJI WATANABE

Watanabe-san and his family grow and sell hostas at their Gotemba nursery, situated at the foot of Mount Fuji at Shizuoka-ken to the south-east of Tokyo, from whose slopes he has collected many variegated forms of hosta species, especially those of *H. montana*. He has been visited by many hosta collectors from the West and has been the source of such plants as *H. fluctuans* 'Sagae' (syn. *H. f.* 'Variegated'), and *H.* 'On Stage' (syn. *H.* 'Choko Nishiki'). In 1985 Watanabe-san published the first book ever written on hostas, *The Observation and Cultivation of Hosta*. Although it has never been officially translated into English, Western growers have been able to glean much useful new information from the photographs.

FRANCES WILLIAMS

Mrs Frances Williams was the first female landscape architect to graduate from the Massachusetts Institute of Technology. She saw the need for plants to grow in the shaded gardens which could be a cool and peaceful antidote to the summer heat of the US. Her most important contributions to the genus are the discovery of *H.* 'Frances Williams', which was named for her in 1963 by the then curator of Oxford Botanic Garden, George Robinson, to whom she sent a plant for the well-known collection of variegated-leaf hostas, and her introduction of many new hostas. Mrs Williams kept accurate records of her acquisitions and the crosses she made, as well as her correspondence with other hosta collectors. These valuable papers are now housed at the library of the Minnesota Landscape Arboretum.

5

CULTIVATION

The art of growing good hostas is to study their needs and then supply them. In general terms hostas need fertile soil, heavier rather than lighter and just a little on the acid side of neutral, plus some shade and shelter from wind. To get the very best from a wide range of hostas, however, it is necessary to look more closely at individual requirements as hostas come from a surprisingly wide variety of habitats and many are more demanding than is generally recognized.

SOIL

Most hostas grow best in rich, friable loam with a pH of about 6. They will grow perfectly well in alkaline soils, but seldom look happy on shallow, chalky soils, which tend to cause the leaves to exhibit chlorotic patches, while the glaucous blues take on a muddy tinge. The soil should be moist but well-drained, and this can usually be best achieved by mixing into the soil at planting time an abundance of organic matter, and then adding more organic matter in the form of a mulch regularly over the years.

Large hostas, such as *H.* 'Great Expectations', will grow well on heavy clay soils, which are rich in plant nutrients, but can be slower to establish themselves and so take longer to reach maturity. They will become established much more quickly if copious and equal quantities of coarse grit and garden compost or well-rotted farmyard manure are worked into the ground, not only where the hosta is to be planted, but for some distance around it, to allow the roots at maturity to spread out beyond the hosta's own leaf mound. The soil can then be maintained in good heart by mulching regularly with more grit and organic matter.

Sandy soils present quite different problems, though the solution is curiously similar. Hostas generally develop good root systems on sandy soils, but they only do this because they have to quest far and wide for nourishment and moisture. Sandy soils are poor soils, and hostas generally look thin and miserable on them unless steps are taken to remedy this. Because sandy soils are free-draining any nutrients that are applied to them are quickly flushed out of the soil by rain and by watering. Hostas will grow very much better in these conditions if plenty of organic matter in the form of farmyard manure or good garden compost is added to the soil at planting time, and the plants are regularly mulched in spring and autumn with the same materials. It may also be necessary to add extra nutrients, and to apply foliar feeds during the spring and early summer months.

Such treatment is not recommended for the smallest hostas, such as *H. venusta*, *H.* 'Shining Tot' or *H.* 'Suzuki Thumbnail'. Mulches are soon scattered by birds and these very small hostas can be completely suffocated by having coarse mulching materials flicked on top of them. Nor are they generally robust enough to compete with other hostas or the normal flora of perennial or woodland borders. In our experience these dwarf hostas are best grown on raised beds, their roots in a mixture of equal parts of peat or a peat substitute, garden compost or extremely old farmyard manure and coarse grit, and given a regular mulch with finely chopped-up leaf-mould. The walls of the raised beds can be made from peat blocks, large decaying tree trunks, railroad ties or bricks. Since such beds need to be sited in shade, these materials will soon develop a covering of moss into which some of the small hostas

will run or seed themselves. On the surface of the beds the moss may grow with sufficient vigour to suppress the hostas, but it can easily be deterred by applying a weak solution of ferrous oxide.

PLANTING

The single factor that most affects whether a hosta (or any other garden plant) will flourish or languish is how well its planting site is prepared. Obviously the size to which the hosta will grow determines the size of the planting hole, but for large hostas such as *H.* 'Sum and Substance', *H. fluctuans* 'Sagae', *H. montana* and its forms and *H. sieboldiana* and its forms, the planting hole should be as large as for a shrub – that is to say, a hole should be dug 91cm (3ft) across and 45cm (18in) deep, and the earth at the bottom of the hole broken up. The bottom half of the hole should be filled with alternating 7.5cm (3in) layers of well-rotted farmyard manure or garden compost and soil, with some grit added to the soil if it is heavy, while the top half should be filled with a friable mixture of the same materials, each layer and the final filling being firmly trodden down with the heel. Ideally the planting holes should be prepared a month or more before planting as freshly worked soil tends to drop somewhat in level. Smaller hostas need proportionately smaller planting holes, but they should never really be less than 45cm (18in) across and 23cm (9in) deep. For dwarf hostas the provision of a suitable growing medium is more important than the preparation of the planting hole.

Hostas may be planted either in the spring just as the new shoots are emerging, which enables them to establish themselves quickly as the soil warms up, or in late summer or early autumn while the soil is still warm from the summer's heat, which again enables them to establish themselves quickly. If necessary, they can even be moved in high summer in full leaf, provided the leaves are then cut down and the plants adequately and persistently watered until they are re-established; they will produce a new flush of leaves which the root system will be able to support. They should never be planted in the dead of winter, when the roots are inactive, since excessive rain or frost is likely to cause any damaged roots to rot. One great advantage of planting hostas while they are visible above the ground is that it enables the gardener to get their placing and spacing right.

When planting hostas that have been grown in pots it will usually be found that the roots have become enmeshed at the bottom of the pot. Such roots should be teased out before planting: it is not a tragedy if in the process much of the compost in which the plant was growing is lost. When planting open-ground hostas it is prudent to remove the old soil so that the roots can make a new start in fresh soil. Any dead or damaged roots should be removed with a sharp knife or secateurs (pruning shears). Once the hosta has been placed in its hole the soil should be replaced in layers, and each layer firmed before the next is added. Once planted the hosta should be well watered in, and particular attention paid to its watering over the following months, especially if planting in the spring. After an initial soaking, a hose very slowly trickling water into the ground beside the hosta for several days is more effective than the occasional swamping with water. After that it is necessary just to keep the ground moist. Large hostas need at least 4.5 litres (1gal/5 qt) of water a day until properly established. A thick layer of organic mulching material should then be placed in a doughnut-like ring around the plant.

MULCHING AND FEEDING

Hostas are generally described as gross feeders, though this is true only of the larger sorts. For any smaller than *H. sieboldii* the provision of the right growing medium and adequate watering is more important. Most other hostas will respond well to liberal applications of manures and fertilizers.

The Kikutii Group. Left to right: top row, *H.* 'Hokkaido', *H. kikutii*, *H. k.* 'Pruinose Form', *H. k.* 'Caput-avis', *H. k.* 'Green Form'; middle row, *H.* 'Shelleys', *H.* 'Spritzer'; bottom row, young leaf of *H. k.* 'Yakushimensis', *H.* 'Green Fountain' seedling, *H.* 'Joy Bulford', *H. k.* 'Albo-stricta', *H. k.* 'Leuconota'.

In this green age organic feeds such as farmyard manure, garden compost or leaf-mould are prized above artificial fertilizers. In reality the nutritional content of these organic materials is often disappointingly low and unbalanced, and varies from batch to batch. Moreover, such organic materials are usually full of weed seeds. What organic materials do contribute to the growth of hostas is humus, which helps to keep soil moisture levels even and provides a good carrier for other nutrients. With artificial fertilizers, and indeed with most packaged, powdered or pelleted plant foods, the nutritional content is known and the gardener can choose whether to apply a high nitrogen or high potash feed.

To grow really sumptuous hostas it is necessary to establish a regular routine of spring and autumn mulching and spring and summer feeding. This applies as much to hostas in pots as to open-ground hostas. The mulch should always be applied in a doughnut-like ring around the crown of the hosta and should never cover it, as otherwise the crown may rot during a wet winter. While nearly all hostas are frost-hardy in the average climate of Britain, in the US and other countries where severe winter frosts are the norm, the crown may be lightly covered with dry fern fronds, straw or, in the US, salt hay. The depth of the mulch should be appropriate to the size of the hosta, which is to say shallower on small hostas and deeper on larger ones. Around large established clumps of some of the *H. sieboldiana* forms and other strong-growing hostas, the mulch may be as much as 10–13cm (4–5in) thick.

Hostas make enormous demands on the available soil nitrogen and will not achieve their sumptuous best unless the supply is adequate. This is especially the case with the larger-leaved ones. Most organic mulches, while they may in the longer term provide some nitrogen, cause short-term nitrogen deficiencies. What happens is that vital nitrogen-converting organisms are attracted from the soil into the mulch, where they play a vital role in breaking it down. For this reason high-nitrogen fertilizers should be used whenever a mulch is applied, and this is especially important in spring. Nitrogen is most vital in spring when hostas are making optimum growth (usually April and May in Britain), and a quick-acting high-nitrogen fertilizer such as dried blood or pelleted chicken manure may be necessary. However, excessive and unbalanced applications of high-nitrogen fertilizers will tend to encourage hostas to produce lush, soft, sappy foliage which is not only easily damaged by wind and weather but utterly delectable to slugs and snails. To prevent this from happening the nitrogen should always be balanced by potassium (potash), which helps to produce firm, crisp leaves. Since hostas also need phosphorus for the development of good roots, it is usually best to use a balanced feed. The various elements in fertilizers are expressed as N for nitrogen, P for potash and K for phosporus. In high-nitrogen fertilizers there may be twice as much N as P and K, while in balanced fertilizers N, P and K are present in equal amounts. Most fertilizers also contain small quantities of trace elements that are essential to plant growth.

Fertilizers can be applied as powder or pellets in a scattered ring round the hosta, as a liquid feed through a can to the root area, or as a foliar feed, applied via a can or through a dilutor attached to a hose. Foliar feeds are particularly appropriate for hostas as they enjoy the extra water this gives them, and it also helps to make the leaves dark and glossy.

Hostas should be fed from early spring until mid-summer (the end of June in Britain). Any feed applied after that, even if it is a balanced feed, will tend to promote soft, sappy growth vulnerable not only to slugs and snails but to disease.

WATERING

The leaves of growing plants remain turgid as a result of the pressure of the water flowing through them. This is caused by the surface of the leaves giving off water vapour, creating a partial vacuum that sucks more water into the plant through the roots in an attempt to replace the water that has been lost. It is this process, which is continuous in daylight, that keeps the leaves plumped up and turgid. Plainly, any plant with leaves as large as those of *H.* 'Snowden' or *H.* 'Sum and Substance'

A superb specimen of *H.* 'Snowden' in the Pergola Garden at Cleave House, Devon.

must give off a lot of water vapour, and must, therefore, need plenty of water to sustain the process. Their leaf size is totally dependent upon their receiving adequate moisture which also accentuates the seersuckering effect. If there is insufficient water available to them, in a drought for example, or when they have been picked, they lose their turgidity, become limp and wither. It is for this reason that the watering of hostas is so essential to their success.

It seems only natural to think that the best way to water plants is by whatever means most nearly resembles rain, but this may not in fact be the best way to water hostas. The main problem is that the droplets falling repeatedly on the leaves of blue-leaved hostas can damage the glaucous bloom for which they are treasured. The use of fine mist sprays avoids this problem. A further problem is that if water is applied overhead and the leaves are then exposed to sunlight, the droplets may focus the sun's rays on to the leaf surface and burn it, causing disfiguring brown and yellow marks. The most effective way of watering hostas is to apply the water directly to the area where the roots are either by can or hose, or, in the case of an extensive planting, by seep hose. In the watering of hostas, the aim is to maintain the soil around them at an evenly

42

moist level and to avoid alternating extremes of wetness and dryness.

Watering should always be done as early as possible in the morning, before the sun's rays get hot. The hostas then have all day to make use of the water, which can only be absorbed in daylight. The problem with watering in the evening is that the moisture tends to attract slugs and snails, which enjoy wet environments.

The same principles apply to hostas being grown in pots and tubs, which are more vulnerable to drying out than hostas growing in the ground.

SHADE

Hostas are often thought of as shade-loving plants, and while this is true of the great majority it is by no means true of all. Given adequate moisture, hostas such as H. 'On Stage' with much yellow and little green in their leaves are a far better colour in some direct sunlight. It is also generally the case that while the leaves may look their best in shade, hostas flower better in sunlight.

In the wild, hostas grow in a variety of conditions that afford them shade. Some grow in open cryptomeria forest, others, such as *H. longissima*, in high-altitude water meadows where shade is cast by taller growing grasses (frequently miscanthus), while others grow on mountains where they are almost always shrouded in cloud. A few grow on rocks or in crevices beside mountain streams where water is always available to them and so the need for shade is compensated for by the availability of the water. However, these conditions are by no means easy to replicate in Western gardens, which is why hostas are usually grown in the shade.

Shade is more than merely the absence of direct sun. It is a modification of the micro-climate, bringing cooler, moister air, often retaining more moisture in the soil if there are not too many competing tree roots.

Filtered shade provides ideal conditions for the National Reference Collection of Modern Hybrid Hostas at Cleave House.

Hostas grow best in light, dappled shade, such as that cast by a high tree canopy. The problem with trees is that when they are young they cast too little shade, and when they are older they cast too much. It is easier to create just the right amount of shade artificially, by building a pergola for example, as at Apple Court, Hampshire, and Cleave House, Devon, or a lath house, as at the Trial Gardens at Weihenstephan near Munich. It is also possible to use pleached limes or hornbeam to cast shade exactly where it is needed, the advantage of pleached trees being that the pleaching limits their height.

Most of us have to make do with whatever shade exists in our garden, but where there is an opportunity to create it a greater variety of shade density can be offered by using three trees rather than one. If the trees are planted in an equilateral triangle whose hypoteneuse is a line running east-west and whose tip lies north of the line (in the northern hemisphere), the most dense shade will occur within the planting triangle itself. The area to the south of the hypoteneuse will be entirely in the sun, but the areas to the north-east and north-west of the triangle will be in light shade for about half the day.

The great advantage of having varying degrees of shade in the garden is that not all hostas require the same amount of shade, and so plants can be tried in different positions until the right one is found. *H.* 'Gold Standard', for example, will scorch in too much sun, yet in too much shade it will not develop its proper colouring.

While trees may seem to provide an elegant and seemingly natural setting for hostas, it should be borne in mind that they compete for the same moisture and nutrients, making the need for adequate feeding and watering all the more essential. Some trees compete with hostas more directly than others. Birches and cherries, for example, are surface-rooting, and such trees invade the space where hosta roots should be, depriving them of goodness. Beeches are also surface-rooting, but oaks are deep-rooted, as are most maples. Trees such as catalpas which come into leaf very late allow hostas beneath to put on growth before the protective shade of their leaves arrives.

SHELTER

When hostas are well-sited they have a sumptuous, well-fed look. Sometimes, though, hostas seem decidedly miserable, their leaves not as large as they should be, not as turgid, even a little limp, and very often this is due not so much to a lack of feeding or watering as to a lack of shelter, when the leaves are exposed to too much wind. Wind not only damages the leaves of hostas by its sheer physical force, knocking and bruising them, but also desiccates them, in extreme cases causing scorching. Wind blowing across leaves dries them just as it dries laundry on the line, and this puts pressure on the plants' roots to supply more water to keep the leaf turgid. In some conditions the roots may not be able to do this and loss of turgidity results, causing the leaves to look tired and withered.

Hostas should never be grown in sites exposed to wind unless steps are taken to reduce its force. In the long term this may mean growing hedges or belts of trees or shrubs, but in the short term fences can be used to reduce or deflect the force of the winds. Modern flexible plastic wind-breaking materials can also be used as a temporary measure. The great advantage of these modern materials, as with hedges and some kinds of fencing, is that being semi-permeable they reduce the force of the wind rather than causing it to go up and over, which often creates turbulence that can be as damaging as the winds it was there to divert.

CONTAINERS

The larger hostas generally do best in containers when planted in a soil-based growing medium rather than in one composed mostly of peat or coir. The problem is quite simply that hostas have a large leaf area and evaporate a considerable amount of moisture. Peat-based composts tend to dry out and are much more difficult to remoisten than soil-based ones, which seem to hold some moisture in reserve for much longer than soilless mixes. Even so, the containers will need to be watered every two or three days at the very least from the time the shoots start to

44

H. 'Wide Brim', one of the best hostas for container-growing, seen here at Hadspen house with *Saxifraga stolonifera* (behind) and *H.* 'Halcyon' (left).

emerge in the spring until the leaves have died down in the autumn. At each watering the growing mix should be soaked: this is far more effective than more frequent sprinklings. The water should be applied beneath the leaves directly to the growing mix rather than over the leaves, which can become discoloured if the water is alkaline. Smaller hostas can be grown very successfully in a peat-based compost with the addition of fine grit to improve the drainage. A layer of broken crocks at the bottom of the container also assists the drainage of excess water.

The hostas will also need regular and ample feeding, but not overfeeding. With large hostas planted in large containers it is often a good idea to put a layer of dung at the bottom of the container before adding the growing mix, and perhaps mulching annually with pelleted chicken manure. Always leave a space of at least 2.5cm (1in) between the surface of the compost and the rim of the pot so that the hosta can be thoroughly soaked. Controlled-release fertilizer pellets placed just below the surface of the compost in early spring will help to produce large and luxuriant leaves, as will foliar feeding every two weeks or so until the end of June.

Even with lavish watering and feeding, few hostas will continue to thrive in containers for more than four years at a time – most of the largest only about two years. After that their leaves begin to diminish in size and sometimes become misshapen, when the plants will need to be divided and replanted into fresh growing mix. Hostas of the Elegans Group, the Golden Medallion Group and the Tokudama Group are usually less successful as container specimens as they seem to develop a fibrous core at the crown, impeding their development if kept in a pot for more than two or three years. Hostas of the Fortunei Group, with their finer root systems, keep their leaf size and shape for many more years.

PESTS AND DISEASES

Hostas are relatively free from disease but slugs and snails can do considerable damage, though gardens vary greatly as to their populations, some being hardly affected at all. A variety of remedies is available, but experience suggests that the most effective regimen is to water a liquid metaldehyde formulation on to the hostas and the ground around them in early spring, just as the emerging shoots start to push through the ground. The timing is crucial because this is when slugs and snails emerge from hibernation. The treatment should be repeated at weekly or fortnightly intervals for six to eight weeks, by which time the liquid metaldehyde will have been applied into the unfurling and expanding leaves in which many small slugs hide by day. Early treatment is particularly effective at destroying the small dark brown or black keeled slugs that live just under the surface of the soil and do most of the early damage to soft young leaves – damage which, in hostas, is all too often visible for the rest of the season.

After that the gardener may resort to slug pellets, but these can be a mixed blessing. Most contain a chemical which actually attracts slugs, and heavy-handed use may exacerbate the problem rather than solving it. It takes very little of the chemical in the pellets to kill a slug, and therefore a lot of pellets are not needed; the art is to find where the slugs hide by day and, very sparingly, scatter the pellets there. Typically slugs like cool, damp places to hide in, and often the gutter between a border and a lawn provides the perfect place. A few pellets scattered in the gutter will be far more effective than a thick ring of pellets poured round a hosta, but they must be applied frequently as they are only viable for about 3–4 days. They are most effective applied after rain, and in damp, muggy conditions when the slugs are at their most active.

Pellets usually contain either metaldehyde or methiocarb, and the latter is generally the more effective, though some people like to alternate them. Both are exceedingly poisonous to humans, and should be treated with respect. It is also possible to obtain pellets based on aluminium sulphate, which are said to be more environmentally friendly: unfortunately they are less effective at destroying slugs and snails. Pellets are usually blue, as it is thought to be a colour which birds cannot see. If there is any reason for concern about pets eating the pellets, place the pellets in the centre of short lengths of clay land drain or plastic guttering or under a piece of slate, where they cannot easily be reached.

The most effective, and cheapest, method of slug control is to go round the garden at dusk with a bucket of salt water; several hundred slugs can be scooped up in a very short time, especially after rain. Many gardeners resort to slug pubs, upturned grapefruit halves, crushed eggshells and other ancient remedies, but these do nothing to improve the beauty of the garden. A method under trial now, both in Britain and the US, is to place a vertical 4cm (1½in) copper strip, fashioned into a collar, around the hosta. Some hosta growers have had success with this method.

Recently a biological control for slugs has become available. A nematode, it is specific to slugs and will do no harm at all to snails. The nematode is mixed with water and applied to the ground around hostas through a watering can. The nematode then parasitizes any slugs that come in contact with it, multiplying in the slug's body and reinfecting any slugs that come to eat the dead slug. Experiments in the US have shown that where the nematode is watered on to a heavy mulch it has little effect, since the slugs tend to be below the mulch rather than in it. What is effective is scraping aside the mulching material, watering on the nematode, and then returning the mulch.

An alternative or complementary way of controlling slugs and snails is to understand their part in the natural scheme of things, and to avoid creating in the garden or around the hostas conditions in which these pests can thrive. Their role is to clear the world of rotting vegetation. If slugs and snails did not exist, gardens would soon be swamped by decaying debris. Keeping the garden free from dying leaves and other garden rubbish such as old bricks and stones under and behind which they can hide will deter them, since such materials provide not only an ideal home for them but also a perfect breeding ground. The leaves of hostas and their companion plants should be removed as soon as they start to turn yellow or show signs of decay. Such a philosophy presents a dilemma for those who like to mulch their hostas, a practice which without doubt helps to conserve moisture and to promote healthy growth, but also tends to provide a cool, damp hiding place for slugs and snails. Regular and thorough cultivation of the borders helps to expose the eggs and the slugs to their natural predators but this precludes the use of a mulch.

The depredations of slugs and snails can be more easily be controlled in pots and containers than in the open garden. These should never be stood directly on the ground since the ground beneath them will be cool and damp, providing slugs and snails with an ideal habitat. Instead they should be raised about 4cm (1½in) above the ground on small feet, broken bricks or broken tiles. Provided this is done and the foliage of the hosta in one pot does not touch the foliage of another hosta, they will very often get through the season with no damage at all, but extra steps may need to be taken. Pellets tucked out of sight around the rim of the pot will prove effective, and are unlikely to be discovered by pets. If a band of petroleum jelly or fruit tree grease about 4cm (1½in) wide is smeared in a circle halfway between the top and bottom of the container this will greatly deter the slugs and snails from reaching the hosta.

Hostas vary greatly in their resistance to slug and snail damage. Those with thick leaves such as *H.* 'Sum and Substance' and *H.* 'Green Sheen' are generally little damaged, while hostas with thin leaves, such as *H.* 'Undulata' and forms of *H. sieboldii*, suffer very badly. (See the list of hostas least prone to pest damage on page 152.)

Vine Weevil

It is the vine weevil grubs that do the real damage to plants, eating the roots. The grubs or larvae are C-shaped, fat, creamy-ivory in colour, and about half the length of a thumbnail. If discovered they should be destroyed at once – they are easily squashed underfoot, and goldfish find them delicious. The adults, which are slow-moving beetles, eat the edges of leaves, leaving characteristic notches. The adults can be controlled by the use of organophosphates, but it is the destruction of the grubs that is really important. A biological control, a parasitic nematode, is now available and is highly effective. As with the slug nematode, it is applied through a watering can.

Vine weevils are usually more of a problem where hostas are grown in pots than in the open garden, though they can become a problem in boggy or ill-drained ground. They tend to infest pots which have contained the same compost for a year or more, so one way of controlling them is to repot all the hostas every year.

Diseases

Given good cultivation, hostas are mostly disease-free, but there are just a few that may occur on occasion. The first is viral infection, which usually takes the form of a yellow mosaic appearing on the leaves, the yellow following the lines of the major and minor veins, but on occasion manifesting itself as large yellow blotches on the leaves or even yellowing of almost the whole of the leaf surface. It may also make the growth of the leaves dwarf and congested. The two viruses which can affect hostas are arabis mosaic virus and tobacco rattle virus and these are usually spread by aphids or by dividing hostas with garden tools which have previously been used on infected plants. Mineral or chromosome deficiency shows up in leaves as blotches or mottling and this is sometimes mistaken for virus infection.

There is no cure for virus infection and only one recommended treatment: affected hostas should be dug up and burned as soon as possible before they infect other hostas. Apart from *H.* 'Crispula', *H.* 'Sea Sprite' and *H.* 'Tardiflora', the most commonly affected hostas seem to be those with glaucous blue leaves.

Another disease found in hostas is crown rot. It usually only affects hostas growing in warm climates or under glass, though over-compacted growing media may also cause it. The leaves turn yellow and fall away from the rootstock. The plants should be dug up and pulled apart, affected pieces being thrown away or burnt and only firm, healthy pieces being retained. Since crown rot is a fungal infection, these pieces should be dipped in a fungicidal solution before being potted up and grown on.

The only other disease to cause a problem to the hosta-grower is leaf spot, which is caused by the fungi *Alternaria*, *Plyllostricta* and *Colletotrichum omnivorum*. The treatment of leaf spot is two or three sprays at fortnightly intervals with Benomyl or Thiram.

However, spots on hosta leaves can be caused by damage from misdirected chemical garden sprays and other air-borne pollutants. Pinhead-sized brown spots sometimes seen on leaves in late spring and early summer are caused by the leaf-cells bursting due to slight frosts which often occur some time after the leaves have unfurled, and this damage is not apparent immediately. Frost damage can also cause the edges to turn brown. Leaf scorch, similar to leaf spotting, is harmless though unsightly, and is caused by small drops of cold water falling on to leaves growing in strong sunlight.

6

PROPAGATION

There are only two means by which hostas can be propagated: seed or division, which includes tissue culture (micropropagation). Of the two, division is generally the most useful.

DIVISION

The usual reasons for wanting to propagate hostas are either that a friend would like one or that the original clump has got too large and you need to start again with a smaller piece. In either of these circumstances the simplest method is to remove a wedge-shaped piece from the clump, rather like a slice of cake, using a spade. The slice can then be planted elsewhere or potted up, and the space from which it was removed refilled with good soil or garden compost (decayed organic matter). The parent plant will grow back into the new soil and in a few weeks it will scarcely be possible to see where the slice was taken. An alternative method is to dig up the whole clump and split it into two or more, using two forks back-to-back. In either case, the operation should be carried out in the spring, just as the noses begin to push through the soil, or in autumn as the leaves are dying down.

If larger numbers of young plants are wanted the best method is either to dig up proportionately larger wedges of the original clump – perhaps as much as three-quarters – and split that into two or three big slices, or to dig up the whole clump and then shake or wash off the earth. Once this has been done the white roots and the rhizomes can be clearly seen, and it is easy to cut them into smaller pieces, each new plant having three or five buds each. The smallest units into which it is normally sensible to divide hostas is single terminal buds, that is to say the buds which occur at the ends of each short length of rhizome. However, if

a still greater quantity is required, it is often possible to coax the latent buds into growth. These are tiny, usually mauve buds that arise on the rhizome just below the terminal bud. The first thing to do is to make sure that there are in fact latent buds on the shoots: having located them, cut the terminal bud off with a very sharp knife and then split the rhizome longitudinally, as if slicing a carrot, each long thin slice having a single latent bud and, if possible, some of the original roots. Dust these plantlets with fungicidal powder and pot them up into a sterilized potting medium. They should then be stood out in a shaded but open position; if they are kept in close conditions the likelihood of fungal attack is much higher. It should be said that dividing hostas into pieces this small is not without its risks, and if the plantlets are attacked by fungal infections all of them may be lost.

There are methods of preparing hostas for propagation which encourages them to make more buds than they would otherwise do, and for the patient this is the more prudent method of producing numerous divisions. The first is a practice known simply as 'mowing'. In about June the leaves of the hosta are cut off about 0.5–1cm (¼–½in) above the ground, depending on the vigour of the variety. This causes the latent buds to break into growth, thereby producing more growing tips. Hostas can be mown twice in a season, if so desired.

Another technique is known as the Ross method, after its American inventor, Henry Ross. The earth is scraped away from around the crown on the hosta, revealing the rhizomes. A sharp knife is inserted into the side of the stem just above the basal plate and pushed downwards through the basal plate to where the roots are located. The knife is then removed and inserted

into the side of the stem again, but at right angles to the original cut. After this the knife is removed and the earth returned around the crown of the hosta, which should then be watered. Over the following few weeks some of the leaves will turn yellow and some blotchy, but the hosta soon returns to looking as good as usual. By autumn it will have produced many more potential buds than the norm. Some growers find this technique is also successful when carried out later in the season. However, grinding the heel of a shoe into the young shoots of hostas just as they are coming through in the spring can be just as effective at producing more buds, and a great deal less trouble.

As a rule of thumb hostas are best propagated in the spring just as the new shoots are coming through, but it is not an inflexible rule. They can be divided all through the growing season, provided their leaves are cut off once they have been divided, they are properly firmed in the ground or growing media, and they are watered properly. Some nurseries actually favour propagating in July and August, because any wounds to the plant will have healed before winter, and the plants very soon put on new leaves.

Hostas grow much faster in sunny conditions, which is why some nurserymen grow them in field rows. However, the leaves of some are liable to become scorched.

An extension of normal division is micropropagation or tissue culture. This is a laboratory technique whereby cells from the tip of a flowering shoot are taken and grown on a sterile jelly in a test tube. By manipulating feeding and lighting, these cells can be made to turn into tiny plantlets that exactly resemble the plant from which the flower was taken. The cells can be divided again and again, so that it is possible to produce huge numbers of plants quite quickly as compared to the older methods. It is this technique that has been largely responsible for many new varieties coming

on the market far faster than would once have been possible, and for far more plants to be put on the market at an early stage, often before they have been adequately trialled in gardens or before unwanted sports have been rogued out. However, it does have the advantage of keeping prices down.

A further reason for wanting to divide a hosta might be if a sport arose on an established clump. The safest procedure is usually to wait until the sport has reappeared for two or three years in succession, and then to lift the part of the plant that has sported, together with some of the surrounding parts of the plant that have not, preferably using the slice of cake technique as described above. The whole slice can then be put on a potting bench to bring it nearer to eye level. The soil should be shaken or washed off. It is then possible to see quite clearly to which piece or pieces of root the sport belongs: the rest can be cut away with a sharp knife, and the sport potted up and grown on. It may take several growing seasons to stabilize the sport as its natural instinct will be to revert to its parent.

SEED

Many hostas produce seed in great quantities, and most of the seed will germinate readily, producing an abundance of seedlings. Indeed, if the seedheads are left on plants in the garden for their decorative winter effect and the seed is scattered, seedlings will usually come up like weeds unless one takes steps to prevent them. It may be best to remove the scapes once the pods have formed to avoid this. Hybrid miniatures usually carry fewer flowers and are more reluctant to set seed.

Generally speaking, hostas raised from seed that has occurred naturally in the garden are unlikely to be of particular merit. In the first place hostas do not usually come true from seed (that is, the seedlings will not normally bear a close resemblance to the parent), apart from *H. ventricosa*, which is apomictic. Secondly, hybridizers pursuing deliberate breeding schemes have so raised our expectations of what a good hosta should be like that few seedlings will measure up. For those who do want to breed hostas, the techniques are discussed in the next chapter.

The Tiara Group. Left to right: top row, *H.* 'Platinum Tiara', *H.* 'Grand Tiara', *H.* 'Emerald Tiara', *H.* 'Diamond Tiara'; bottom row, *H.* 'Golden Tiara', *H.* 'Golden Scepter', *H.* 'Emerald Scepter'.

7

BREEDING HOSTAS

The breeding of good plants requires the eye of a painter, the inspiration of a poet, the vision of a seer and the disciplined and methodical approach of a scientist. Beyond that it is quite easy.

The essence of plant breeding is to bring pollen from the chosen male parent into contact with the receptive organ of the chosen female parent, while at the same time preventing any other agent from introducing pollen to the female. The mechanics of this are quite simple, although a minimal understanding of the structure of the flower concerned is required. A hosta flower is quite simple from this point of view, typically having one female organ (the stigma) and several (often six) male organs, or anthers, which surround it. The stigma is longer and thicker than the stamens, which bear a remarkable resemblance, especially in diagrams, to long eyelashes curling up at the tips.

PREPARING THE POD PARENT

In order to prevent the pollination of the selected flower by natural agents such as bees the plant has to be emasculated. Before attempting this it is essential to study hosta flowers in order to know exactly when they are going to open, because it is necessary to catch the flower in the late afternoon of the day before it opens – that is, while it is still in bud but almost ready to open. The procedure is first to slit open the bud carefully, exposing the sex organs without damaging them, and then to cut away the petals and sepals. The final step is to locate the anthers and to cut them away without damaging the stigma. The removal of the petals and sepals deprives insects of a landing platform and makes it most unlikely that they will try to effect pollination, while the removal of the anthers eliminates any likelihood of self-pollination. Wind pollination is unlikely anyway since hosta pollen is heavy.

GATHERING AND STORING POLLEN

Pollen is the medium in which the male gamete is transferred to the female. It is by its very nature short-lived and sensitive to changes in temperature. When the pollen of hostas is ripe and ready to use it has a powder-like texture. What governs its viability is enzyme activity, which is mainly temperature-controlled: the pollen needs a reasonable amount of heat to ripen, but in too much heat its viability deteriorates rapidly. The workable range would seem to be between 18°C (65°F) and 29°C (85°F), with an optimum of about 24°C (75°F).

Because it is so sensitive to temperature, it is important that pollen is gathered at the right time: too early in the day and the ambient temperature will not be high enough, too late in the afternoon or evening and the temperature will have fallen too low again. Mid-morning seems to be the time of optimum enzyme activity, but by this time of day the bees may have already got there and taken the pollen. For this reason it is better to gather the anthers, bearing their pollen, reasonably early in the day. The anthers should then be taken indoors, placed in the dark and allowed to come up to the optimum temperature before being either harvested or used.

Pollen may be used as soon as it has reached a suitable temperature, or it may be stored in folds of low-grade white paper, on which the source of the pollen can easily be written. It helps to fold the paper first and then open it out, tap the pollen into the middle section and refold it. The paper containers can then be stored in a refrigerator (not a freezer, which is far too cold) and will remain viable for the rest of the season and often into the early part of the following one. This of course means that one can mate hostas that do not naturally flower at the same time.

TRANSFERRING THE POLLEN

The actual moment of mating is achieved when the pollen from the male anthers is transferred to the female stigma, which becomes moist and slightly swollen when it is at its most receptive: once it forms a dew-drop it is too late. The simplest and most natural way to do this is to brush the pollen-laden anthers across the slightly sticky stigma, thereby leaving a deposit of pollen on it. This of course is only possible when the anthers and stigma are in season at the same time.

Where stored pollen has to be used, a fine camel-hair or sable brush will be needed. Pollen is delicately taken on to the tip of the brush, which is then wiped across the stigma. Each cross should be made using a different brush, and the brushes should be cleaned afterwards in methylated spirits. As the brush then has to dry before use, it is practical to have a whole batch of brushes to work through before having to clean them. Another technique is to use a wisp of cotton wool held by tweezers to transfer the pollen, using a fresh piece of cotton wool for each mating.

Whichever technique is used, it is important to repeat the cross two or three times in the same day to make sure that pollination has been carried out at the right time, or as near to it as possible. When selfing – that is, pollinating a flower with its own pollen – the pollen and the stigma may not ripen at the same time so the pollen will have to be stored.

SUCCESSFUL CROSSING

Some hostas are much more difficult to cross than others. *H. plantaginea* and some of its offspring are notorious for rejecting the pollen of other hostas. One technique that has been found successful is to use *H. plantaginea* pollen round the rim of the stigma, and the pollen of the parent you want to cross in the centre of the stigma.

Many breeders believe that there is no need to do anything further to defend the stigma once the cross has been made as the pollen takes only an hour and a half to reach the ovary. However, it is not unknown for bees to come and steal the pollen off the stigma after it has been put there. The simplest defence against this is to slip a short length of drinking straw over the anther. This can be removed the next day.

There are a number of factors which may inhibit pollen from taking. Timing may be critical. *H. plantaginea*, along with most of its fragrant offspring, is a notoriously difficult hosta to encourage to set seed. Part of the problem would seem to be that it is a nocturnal species, opening its flowers in the evening just as the dew is descending; dampness on the stigma may prevent the pollen taking. This may explain why crosses made at 4pm the day before the flower opens may be successful, while those made the following morning may not be.

Watering and soil fertility may also be contributing factors. Plants growing in poor soils seldom produce a good set of seed, and the same is true of plants starved of water. A further consideration may be how long a plant has been growing in the same place: hostas seldom set good seed when newly planted and are much more likely to do so when they have been growing in one place for several years. Finally, early- and late-season crosses may be easier to carry out if the pod parent is removed to a greenhouse or windowsill as the vagaries of the weather may prevent successful mating.

LABELLING AND RECORDING

It is important to label crosses and keep records of them in order to be able to make the same cross again – or just possibly, having seen the progeny, to avoid making it again. Alternatively, it may be desirable to make the reverse cross, or to back cross, or to use a different pollen parent, and so on.

The first step is to label the pod parent. The label should be tied to the pedicel (the short flower-bearing stalk) where it joins the scape – if it is tied to the pedicel alone the swelling pod may push it off. Plastic labels are generally too heavy, bending the scape sometimes to breaking point. Jewellery tags are better, but the ink must be indelible. An alternative is to use coloured wire or wool. The name of the pod parent should always be written first, followed by an 'x' and then the name of the pollen parent. Some people prefer to use numbers rather than names, and while this may be useful if secrecy is important, it does necessitate keeping a separate record of what the numbers stand for. It is extremely important to record each cross immediately, especially when making several crosses, in order to avoid confusion.

The information on the label tied to the pod parent should follow the progeny through all the different stages of seed sowing, pricking out and growing on and all the way to maturity.

HARVESTING AND STORING

It takes some six to eight weeks from the time the cross is made for the seed to ripen, and most early varieties can be left to ripen their seed on their own, out in the open. It is however important to clean the spent flower off the ripening pod: if it is left there it might become a source of disease. Many mid-season and late varieties will not fully ripen their seed out of doors, especially in Britain and other cooler climates, and they must be brought indoors and ripened in sugar water. This can be made by adding ¼ teaspoon sugar to 600ml (1pt/2½ cups) water, stirring until thoroughly dissolved and then leaving to cool before use.

When the pods go brown and begin to split, they are ready for harvesting. All the pods of the same cross should be gathered and placed loosely in a bag, preferably a brown paper bag to permit the pods to ripen. On no account should the bag be a plastic one, since this will retain any moisture that may be left in the pods and is likely to cause the seeds to rot. The paper bag should be sealed with staples or paper clips and clearly labelled. A lot of pods do not split open properly and have to be assisted: coax the seeds out of the pod by gently stroking them with the tip of a pencil. The seeds should then be winnowed from the husks by blowing on them lightly. The importance of removing all husks and husk fragments (which may have to be picked away with tweezers) cannot be over-emphasized, as any unwanted debris may harbour disease. Unless you have special facilities, keep only fully ripened seed and discard the rest.

Unless the seed is going to be sown straight away, which is often very successful, it will need to be stored, but only when it is thoroughly dry and clean. It should always be stored in a cool, dry place, and in a refrigerator if it is going to be kept for more than about a month. It can also be stored in a freezer, though most breeders do not favour this.

Most hosta seed will remain viable for six months or so stored in the correct conditions, though viability does differ from one variety to another. One notable exception is the seed of large-flowered fragrant varieties, which should be sown within a month of harvesting.

In Britain, seed of streaked varieties should be sown by February or March at the latest, as the growing season is not long enough for plants sown any later to have become strong enough to survive the following winter. This is particularly true of medio-variegated varieties, which are very slow to grow into viable plants. One way of circumventing this problem is to grow the seedlings on in a closed case under daylight fluorescent tubes. Under such conditions they can be kept growing for 24 hours a day until they are large enough to harden off and transfer to less pampered conditions.

Modern hybrid hostas. Left to right: top row, *H.* 'Fragrant Gold', *H.* 'Brim Cup', *H.* 'So Sweet', *H.* 'Mildred Seaver'; middle row, *H.* 'El Capitan', *H.* 'Don Stevens', *H.* 'Bold Edger'; bottom row, *H.* 'Abby', *H.* 'Christmas Tree', *H.* 'Snow Cap', *H.* 'Sea Dream', *H.* 'Bold Ribbons', *H.* 'Wide Brim', *H.* 'Fascination'.

SOWING THE SEED

Seed generally germinates very easily, whether it is sown fresh or taken out of storage. Many people like to raise seed under glass because they feel they have more control over it, but this is really not necessary. Hostas and their seeds are perfectly frost-hardy, and seed can be sown directly into prepared seedbeds in the open garden, preferably in a shaded position. A greater degree of control over pests can be achieved if the seed is sown in cold frames, either directly into the ground or in pots or seed trays (flats). If frost causes the ground to heave, it may need to be firmed down from time to time. Obviously, precautions need to be taken against slugs and snails (see pages 44–6).

Once the seeds have germinated the seedlings need to be kept watered and shaded until they are ready to be pricked out into small pots, an operation which is best carried out when they have four or five true leaves. They can then be set out in nursery rows once they have about 15 leaves. If the rows are spaced 45cm (18in) apart, and the plants are set out 20cm (8in) apart, this will enable them to reach sufficient size for their merits to be assessed.

EVALUATION

The first and most essential quality needed for successful hybridizing is the ability to discard most of the seedlings that have been so carefully raised in order to avoid being swamped with a plethora of second-rate seedlings. The breeder who thinks a young seedling that has no special merit may improve with age is already on the road to ruin, because the probability is that it will not. The chances are that fewer than 5 per cent of seedlings will be worth growing on to maturity and some crosses may yield nothing worthwhile at all.

The art is to have a yardstick against which to measure the seedlings, and that in turn means having a definite aim in mind when making the cross. When breeding for variegation it is possible to make an initial evaluation quite early on,

when the seedlings have about four true leaves. A magnifying glass will usually be needed at this stage to see whether the seedlings are variegated, and how well. The probability is that if no variegation is showing at this stage it will not develop later, so all non-variegated seedlings should be eliminated at this stage, and also all the inferior variegated ones. Unwanted seedlings do not need to be pulled up, which might disturb other seedlings: they should merely be cut through just below the collar, where the leaves and the roots meet. When breeding for flower a larger sample of seedlings should be kept at this stage, since the important evaluation cannot be made until the seedlings flower. At the first flowering it is essential to discard everything that does not match up to the breeding objective.

Seed of streaked pod parents will produce a modest percentage of streaked plants. It is necessary to wait for those plants to settle out into margined or medio-variegated. Reversions to plain colour should again be removed by cutting vertically right through the collar and discarding the unwanted section with its roots. Where the plants remain streaked, they will usually, when of flowering size, produce a future generation of streaked seedlings.

The seedlings that have been retained as having promising variegation should be grown on until they have 15 leaves, when a further purge should be made of those that do not measure up. Those that remain will probably be worth growing on for a further season or two, before discarding those that are not good enough. This business of ruthlessly discarding all but the most desirable is most important, not only because time, energy and even money should not be expended on seedlings that are not worth it, but also because they will occupy the space which is needed to raise future generations of crosses.

The Tokudama and Golden Medallion Groups. Left to right: top row, *H.* 'Aspen Gold', *H.* 'Love Pat', *H.* 'Tokudama Flavocircinalis'; middle row, *H.* 'Buckshaw Blue', *H.* 'Golden Medallion', *H.* 'Little Aurora'; bottom row, *H.* 'Tokudama', *H.* 'Lime Krinkles', *H.* 'Bright Lights', *H.* 'Blue Shadows', *H.* 'Rough Waters'.

ESTABLISHING CRITERIA

It is important to have clear objectives when breeding hostas, as they produce seed in such abundance it is easy to become overwhelmed with a wealth of worthless seedlings. Breeding variegated hostas may not be a sufficient objective in itself, for example; it may be advisable to think as well in terms of increasing the thickness of the leaf, which will reduce the amount of damage done by slugs and snails, or of using relatively sun-tolerant parents to produce relatively more sun-resistant variegated hostas, or of trying to introduce fragrance into hostas of the quality of *H. fluctuans* 'Sagae'. Other desirable breeding lines include attempting to bring the red-dotting on the petioles inherent in some species right up into the leaf – the ultimate objective being hostas with seemingly red leaves – and to breed a race of hostas with branched scapes in tones from palest lavender to deep purple. There is still no first-class pure white-flowered hosta with foliage of the quality of *H. sieboldiana* 'Elegans', and trying to produce one would be another worthwhile objective.

Not all breeding lines are productive, however; for example, crossing dwarf hostas with other dwarf hostas results in hostas of ever-decreasing vigour. Take care to avoid embarking upon such self-defeating programmes.

THE INHERITANCE OF VARIEGATION

Mendelian laws provide a means of predicting the outcome of crosses made for flowers, but they offer no help at all when it comes to variegation, where other rules apply. In the inheritance of variegation it is the pod parent that is dominant and the highest chance of raising variegated hostas comes from using streaked or splashed pod parents. This is not to say that every seedling from a variegated pod will necessarily be variegated, but rather that if the pod is not variegated the chances of obtaining a variegated seedling are very remote indeed. They are remote even where the pollen parent is variegated, so little does the male parent contribute to the inheritance of variegation.

NAMING AND REGISTRATION

It is always tempting to name a new hosta just as soon as it appears to be a worthwhile plant, but this is a temptation to be firmly resisted: there are already well over 1,000 cultivars registered with the International Registration Authority for *Hosta*, and the new plant may in time turn out not to be as good or distinct as first thought. Young hostas, whether they are seedlings or sports, should always be grown on for five or even seven years to establish whether they are stable and really worthwhile. If they are, they may well be worth naming, but there are clearly established criteria in this regard: the hosta must be clearly distinct from all other hostas, it must be uniform and stable in its characteristics and these must remain constant when it is propagated.

If you have raised a hosta which does measure up to these criteria, it probably is worth naming. For details of how to go about this procedure, see Chapter 3.

8
THE GARDEN USES OF HOSTAS

So much have hostas come to the fore in modern gardens that it is difficult to imagine gardening without them. Their contribution is unique. No other hardy plant has such sumptuous and richly coloured foliage, nor is so distinct both in leaf outline and clump shape. Not only do they look good as individual specimens, they also lend themselves to planting in drifts of the same variety, or of mixed varieties. They enhance the hard, sharp-cornered features of buildings and the brick, stonework and paving of gardens as well as being at home in relaxed, unstructured woodland gardens and in the whole gamut of gardens in between. They can be the ultimate adornment of small courtyard or terrace gardens and many flourish in pots, tubs and other containers. There are even miniature species suitable for rock gardens, raised beds or sinks.

The important thing is to choose the right hosta for the right place, for plainly the hostas which in the wild enjoy hot, sunny positions will scarcely survive in shade at the pond- or stream-side or in a bog, while the moisture-lovers will not last long in hot sunny places. Fortunately most hostas have cultural requirements that fall midway between these extremes and are relatively easy to suit in the garden.

SETTING THE SCENE

To a garden designer hostas are merely one genus among myriad plants from which the rich and varied tapestry of a planting may be made, while to a large number of hosta enthusiasts the hostas are everything: nothing else matters. The best hosta plantings are probably made by gardeners who hold views somewhere between these extremes, paying enough attention to the overall design to set the hostas off to perfection, just as a jeweller, while recognizing the intrinsic beauty of a jewel, knows that the value will be infinitely increased if it is provided with a beautiful setting.

The best way to create a setting in which to display hostas is to work on the winter shape of the garden, for the ultimate test of a garden is what it looks like bereft of flowers and foliage on a dull, damp, grey day. If the garden can pass that acid test with honours it will look superb in summer, the winter shape filled out with the colours of leaves and blooms. Such structural plantings are not merely aesthetic; they modify the microclimate, casting shade, breaking the force of the wind and encouraging high atmospheric humidity. They also divide space into smaller, more manageable compartments in which hostas and other plants can be composed into pictures.

The structural planting should be subdued and should not compete with the hostas, though a few deciduous shrubs such as *Hamamelis mollis* or *Edgworthia papyfera* can be the stars in the winter when the hostas are dormant. In general, the winter shape is best composed of evergreens such as *Viburnum tinus* and *Camellia japonica* with its glossy leaves, as well as the occasional conifer. With rhododendrons it is necessary to choose the effects with care: the most jazzy of rhodendron flowers can however be cooled down with an underplanting of green-leaved

hostas, while the quietest of rhododendrons may emphasize the glorious colouring or variegation of hosta leaves.

Most hostas form rounded domes of foliage, so it is important to use supporting plants that are quite different in shape. Fastigiate shrubs and conifers such as *Taxus baccata* 'Fastigiata' and *Juniperus virginiana* 'Skyrocket' will provide a vertical accent, while *Viburnum tomentosum*, though deciduous, creates a strongly horizontal emphasis, as do *Cornus controversa* and *C. alternifolia*.

It is also important to vary the size, shape and form of the leaves of supporting plants. *Azara microphylla* and *Lonicera nitida* both have conspicuously small leaves, while those of *Fatsia japonica*, *Viburnum rhytidophyllum* and most evergreen magnolias are conspicuously large.

The Tardiana Group. Left to right: top row, *H.* 'Halcyon', *H.* 'Blue Diamond', *H.* 'Blue Danube', *H.* 'Happiness'; middle row, *H.* 'Blue Skies', *H.* 'Harmony', *H.* 'Hadspen Heron'; bottom row, *H.* 'Blue Dimples', *H.* 'Blue Moon', *H.* 'Hadspen Hawk', *H.* 'Dorset Blue', *H.* 'Blue Wedgwood'.

Shrubs with compound leaves, such as *Mahonia* 'Charity', create a different effect.

If trees are needed to cast shade, deep-rooted trees such as oaks are the most satisfactory. A problem with trees is that they cast too little shade to begin with and too much later. It is always worth considering whether it might be better to use structures such as colonnades, pergolas or arbours to support climbers to cast shade rather than trees since then the area of shade can be predetermined.

Most hostas mix happily with most other hostas, though as a rule of thumb, yellow-leaved hostas and those with yellow variegation will take more sun while those with a white variegation need most shade. Hostas with glaucous blue or grey leaves will lose their glaucous bloom if grown in too much sun or in shade which is too dense. Many hostas will grow in more sun if there is sufficient moisture available at their roots. All

60

hostas flower better in sun than in the shade, and hostas grown for their flowers rather than their foliage should always be planted in more rather than less sun, though too much will usually damage their leaves.

As a rule the tallest plants should be placed at the back of the border, the smaller at the front, and this applies as much to the supporting shrubs as to the hostas themselves. However, it creates more interest if just occasionally a large shrub or hosta is put near the front. In deep borders where it is possible to use hostas as large as H. 'Green Acres' or H. 'Colossal' at the back, with medium-sized hostas in the middle and small hostas at the front, it may be found best to plant the small hostas in drifts or groups of threes or fives to maintain a visual balance.

The foreground of a planting – that is to say, the place where the planting meets the lawn or other contrasting surface – generally draws the eye more strongly than the rest of the planting. If a rhythm and pattern is created here by repeating particular plants or groupings of plants at more or less regular intervals it will help to hold the planting together in the mind's eye, no matter how disparate the rest of the planting. Such rhythms are most easily established by using plants with very dark leaves such as *Viburnum davidii* or grey- or blue-leaved hostas such as *H.* 'Halcyon' or, on a larger scale, hostas of the Elegans Group.

WOODLAND GARDENS

Hostas are often grown in woodland conditions because the shade cast by the trees ensures that the leaves remain in good condition far longer than they would were they to be grown without shade. The disadvantage of woodland is that the ground often becomes very dry in summer and before planting some thought should be given as to how the hostas will be watered. If it is necessary to install underground irrigation pipes, this is best done before planting begins. Some consideration should also be given to the density of the woodland and to the amount of shade cast by the trees. Hostas grow best at the edge of woodland or in

H. 'Gold Standard' at Bosvigo House in Truro, Cornwall, with *Cornus controversa* 'Variegata'.

woodland glades or clearings where the shade is not too deep. It is often necessary to thin the trees and to raise the canopy by removing lower branches. However, raising the canopy may produce the odd effect of the woodland consisting mainly of relatively thin stems all pointing straight up to the sky and may also let in destructive winds. Both problems can be solved by planting an understorey of shrubs and small trees. Stewartias and halesias are ideal for this, as are the Japanese and other ornamental maples, as well as some magnolias. To cut down the flow of wind through the woodland a structural planting mainly of evergreen shrubs is usually necessary. Many hollies are ideal, as are viburnums, aucubas (especially the narrow-leaved forms), skimmias and such deciduous shrubs as corylopsis, fothergilla, summer-sweet (*Clethra alnifolia*) and disanthus. Rhododendrons may also be suitable, especially those with distinct foliage, such as *R. makinoi*, *R. yakushimanun*, *R. smirnowii* and *R. hyperythrum*, with rolled leaves and rusty indumentum, *R. orbiculare* and *R. williamsianum*, with round leaves, or *R. falconeri* and *R. macabeanum*, which have huge, almost tropical leaves.

Woodland areas are among the most inviting of places to plant. Since they are often larger than manicured gardens they tempt the gardener to plant in bold drifts and groups, often following the contours of the land. This rather restful style is particularly well-suited to woodlands. While most hostas grow into dense, rounded mounds, there are quite a number that naturally grow into drifts or seed themselves without losing their identity. *H. clausa* is stoloniferous in all its forms. *H. c.* 'Normalis' is the form whose flowers open normally; they are deep lilac-purple and among the best in the genus. *H.* 'Tapis Vert', another *H. clausa* selection, is, as its name suggests, a green carpeter. *H.* 'Birchwood Parky's Gold', with its greyish-yellow heart-shaped leaves and pleasing lavender flowers, is another that spreads, as does the muted, yellow-margined *H.* 'Fool's Gold'. Several variegated hostas with strap- or lance-shaped leaves soon make good ground cover: *H.* 'Resonance' is excellent for this purpose, as are *H.* 'Bold Ribbons', *H.* 'Neat Splash', *H.* 'Yellow Splash', *H.* 'Yellow Splash Rim' and *H.* 'Ground Master'. Many forms and selections of *H. sieboldii* both run and seed themselves. *H. s.* 'Alba', with white flowers, is particularly effective in woodland, as is *H.* 'Purple Lady Finger', whose deep purple flowers never open, and *H.* 'Tall Twister', also with dark flowers. *H.* 'Lancifolia' is another with narrow leaves and dark flowers that spreads quite quickly, making a dense ground cover of glossy leaves. Similar effects can also be created by using clump-forming hostas in drifts. Larger clump-forming hostas such as *H.* 'Big Mama' or *H.* 'Krossa Regal' can be used as specimens in the midst of these drifts.

Having established this style it is usually best to continue it in the supporting planting. Most of the plants that seem to be the natural garden companions of hostas also lend themselves to planting in drifts: ferns, epimediums, tiarellas, × *heucherella*, heucheras, primulas, liriopes, sedges and grasses.

The whole scene will take on an extra dimension if a series of pictures is planted. The gardener might, for example, make a late autumn picture using *H.* 'Tardiflora' and *Saxifraga fortunei* (preferably in one of its red-leaved forms) together with some liriopes, all of which flower at the same time. A spring group might use viridescent yellows such as *H.* 'Fortunei Albopicta', *H.* 'Golden Haze', and green and yellow mottled *H.* 'Nancy Lindsay' in the midst of a drift of grape hyacinths (*Muscari*) backed up by drifts of *Carex elata* 'Bowles' Golden Sedge', *Millium effusum* 'Aureum' or with low-growing yellow- or blue-flowered rhododendrons behind.

Other plants that lend themselves readily to mixing with hostas in a woodland setting include martagon lilies (*Lilium martagon*) and ginger lilies (*Hedychium*), arisaemas, toad lilies (*Tricyrtis*), lily-of-the-valley (*Convallaria majalis*), columbines (*Aquilegia*), Solomon's seal (*Polygonatum*) and the annual smyrniums, astilbes (where there is enough moisture) and ajugas, as well as sedges and woodrushes whose narrow leaves emphasize the sheer width of hosta leaves.

WATERSIDE PLANTING

Most of us expect the vegetation at the water's edge to grow more lushly than vegetation elsewhere, because that is what happens in nature. However, the ground surrounding a pond that has been created using a liner is usually no wetter than the soil anywhere else in the garden.

Most of the hostas that grow in the wild in very wet ground such as *H. alismifolia* and *H. atropurpurea* are extremely rare in cultivation or difficult to grow, or else too small to achieve a luxuriant waterside effect, while those hostas which best create a lush appearance will mostly not thrive in places where their roots are permanently wet. The strategy is therefore either to plant the hostas on mounds at the water's edge, or to plant them a little further away from the water where the soil is drier, so that the crowns are dry but the roots have access to plenty of water. Which are used will depend on whether the planting is in sun or shade.

In sun most of the best are hybrids derived from *H. plantaginea*, such as the green-leaved,

H. 'Mira' by the lily pond at Hadspen House with white Siberian irises and *Gunnera manicata* and *Astilboïdes tabularis* behind.

white-flowered H. 'Royal Standard', the lilac-tinted, white-flowered H. 'Honeybells' and the lavender-flowered H. 'Flower Power', all of which are reasonably priced enough to group in large drifts. Similarly easily available, if a yellow-edged hosta is wanted, is H. 'Fortunei Aureomarginata', which is vigorous enough to clothe long stretches of a sunny streamside and bears its tall spires of lavender flowers for weeks on end.

Moisture-loving irises such as *Iris laevigata*, *I. sibirica* and *I. pseudacorus*, with their stiffly upright, narrowly sword-shaped leaves, make an excellent foil to the rounded shapes of the hostas, while astilbes with their lacy foliage and fluffy flowers create a soft haze which throws the well-defined foliage of the hostas into even sharper focus. Daylilies, now available in an ever-wider range of colours, will also flourish at the waterside. As a rule of thumb the planting of bog and

waterside areas is usually most effective when it is done in bold groups and drifts, with the plants set quite close together, in the way that bog plants tend to grow in the wild.

In shade the range of hostas and other plants that can be grown beside water is far greater. Indeed, most hostas will be happy in such a situation, though many yellow-leaved sorts will remain chartreuse-green rather than yellow. Many large hostas look particularly good in such situations: for example, the various forms of H. *montana* and H. *sieboldiana* 'Elegans', with drifts of hostas with very tall flower scapes behind them, such as H. 'Krossa Regal', the dignified H. *nigrescens*, the showy H. 'Tall Boy' and, tallest of all, *H.* 'Tenryu', with its 2.1m (7ft) spikes. In the foreground, the picture can be completed with drifts of smaller hostas such as *H.* 'Undulata' in almost any of its forms; they all seem happy planted just above the waterline and hostas with strap-shaped leaves such as *H. rectifolia* 'Chionea' or *H.* 'Neat Splash Rim' are stoloniferous and will soon form long drifts.

There is a wealth of moisture-loving plants to grow with hostas in moist shade. Others with bold but contrasting foliage include the ornamental rhubarbs (*Rheum*), which have leaves as large as or larger than those of the hostas but often tinted red or maroon and with jagged edges, and rodgersias, which have equally bold, lobed foliage of varying textures in shades of green and dark red. Much finer foliage can be provided by ferns such as the ostrich fern (*Matteuccia struthiopteris*) and the sensitive fern (*Onoclea sensibilis*), which are only happy in very wet conditions, and by some bamboos which also like it wet, *Fargesia nitida* and *F. spathacea* being particularly good: both are densely clump-forming and make fountain-shaped plants. The exotic South American chusqueas enjoy equally wet conditions but are stiffly upright. Candelabra primulas make a lovely show when massed on the wetter ground between the hostas and the water's edge and flower for several weeks at midsummer, as do the moisture-loving Bellingham hybrid lilies which follow on in flower.

The more obviously structured the waterside planting the more suitable are the hostas with brightly coloured or variegated leaves. A charming cameo of the brilliant acid-yellow bamboo *Arundinaria viridistriata* or the sedge *Carex elata* 'Bowles' Golden Sedge' planted next to burgundy-pink *Rodgersia pinnata* 'Superba' with *Hosta* 'Big Daddy' to echo the knubbly leaf of the rodgersia, grown beside paving and a formal pool, would illustrate this point. For a wholly glaucous grey effect in a boggy border, the low-growing, soft, furry or ribbed leaves of *Salix lanata* or *S. helvetica* nicely pick up the glaucous tones of *Hosta* 'Rough Waters' or *H.* 'Pearl Lake'.

Water features do not have to be large to be effective. In a courtyard garden a circular pool no more than 45cm (18in) is enough to draw the eye, and certainly excuse enough to grow a hosta or two. In such a situation the hostas would probably be best growing in pots (see page 71).

SUNNY BORDERS

As little as 10 years ago a hosta border in the sun would not even have been contemplated because there were only two or three hostas that could be grown successfully and all had green leaves and white or near-white flowers. Now there is not only a sufficient number to make it worthwhile but also a sufficient variety to make it interesting.

The starting point for these has been the sun-loving *H. plantaginea* from China, which is unfortunately one of the most difficult hostas to breed from. Both Paul Aden and Kevin Vaughan, who set out to raise hostas with larger, more interesting flowers, used *H. plantaginea* to put an infusion of new genes into the process and found that when crossed with normally shade-loving hostas they not only became tolerant of sun but also inherited some of the exotic, heady fragrance of *H. plantaginea*.

Previously unthought-of late-summer effects can be achieved with these new hostas in the sun. At the foot of a sunny wall they can have an almost tropical appearance, especially the larger sorts, when grown with the spiky foliage of phormiums, yuccas and kniphofias, the strap-shaped leaves of agapanthus and daylilies, and the grass-like foliage of crocosmias. Such plantings will provide not only colour but also interest and shape in the border at a time when more traditional border plantings are past their best. The garden in late summer has quite a different light from earlier, and more exotic plantings seem quite in keeping with even the most tranquil of summer gardens.

The gardener can exploit not only the tropical mien of the leaves of these hostas but also their colouring and that of the other plants in the scheme. For example, the pink and greyish-bronze *Phormium* 'Sundowner' and the clear pink daylilies *Hemerocallis* 'Edna Spalding' and *H.* 'Millie Schlumpf' might be used with the creamy-white margined *Hosta* 'Summer Fragrance', whose excellent deep mauve, fragrant flowers would pick up the pink of the daylilies, and the green-leaved lightly fragrant *H.* 'Sweet Susan', whose lavender-pink flowers are often remontant in hot weather. The sprays of pink *Tritonia rubrolucens* would also fit in here with grey-blue *Agapanthus* 'Blue Moon' and *A.* 'Superstar', caerulean *Elymus hispidus* and the dull metallic blue of *Panicum virgatum* 'Heavy Metal'.

Still hotter effects could be created using some of the yellow-leaved hostas which colour best in sun, such as *H.* 'August Moon', *H.* 'Fragrant Gold', *H.* 'Midas Touch', *H.* 'Super Bowl' and *H.* 'Golden Medallion', their matt leaves perhaps contrasted with the glossier green leaves of *H.* 'Invincible' or

the satiny-textured *H.* 'Sweetie', which is chartreuse to yellow with a white margin. These could be mixed with clumps of yellow-variegated yuccas such as *Yucca filamentosa* 'Bright Edge' or *Y. flaccida* 'Golden Sword', or with yellow-striped phormiums such as the upright *Phormium tenax* 'Radiance' or the recurving *P.* 'Yellow Wave', and with crocosmias such as *Crocosmia* × *crocosmiiflora* 'Solfaterre', *C.* 'Dusky Maiden', *C.* 'Star of the East' and the marmalade-coloured

The Yellow Hosta Walk at Apple Court with *Persicaria filiformis* 'Painter's Palette' (front), *H.* 'Sum and Substance' and *H.* 'Gold Standard'; *Jasminum officinale* 'Aureum' and *Fuchsia magellanica* 'Aureomarginata' twine up the brick pillar.

C. × *crocosmiiflora* 'Emily Mackenzie'. Kniphofias such as the sultry *Kniphofia* 'Nancy's Red' or *K.* 'Atlanta' would complete the picture.

HOSTAS IN A WHITE GARDEN

Hosta plantaginea 'Grandiflora' and *H.* 'Royal Standard' will provide scented white flowers for a sunny white garden, the latter flowering from July and the much larger-flowered *H. plantaginea* 'Grandiflora', the August lily of cottage gardens, from mid-August given the heat of a south wall; the lily-like fragrance becomes more pervasive as evening approaches.

In our own white garden we also use hostas for their foliage interest, removing the flowers if they are other than pure white. *H.* 'Francee' and *H.* 'Patriot', with their cleanly defined white margins and dark green leaves, make a substantial contribution to the whiteness of the garden and we grow them in the shade of *Sambucus nigra* 'Pulverulenta' and glossy green-leaved *Parasyringa sempervirens*, a lovely contrast of leaf size. Several glaucous blue-leaved hostas in deeper shade provide patches of blue-grey to balance the Mediterranean greys that are so easily grown in the sun elsewhere in the white garden. *H.* 'Nonsuch', a huge, furrowed glaucous *H. montana* seedling, even more majestic in size and habit than *H.* 'Snowden' and bluer in colour, is outstanding here, especially as its long-leaning scapes of flower are virtually white. So is stiff and stately *H.* 'Bold Ruffles,' whose flowers are, alas, mauve and must be removed. We have found that the perfect small tree to provide the necessary shade is the mottled, late-to-leaf *Catalpa ducluxii* 'Pulverulenta', giving the hostas plenty of light when they most need it to put on good leaf. One anomalous hosta here in front of the border is the invalidly named *Hosta kikutii* 'Albo-stricta', whose leaning-scaped white flowers revel in sun for most of the day. Its companions in flower in late July

and August are *Astrantia major* ssp. *involucrata* 'Shaggy' and *Phlox paniculata* 'Fujiyama', all three plants lapping up moisture.

These hostas all contribute more than merely their leaf or flower colour: the size and opulence of their leaves emphasizes the contrasting leaf shapes of the other plants in a white garden, a most noticeable combination being the tiny, shiny pointed leaves of *Sarcococca confusa* and the elegant, thread-like foliage of *Miscanthus sinensis* 'Morning Light'. The tiered, shrub-like mound of *Hosta* 'Blue Angel' grows in the shelter and shade of the white-margined *Aralia elata*, whose huge tripinnate leaves do not unfurl until late May when the hosta leaves start to need protection.

SHADED BORDERS

The best shaded borders in which to grow hostas are those at the foot of a north wall (in the northern hemisphere). Hosta leaves look wonderful when planted against or near walls of whatever

A beautiful blending of variegated and plain-leaved hostas displayed in the Pergola Garden at Cleave House, Devon.

A piece of classical statuary at Sun House in Long Melford, Suffolk, is complemented by ferns and *H.* 'Blue Diamond'.

disadvantage of walls is that they may cast a rain shadow, and the taller the wall the more of a problem this can be, so some provision needs to be made to ensure sufficient moisture: seep hoses are ideal in this situation.

Not all walls are beautiful, and it sometimes helps to break them up visually with a foundation planting of trees, shrubs or climbers. Not only will such planting provide a setting to show off the hostas, it will break up the flow of wind along the wall and this can be most important because when wind hits a wall obliquely, which it usually does, it tends to accelerate.

At ground level evergreen ferns such as *Polystichum setiferum* and its forms can help to provide a setting for the hostas, as can both the Christmas and the sword ferns, *P. munitum* and *P. acrostichoïdes*, which look charming with snowdrops and help to cover their dying foliage. Deciduous ferns can also help to set the stage, especially the silver-grey Japanese painted fern *Athyrium niponicum* var. *pictum* and the claret-midribbed *Athyrium otophorum* var. *okanum*, while the delicately fern-like woodland rue, *Boenninghausenia albiflora*, thrives on retentive soil and light shade and looks marvellous enveloping either *Hosta* 'Francee' or *H.* 'Patriot' in the soft haze of its dark-green foliage.

Among the best companions for hostas in the shade are the dicentras, pulmonarias and heucheras. The mulberry-coloured lockets and pale glaucous grey lacy leaves of *Dicentra* 'Bacchanal' and *D.* 'Luxuriant' accentuate the intense frosty blue hues of *Hosta* 'Betcher's Blue' and *H.* 'Blue Vision'. The pulmonarias, with their hairy, rough-textured leaves, enjoy just the same conditions of dappled shade and well-worked, moisture-retentive soil as hostas, and their intricately marked leaves make the glaucous-blue foliage of hostas such as *H.* 'Blue Skies' or *H.* 'Devon Blue' look positively restful. We grow the glossy spinach green *H. ventricosa* with the

construction. The great advantage of walls (and indeed of fences) is that although they cast shade the hostas are still open to the sky above, which means that they are growing in good light. The green-leaved, evenly spotted *Pulmonaria saccharata* 'Leopard' in the shade of *Cornus controversa* 'Variegata', its silver-edged delicate leaves picking up the silver spots of the pulmonaria. More dramatic would be the silver-encrusted leaves of *Pulmonaria saccharata* 'Cotton Cool', or of *P. s.* 'Majestée' from France, with *Hosta* 'Blue Wedgwood', or the huge silvery-leaved *Pulmonaria* 'Excalibur' with drifts of tiny *Hosta* 'Blue Moon'. Little groups of pink, yellow or white flowered erythroniums, flowering with the pulmonarias, would add a lift to any of these schemes.

Thanks largely to the efforts of Dan Heims and his Terra Nova Nursery, heucheras are rapidly becoming almost as collectable as hostas. We particularly like growing the marbled silvery-burgundy-leaved heucheras such as *Heuchera americana* 'Persian Carpet' and *H. a.* 'Pewter Veil' with blue-leaved hostas such as *Hosta* 'Buckshaw Blue', *H.* 'Silvery Slugproof', *H.* 'Big Daddy' or *H.* 'True Blue', while the silvery-mottled, scalloped green-leaved *Heuchera americana* 'Ecomagnififolia' and *H. sanguinea* 'Jack Frost' seem to go better with white-variegated hostas such as *Hosta* 'Ginko Craig' and *H.* 'Gloriosa'. There are several bugles (*Ajuga reptans* forms) which pick up and echo the leaf colours of the heucheras, in particular *Ajuga reptans* 'Burgundy Glow' and *A. r.* 'Delight' (a delight also to lurking slugs), which are useful as a ground cover among the heucheras and the hostas. Some of the smaller astilbes, such as *Astilbe* 'Perkeo' with its intricate, beetroot-coloured foliage, are in keeping with hostas of the Tardiana Group both in colour and size, and the picture could be completed with dark green, scallop-leaved *Asarum europaeum* and the long-flowering *Viola* 'Maggie Mott'.

On the yellow side of the spectrum a magical effect has been achieved in a small town garden where space is at a premium. A narrow, 3m (10ft) long border against a white wall has been closely planted with *Hosta* 'Fortunei Aureomarginata', over which is growing a laburnum on a one-sided trellis arch attached to the house. The drooping ropes of yellow laburnum exactly pick up the colour in the variegation of the hosta leaves. This arresting picture is positioned at the end of a blue and yellow garden designed to peak in early summer. Similar effects could be achieved using white-flowered wisteria with white-margined *Hosta* 'Francee' or *H.* 'Carol' and blue-mauve wisteria, underplanted with *H.* 'Blue Shadows' or *H.* 'Blue Vision', the wisteria coming into leaf in time to protect the hostas from scorching.

Still on the yellow and blue theme, soft yellow-leaved hostas such as *Hosta* 'Piedmont Gold' and *H.* 'Fragrant Gold' with shade-loving *Heuchera* 'Snow Storm' or *H.* 'Taff's Joy', yellow cottage tulips, *Roscoea cautleyoïdes* 'Kew Beauty' and *Astrantia major* 'Sunningdale Variegated' make a cheerful late spring scene, contrasting well with some of the early-flowering hardy geraniums such as deep mauve-blue *Geranium* × *magnificum* or *G.* 'Spinners'. Shiny-leaved *Hosta* 'Bold Ribbons' or *H.* 'Neat Splash Rim', can be emphasized by the linear-leaved sedge *Carex morrowii* 'Fisher's Form', their colouring intensified with a scattering of light powder-blue *Muscari* 'Baby's Breath'; or try blue and white *Omphalodes cappadocica* 'Starry Eyes' with the brilliant searing yellow early foliage of *Hosta* 'Fortunei Aurea' before it dulls to a softer green. Just as lovely an effect can be created with the deeper blue of *Muscari armeniacum* 'Heavenly Blue' with soft sage green *Hosta pycnophylla* or huge-leaved *H.* 'Green Sheen'. *Muscari* (grape hyacinths) make excellent companions for young hosta foliage, their dying leaves increasingly disguised by the maturing hosta leaves.

There is a tendency for plantings in the shade to be dominated by rounded shapes such as those of hostas, if only because there are relatively few plants of vertical habit which thrive in shade. Astilbes, with their upright spikes of flowers, are one obvious solution, but only if it is relatively damp. Irises provide another, especially *Iris foetidissima* in its various forms, the 1.2cm (4ft) tall, white-flowered *I. orientalis* and the shorter *I. spuria*; most forms of *I. sibirica* will take some shade, but not too much. Another possibility is to use foxgloves, which are nothing if not vertical, and Japanese anemones, whose flowering stems are again strongly vertical.

COURTYARDS

H. 'Bressingham Blue' growing with wild fumitory outside the Old Kennels at Nunwick, near Hexham, Northumberland.

Because hostas look so good growing against buildings and architectural or hard landscape features, courtyards and terraces can provide ideal settings for them. However, the gardener needs to be discriminating in the choice of hostas since they will be looked at minutely and frequently. Brightly variegated hostas might well create an inappropriately restless feeling, as would a great variety of different sorts of vegetation. It might also be tempting to plant larger numbers of smaller hostas, rather than fewer larger ones; again this might create a restless feeling rather than a calm one. Restraint is the essence of good

planting, and the effects that can be achieved with four or five different sorts of vegetation in a small courtyard will be far more satisfying than those created with a multitude of different plants. Indeed, planting a courtyard with nothing but hostas may be the most pleasing way of all, and a single *Hosta* 'Yellow River' or *H.* 'Devon Giant' better than a dozen lesser ones. Plant *H. fluctuans* 'Sagae' in an unpainted wooden barrel, the plainness of its container setting off to perfection the exquisite shape and poise of its strongly variegated leaves.

The best forms of hostas to grow in small courtyards are generally those with plain leaves. Among the best of the green-leaved forms for this purpose are *H.* 'Green Acres', which grows waist-high and 1.2m (4ft) across, its huge, deeply corrugated green leaves hanging almost vertically from the tips of the petioles, or the much smaller *H.* 'Invincible', whose stiff, olive-green leaves are held nearly horizontally and appear almost polished. Grey or blue-leaved hostas may be preferable, since these colours have a receding effect, making small spaces seem larger. First choices in this case would be *H. sieboldiana* 'Elegans', *H.* 'Big Daddy', *H.* 'Snowden' or, on a smaller scale, *H.* 'Halcyon', *H.* 'Tokudama' or *H.* 'Buckshaw Blue'. In some contexts, perhaps depending on the colour of the walls, it might be right to use yellow-leaved hostas such as *H.* 'Golden Medallion' or the larger *H.* 'Zounds'.

In sunny courtyards the fragrant hybrids of *H. plantaginea* will flourish, the enclosing walls trapping the exotic scents of the flowers. Their bold leaves would contrast well with the small, complex leaves of *Jasminum officinale*.

TERRACES

Terraces are essentially rooms without walls. What gives them this feeling is that they are paved underfoot, this paving establishing a clearly delimited area, the analogy with a room being further emphasized if the terrace is furnished, if only in summer, with chairs and tables.

As with courtyards, the building materials of which the terrace is made, as well as any building behind it, make it an ideal place to grow hostas,

In the Old Kennels at Nunwick, hostas reach their full potential. The walls are draped with *Erinus alpinus*.

A thriving specimen of *H.* 'Fortunei Albopicta' at Kirkley Hall in Northumberland, showing how the leaves fade from their spring colour to summer green.

but the particular varieties chosen will depend upon whether the terrace is in the sun or in shade. The range of hostas grown can be greatly increased if they are also grown in pots or large containers on the terrace (see below).

CONSERVATORIES

Conservatories are par excellence the place to grow *H. plantaginea* and its various forms and modern fragrant hybrids. It was Gertrude Jekyll who first advocated growing hostas as conservatory plants. Her practice was to grow them in large Italian terracotta pots to hide what she termed the 'common flowerpots' ranged behind. As companions to the hostas she would grow in nearby pots the male fern *Dryopteris filix-mas* and aspidistras as well as such flowering plants as lilies, as much for their fragrance as their flowers, and hydrangeas.

POTS, TUBS AND CONTAINERS

Hostas and pots go extraordinarily well together, the rounded, domed shape of the hostas seeming to be the natural complement to the shape of a typical pot or container. In addition, many gardeners and flower arrangers find that they can grow their hostas in pots or other containers without them suffering as much damage as is done to them by slugs and snails when they are planted in the ground.

As much care should be given to choosing the pots or containers as to choosing the plants to go in them. Since the containers are playing only a

supporting role they should be as simple as possible, especially if variegated-leaf hostas are to be their occupants. Terracotta and stone pots keep the plant's root system cooler, but as they are porous the moisture evaporates faster. If plain-leaved hostas are to be grown, the containers can be more highly patterned or decorated – the glaucous blue-leaved forms look stunning in dark green or blue glazed oriental pots. If a number of pots are grouped together, they look better in the same style (though perhaps in different sizes), especially if an assortment of hostas is to be grown in them; a miscellany of pots planted with a miscellany of hostas tends to look unrestful. Matching hostas in matching pots can be sited to great effect along a wall, at the head of a flight of steps or round a formal pool.

If formal wooden tubs or *caisses* are to be used, thought must be given to their colouring. Very often these containers are painted white, but white, as the most luminous of all colours, will draw the eye more strongly than any hosta that could be grown in it, thus defeating the object (unless of course the *caisse* rather than the hosta is the star). Natural wood colours, which tend to fade to an ashen grey, are preferable, though sombre greens run them a close second.

The question then arises as to whether it is better to grow the hostas in the pots themselves, or to treat the pots as *jardinières* or *cache pots*, the hostas actually being grown in plastic pots of a slightly smaller size slipped inside. One disadvantage with the latter method is that the space between the pots provides an ideal hiding and breeding place for slugs and snails. However, the problem with growing hostas in precious pots is that hostas usually increase in size rapidly and if at all vigorous may actually break the pot or fill it so well that the pot gets broken in an effort to get the plant out.

9

GROWING HOSTAS FOR EXHIBITION

Richard Ford

The same criteria apply to growing hostas for exhibition as to growing them just for enjoyment. All the hostas that we grow for our 20 shows each year are in pots. This gives us greater control over the growth and condition of the plants than those grown in the open garden. It does not preclude the selection of a plant from the garden for transfer to a pot for showing, but this is not practical where a wide selection and a large number of plants are required.

Most hostas grow well in pots, although some of the Tardiana Group, some *H.* 'Tokudama' forms and some forms of *H. sieboldiana* do not always perform as well as others. Within these constraints we aim to grow a wide range of varieties, including as many new ones as possible, because:

1 Variations in the weather will favour certain varieties over others.

2 The foliage of some will be better than others.

3 We don't like to force varieties for early shows, but some do accept this more readily.

4 Some individual plants can be exhibited over and over again, but others (particularly those with glaucous leaves) can only be used for a single show.

5 A few varieties are particularly attractive to pests. For example, we find that adult vine weevils just will not leave alone our *H.* 'Spritzer' and *H.* 'Green Fountain'. Fortunately we never have trouble with the larvae.

6 Accommodation in the nursery and transport to the show have to be borne in mind, so we don't go overboard on the largest varieties.

It is essential to exhibit plants which are mature, well-grown and well-balanced. With dwarf and medium-sized varieties this is relatively easy and can be achieved by growing them in pots of 3 litre (3qt US) volume. With large varieties a well-balanced plant cannot be grown in a pot of less than 5 litres (5^1/$_2$qt US) and more usually a 7.5 or 12 litre (2 or 3^1/$_2$gal US) pot is required. For all these we use standard round black plastic pots. Occasionally we grow larger plants in correspondingly bigger pots, but then we use terracotta. However, prospective exhibitors should remember that the bigger the pot, the heavier it is to lift and carry and the more space it takes up.

Well-grown plants do not appear over a single season. We select good-looking, typical plants from our sales stock when they are still in 0.5–1.5 litre (1–3^1/$_4$pt US) pots. These are potted up through increasing pot sizes over two to three years. Once they have achieved a satisfactory size and are threatening to outgrow their container, we split the plant into two or three equal-sized pieces and repot in the same size pot. This brings us a surplus and some plants are sold after the majority of our shows.

We do all our hosta potting from the end of October to the end of December. Apart from any other considerations, it means that we can ensure that any vine weevil larvae and slugs and their eggs are removed from the growing medium at the most appropriate time.

Many widely different composts, from loam-based to soilless, are recommended for hostas.

We have not tried them all, but I favour a peat-based compost and, within reason, we use whatever manufacturer's product is best priced at the time. A coarse compost, on the acid side of pH7, with a moderate nutrient level is best. To this we add about 10 per cent in volume of grit. This gives a bit of weight to the pot, making it less liable to topple over, and also improves the drainage so that the compost does not become slimy or sour. We also add a controlled-release fertilizer, usually 'Ficote' or 'Osmocote', which releases nutrients over a 12-month period. We do not believe in the need for the very complex mixes recommended by some and nor do our hostas receive any further fertilizer treatment – our results testify that neither is necessary.

All our hostas for exhibition are grown in net-sided tunnels covered with white polythene. Some of our tunnels are shaded for part of the day by trees and therefore we allocate hosta varieties to individual tunnels on the basis of the light intensity required for the best plant growth and leaf colour. They are further divided according to the method of watering. Most have overhead irrigation, but not the glaucous-leaved varieties –

these are all watered individually directly into the pots, using a hand lance.

Finally, slugs: all our tunnels are completely cleared annually and swept through to remove resident slugs. The other treatment required – mainly for insurance – is the application of a few slug pellets based on methiocarb (not harmful to birds, frogs or hedgehogs when used as directed) to each pot just as the new shoots are emerging in early spring. During the summer we also have slug and vine weevil patrols at dusk.

There are those that recommend talking to the plants. We don't talk to them, but I do recommend looking at them daily. If trouble threatens, counter-measures can quickly be taken.

Together with his wife Mary, **Richard Ford** runs Park Green Nurseries at Stowmarket in Suffolk, specializing in hostas. He is Hon. Editor of the *Bulletin of the British Hosta & Hemerocallis Society*.

H. 'Sum and Substance' dominating the foreground of Park Green Nurseries' exhibit at the BBC Gardeners' World Live Show, 1995.

10

HOSTA COLLECTIONS

One of the basic urges of most gardeners is to collect, and since hostas are among the most collectable of garden plants many excellent collections in different parts of the world have come into being over the years. However, many of these collections now have added point and purpose due to the activities of the National Council for the Conservation of Plants and Gardens (NCCPG).

The NCCPG was founded in Great Britain in 1978 as a consequence of a growing awareness that many plants that had once been grown in gardens could no longer be found. Its prime aim was to prevent more garden plants from becoming extinct. To do this it was first necessary to establish what plants are actually being grown in gardens, and this led to the establishment of National Reference Collections of all the major horticultural genera in Britain. An essential part of the work of every collection holder is to document the source and true identity of every plant, which often means obtaining from many different sources all the plants in cultivation under the same name, a technique which is most revealing. Similar work is now being done by collection holders in other countries which makes these collections a vital living reference resource, with access for the public, and there is now much co-operation between the collection holders in Great Britain and abroad. In Britain there are four designated National Hosta Reference Collections.

LEEDS CITY COUNCIL PARKS DEPARTMENT

The Collection of Large-leaved Species and Cultivars is held under the curatorship of Sam Hicken of the Parks and Leisure Department. It was designated a National Reference Collection in 1987 and contains over 200 species and cultivars. The curator at the time felt that with the large amount of land he had under his control it would be prudent to grow hostas which would be in scale with the large plantings he envisaged. The hostas are growing at Golden Acre Park, an area of some 55ha (137 acres) at Bramhope, 9.5km (6 miles) north-west of the city of Leeds, West Yorkshire. It lies at an altitude of 120m (394ft) above sea level. The soil is thin and acid overlying sandstone rock on the hillside, and a heavy acid loam overlying clay on the low-lying ground. The average rainfall is 750mm (30in).

The hostas are planted along the edges of the ponds and the streamsides, along the woodland walks and in the hardy plant borders. More hostas will also be planted in association with hemerocallis and phlox from the other National Reference Collections held in Leeds, together with primulas, astilbes and irises. It is felt that by planting the hosta collection around the park in association with other plants, rather than altogether in one particular area, more interest and diversity will be created for visitors. The park is open to the public daily.

APPLE COURT

Apple Court lies about 1.6km (1 mile) from the south coast of Hampshire, at about 30ft (9m) above sea level. The garden is sheltered by 2.4m (8ft) walls and even further protected from southerly gales by the Isle of Wight. However, much of the rain from the south is dissipated on the hills of the Isle of Wight so the necessary moisure for our hostas has to be supplemented by a heavy watering programme. We have also planted many internal hedges which are now giving us the necessary warm and humid micro-climate. The soil is a heavy neutral loam.

As our garden is only 0.4ha (1 acre) in extent we do not have sufficient space to grow a comprehensive collection of the larger-leaved hostas, and so in 1988 we were honoured to be invited by the NCCPG to hold the Reference Collection of Small and Dwarf Hostas. Since the terms large and small are not only relative but subjective, and since the growth of hostas varies greatly with both cultivation and climate, we decided to choose a particular hosta rather than a measurement as the dividing line between large and small. The hosta we selected is the roughly medium-sized *H.* 'Gloriosa', which is one of the smaller-growing of the *H.* Fortunei Group, and any hosta the same size or smaller belongs in our collection. Taking on the small-leaved Reference Collection is a decision we have never regretted, because in the last 10 or so years the range of small and dwarf hostas has increased enormously, with new and variegated forms being found in the wild and many breeders, such as Bill Zumbar of Alliance, Ohio, working solely on these smaller sorts. We now have approximately 350 small and dwarf hostas, a number we would never have foreseen when we took on the Collection.

The hostas are grown in different types of garden setting to show visitors and potential growers how small hostas respond to a variety of garden habitats. In the 24m (80ft) long Hosta Walk, divided into 'yellow-leaved' and 'blue-leaved' areas, the smaller hostas are planted towards the front of the border with the larger specimens in the background as a size comparison. At the entrance to the garden, on the shaded side of the Lime Walk, hostas mainly of the Tardiana Group such as *H.* 'Hadspen Heron' and *H.* 'Blue Wedgwood' are growing with snowdrops, helle-bores, paeonies, and asters for late summer colour. The latter associate well with the later-flowering *H.* 'Tardiflora' and *H.* 'Hydon Twilight', a seedling from *H. rupifraga*. On the north-facing nursery wall, some of the dwarf hostas are grown in light friable soil contained in

curved peat beds with small, delicate ferns to accompany them. Some of the smaller *H. kikutii* forms, including the recently named *H.* 'Joy Bulford', lean out over the peat blocks so that their flowers can catch the sun. Here we are making a collection of all the *H. sieboldii* forms with white flowers; so far, *H.* 'Weihenstephan' is the best of these. We also grow miniature hostas such as *H. gracillima*, *H.* 'Masquerade' (formerly *H. venusta* 'Variegated'), *H.* 'Ko Mame' and *H. pulchella* 'Kifukurin' in antique stone sinks placed around the north-facing courtyard of the house.

CLEAVE HOUSE

At Cleave House in Sticklepath, a small village 213m (700ft) up on the edge of Dartmoor, Devon, leading hosta growers Ann and Roger Bowden were granted National Reference Collection status in 1990 for their comprehensive collection of modern hosta cultivars and hybrids. The Collection now houses over 500 plants.

The low April temperatures of around 7°C (45°F) mean that the hostas come into leaf about six weeks later than average, but more than make up for their tardy emergence in the balmy micro-climate of this densely planted garden in mid-summer. However, there is not sufficient late summer heat for *H. plantaginea* and its hybrids to flower reliably. The soil is slightly acid and there is a rainfall of 140cm (55in).

The hosta collection grew in part from nursery stock acquired from the late John Goater and was replanted into the specially constructed, artifically shaded and gently curved Pergola Garden, which is sheltered by an ancient stone wall. This has become an outstandingly attractive feature of the garden. Most of the hostas grown here are the larger sorts, including *H.* 'Snowden', *H.* 'Piedmont Gold', *H.* 'Golden Sunburst', *H.* 'Gold Standard', *H.* 'Devon Blue', *H.* 'Antioch' and *H.* 'Francee', giving a useful guide to visitors as to how large some hostas actually grow when given optimum conditions. Another area of the 0.4ha (1 acre) garden is devoted to the Bowden's extensive collection of hostas of the Tardiana Group raised by Eric Smith between early 1960 and mid-1970 which have since

become classic hostas in view of their suitability for growing in smaller gardens, the best-known being *H.* 'Halcyon', *H.* 'Blue Wedgwood' and *H.* 'Hadspen Heron'. Almost all of the other hostas Eric Smith is known to have raised, many of which created great interest at the time of their introduction, also grow here, including *H.* 'Golden Haze', *H.* 'Golden Isle' and *H.* 'Emerald Isle'. These are now mainly collectors' plants, but others such as *H.* 'Granary Gold' and *H.* 'Goldsmith' can hold their own among today's best and are still sought after by flower arrangers for the seasonal colour-changing properties of their yellow-gold leaves.

From a National Collections point of view it is probably the 418m² (500sq yd) area of hostas grown as specimen plants under a cover giving half shade, half sun, mulched with neutral-coloured pebbles and watered by overhead sprinklers, that is most valuable for students of the genus, and for nurserygrowers wishing to verify

Feverfew and aquilegias blend with *Hosta* 'Wogon's Boy', *H.* 'Tokudama' and *H.* 'Tokudama Flavocircinalis' in the Barn Bed at Cleave House with *Hydrangea petiolaris* and *Hosta* 'Eldorado' in the background.

the provenance of their own stock plants. The hostas are grown in a pleasing assemblage emphasizing the wide range of different leaf sizes, shapes and colours and include specimens of the very latest work of hybridizers from all over the world, among them *H.* 'Gaiety', *H.* 'Spilt Milk' and *H.* 'Patriot' from the US, which will be new to most visitors to Cleave House. Also grown here are some British hybrids – *H.* 'Sheila West', *H.* 'Silver Spray', *H.* 'Anthony Gattrell' and *H.* 'Vicar's Mead' – and the Bowden's own introductions, *H.* 'Devon Giant' and *H.* 'Lemon Delight', which are being trialled for their gardenworthiness and their differences from other named cultivars.

KITTOCH MILL HOSTA GARDEN

Records of this historic mill, situated at the bottom of a narrow lane outside the village of Carmunnock, Glasgow, go back to the 14th century, appearing in the Great Seal. The mill is thought to have once belonged to Paisley Abbey and first featured on a local map in 1600, made by one Timothy Pant. It ceased to be a working meal mill in 1907/8.

It is now the home of the Scottish National Reference Collection of the genus *Hosta*, amassed by Howard and Pat Jordan in their 0.8ha (2 acre) garden since 1985. It currently contains about 300 species and varieties specifically chosen to suit the climate, which is a frost pocket dipping down to −16°C (3°F) although the average is 5–6°C (41–43°F), with an average summer temperature of 20°C (68°F). The garden lies at an altitude of 137m (450ft) above sea level and contains a waterfall with a dramatic drop of 7.5m (25ft), forming the southern boundary. The prolonged cold, wet winters can kill off young hostas, so most are grown on in pots until they are considered sufficiently mature to withstand the rigours of this harsh climate, which has an annual rainfall of 1500mm (59in).

The soil is heavy clay with a pH of 6.5 and most of the hostas are planted on the south-facing slope, kept moist by the Pedmyre burn which trickles through the garden down to the Kittoch Water. Most of the garden is surrounded by light woodland, a Site of Special Scientific Interest (SSSI) providing shelter and shade for the hostas.

Many of the hostas have been acquired from the nursery of Heinz Klose in Kassel, central Germany, and they have eventually adapted well to the particular growing conditions of this unusual site. Heinz Klose named some of Eric Smith's Tardiana Group only previously identified by number. These include the little-known *H.* 'Blaue Venus', *H.* 'Saarbrucken', and *H.* 'Tomoko' – the latter name, according to W. George Schmid, honouring Tomoko Kamo, the daughter of an associate of Maekawa, a hosta nurseryman near Mount Fuji in Japan. Pat Jordan has amassed a very comprehensive collection of hostas raised by American hybridizer Mildred Seaver of Boston, Massachusetts. These include *H.* 'Sea Lotus Leaf', *H.* 'Sea Fire', *H.* 'Sea Sapphire', *H.* 'Mildred Seaver', *H.* 'Sea Mist', *H.* 'Sea Monster', *H.* 'Sea Yellow Sunrise', *H.* 'Sea Drift', *H.* 'Sea Gold Star', *H.* 'Sea Octopus' and *H.* 'Sea Dream'.

Other areas of the garden are gradually coming under cultivation and the wilder reaches of the property nearest the river are becoming home to the largest forms of hosta, mostly *H. montana* and its hybrids 'Green Acres' and 'Frosted Jade', which are accompanied by a collection of ligularias which can cope with the competing vegetation revelling in the humid summer microclimate. In complete contrast there are attractively arranged pots of hostas placed in groups all round the house, with a selection of the tiniest sorts growing in a terracotta strawberry pot.

FRANCE

National and Regional collections doing similar work to NCCPG operate under the auspices of the CCVS (Comité des Collections Végétales Specialises). A Collection Agrée is held by the horticultural journalist and photographer Didier Willery, near Bruay-la-Buissière and Béthune, Pas de Calais. The collection is housed in an area of 1500m² (1800sq yd) surrounded by tall trees. The average temperature over the year is 11°C (52°F)

H. 'Sugar and Cream', one of the modern sun-loving hostas that increases rapidly: the fragrant flowers are palest lavender.

with an average minimum of 2°C (35°F) and there are usually 20–40 days when there is frost. The average rainfall is 800–900mm (31–35in).

The collection was started in 1987 and now contains about 112 species and cultivars. M. Willery particularly likes variegated hostas with fragrant flowers, and *H*. 'Sugar and Cream' in particular as it increases very readily. The aim of the collection is to select varieties for their garden value and their ease of cultivation. The hostas are planted, with companion plants, according to colour and the quantity of light required.

The French National Collection is held by Jean Thoby at Le Jardin Botanique, in Vendée. M. Thoby has about 250 hosta species and cultivars, most of which he obtained from American and French nurseries.

HOLLAND

The Dutch National Hosta Collection is housed at Trompenburg Arboretum, an area of 5ha (13 acres) tucked away in the outskirts of Rotterdam, 4m (13ft) below sea level and sheltered by a dyke. Although not yet as comprehensive as some other national collections, it has a particular importance since many of the hostas there are believed to be plants that came from von Siebold's nursery and may possibly be some of his original introductions.

Trompenburg Arboretum went out of private hands and became a foundation in 1992, when Gert Fortgens was appointed curator: up until that time all the work had been done by the owners, the van Hoey Smith family. Mr van Hoey Smith was awarded the Royal Horticultural Society's Veitch Memorial Medal in 1984 for his work on oaks.

The top summer temperature is 30°C (86°F) and there can be frost down to –15°C (5°F). The rainfall is 700mm (28in). The Hosta Collection was started in April 1993 in co-operation with the Dutch Hosta Society (Nederlandse Hosta-vereeniging), which is supplying many of the plants. The plan is that it will house about 300 species and cultivars by the end of 1995. Hostas are used elsewhere in the garden, but the collection itself is located along the Long Lane beside a

Hostas lining a path at Trompenburg. Many have been donated by the Dutch Hosta Society.

Hosta 'Tokudama Aureonebulosa' at Trompenburg.

canal in the middle section of the garden, planted under the shade of trees and shrubs. There are many cultivars dating back to the 1960s and 1970s which are not yet in the British collections, such as *H.* 'Evelyn McCafferty', an excellent *H. sieboldiana* selection, and *H.* 'Zager's White Edge', of the Fortunei Albomarginata Group, making this collection an extremely valuable record. Many of the hostas came from the canal-side garden of Arie van Vliet in Boskoop. Soil conditions vary from moist peaty clay along the side of the canal to dry, humus-rich soil underneath the trees. The hostas are only fed to get them started in the first two years after planting.

At the Agricultural University of Wageningen there is an historic collection of hostas that was originally amassed and studied at the Botanic Garden of Uppsala University in Sweden by Dr Nils Hylander for his 1954 monograph *Hostas in Swedish Gardens*. In the 1960s the hostas were sent to Wageningen, where they were studied by the resident taxonomist, Dr Karel Hensen. The collection included a comprehensive range of *H.* 'Fortunei' forms.

These hostas, together with others such as *H.* 'Elisabeth' raised by Dr Hensen, are grown in order beds for ease of reference.

BELGIUM

Although there is no official hosta collection in Belgium as yet, the distinguished collector and nurseryman Igace van Doorslaer has amassed at his home near Ghent a comprehensive and well-maintained collection of over 500 species and cultivars, ranging from the European form of *H. plantaginea* and Karl Foester's *H.* 'Semperaurea' to the most modern hybrids, including *H.* 'Mountain Snow', *H.* 'Knockout' and *H.* 'Fresh'. These hostas are being grown on and trialled for European conditions before distribution. They are grown in 50 per cent net shade tunnels and watered every day throughout the summer from overhead sprinklers. M. van Doorslaer is a well-known figure at plant sales in Belgium, France and Holland, where he offers probably the largest range of hostas in Europe.

UNITED STATES OF AMERICA

Large and comprehensive hosta collections in the US can be designated Display Gardens by the American Hosta Society, which issues an invaluable booklet entitled *Display Gardens of the American Hosta Society*. As there are so many climatic differences in the large land mass covered by the United States these gardens are extremely valuable, giving useful guidelines to visitors on how hostas perform in different temperatures, soil, amount of rainfall and other growing conditions. The private collections reflect the personal tastes of the owner, often promoting the work of a local hosta breeder or breeders. Of particular note are the gardens of Shirley and Van Wade in Bellville, Ohio; Jim, Jill and Shirley Wilkins of Jackson, Michigan; Warren and Ali Pollock of Wilmington, Delaware, Alex and Gene Summers of Bridgeville, Delaware; and Judy Springer, just south of Washington, DC, in Great Falls, Virginia. The American Hosta Society itself has an extensive collection planted in the Hosta Glade at the Landscape Arboretum, University of Minnesota, the university being the designated International Registration Authority for the genus *Hosta*. Many of the regional chapters of the American Hosta Society are planting hosta display gardens in large public gardens and educational establishments such as the Scott Arboretum at Swarthmore College, Pennsylvania.

11

HOSTAS IN JAPAN

William Burto

Ever since the 17th century Westerners have sought to study and collect Japanese plants, including hostas. The German physician Englebert Kaempfer, who sailed for Nagasaki in 1690, was the first European to publish an account of hostas; next were the Swedish botanist Carl Peter Thunberg, who landed in Japan in 1775, and the German Philipp Franz von Siebold, who arrived in Nagasaki in 1823 and left in 1830 with numerous live specimens of hostas. The Englishman Robert Fortune and the American Thomas Hogg Jr. also contributed to the number of Japanese hostas made available in the trade.

In the footsteps of such notable visitors, a small group from the American Hosta Society recently demonstrated that the story is by no means finished. For two weeks in the summer of 1995 the group traversed Honshu from Nikko in the north to Iwakuni in the south-west, with a side trip to the island of Shikoku. Our aim was to see hostas in the wild, and happily we were not disappointed with what we found.

In March 1973, Alex Summers noted in the *Bulletin of the American Hosta Society* No. 5 that he saw very few hostas in his travels throughout Japan in 1972 except for a small number in pots in the cities, but hostas are indeed to be found. Far from the cities we saw colonies of species growing in conditions that were both beautiful and breathtaking. Two hours north of Tokyo, for example, at Nikko, we found small hostas growing beneath towering cryptomeria on the beautiful precincts of the Tosho-gu, the shrine-mausoleum consecrated to the 17th-century shogun Tokugawa Ieyasu. Unable to identify this hosta, we wondered if it might be some offspring of hostas that Roy Davidson had seen in his walks around Nikko in the early summer of 1969 (reported in the *Bulletin of the American Hosta Society* No. 2, 1970).

The most spectacular setting for any hosta that we saw in the wild was at Chiiwa in the mountainous region around the town of Horai in Aichi Prefecture, the home of *H. hypoleuca* (Urajiro giboshi), or white-backed hosta. Led by our knowledgeable guide, Mr Hiroo Ishiguro, we made a half-hour steep climb up a narrow path bordering a swollen stream filled with huge boulders. We ascended through the forest, at times up an almost vertical trail that included entirely vertical ladders. At the top of the trail, we were able to see clumps of *H. hypoleuca* clinging to the sheer rock face of Chiiwa hundreds of feet above our heads. Although the hike was arduous (not all of our group made it to the top), it was thrilling to see the hostas luxuriating in such a hostile environment, grasping at the slightest bit of soil in the smallest fissures in the rock. Propagation can only result from chance germination of seed scattered as the seed pods open in the autumn. Although Hajime Sugita claims that this species grows only near Chiiwa (see Hajime Sugita, 'Wild Hostas and Little-known *H. alismifolia* in Aichi Prefecture and the Surrounding Areas', *The Hosta Journal*, Vol. 25, No. 1, 1994, pp51–2), we heard unconfirmed reports of other sightings in Aichi Prefecture. We also became sceptical of the old adage that the white back of *H. hypoleuca* was to protect it from the sun reflected from the hot surface of the rock on which it grows, since in other locations lower down the mountain we saw clumps growing in the dense shade of overhanging trees with equally white backs.

Because of our tight schedule we were unable to visit other colonies of wild species in Aichi Prefecture and surrounding areas. We therefore did not see *H. longissima*, described by Sugita as growing in wetlands and which, he says, depending on whether it grows in the sun or in the shade, can look like two different species, *H. aequinoctiiantha*, which grows in a restricted area around the rocks of Yoro Waterfall in Gifu Prefecture, or *H. longipes* (Iwa giboshi, or rock hosta), which grows between rocks or on cliffs near rivers and flourishes in Aichi, Gifu and Shizuoka prefectures.

In Matsuyama, a city in the western part of the island of Shikoku, we were scheduled to visit the Katsuragawa (Katsura River) Valley near the town of Nomura in Ehime Prefecture to see a stand of a special local hosta that so far has no botanical name. Unfortunately, the torrential rains that had been plaguing the region for a number of days caused mud slides that closed the roads and prevented us from making the trip. We did, however, see a special and outstanding form of the plant later at Mr Yoshimichi Hirose's home in Iwakuni, and we were presented with a number of specimens to bring back for propagation. This new hosta has a medium-sized green leaf with petioles richly covered with purple dots that spread on to the leaf and into the veins; there is no pruinose on the back. Some thought it might be a form of *H. longipes* f. *hypoglauca*; others suggested that it might be a singular form of *H. kikutii*, but whether it is a new species or a hybrid form must await the taxonomic report of Mr Noboru Fujita, who is currently studying it. Mr Hirose told us that when it is registered he hopes to name it *Hosta* 'Katsuragawa' after the valley where Mr Hirose Masaoka discovered it a few years ago.

Another especially interesting site of wild hosta was the colony of *H. pycnophylla* on Mount Genmei on Yashiro-jima, a large island between

H. gracillima, shown growing in the wild on Shikoku Island, Japan.

western Shikoku and the mainland of Honshu. Reached by a narrow path that forced us to cross a raging torrent by jumping from one slippery boulder to another, the hostas grow in thick underbrush on the steep mountainside. In the darkness of the forest the white back on the piecrusted leaves was intense. As has been noted by others, the combination of the piecrust edging and the white pruinose on the back of the leaf of *H. pycnophylla*, along with its purple-dotted petioles, make this an interesting plant for selective breeding.

Vast stands of *H. montana* in full flower were growing on the steeply raked banks along the roadside outside the city limits of Iwakuni. (A sighting of large colonies of the same plant in the mountains near the north-western city of Nigata on the Sea of Japan side of Honshu was recently reported.) Nearby, in Kuga, helped by Mr Toshiro Shimizu, our machete-wielding guide, who cut a path through the underbrush for us beside a rushing stream, we saw many clumps of *H. longissima* clinging to the exposed rocky surface of a small waterfall, drenched in the spray. From there it was only a short distance to a more open position near some cultivated rice-paddies where a stand of *H. longissima* var. *brevifolia* had survived a partial mowing by local farmers. Not many of us, however, could see the difference between the two hostas – an opinion shared by W. George Schmid, who, in *The Genus Hosta*, wrote that 'there is no macromorphological difference between it and the species'.

Besides trekking for hostas in the countryside, we visited three nurseries and two private collections where we saw numerous varieties, many imported from the United States, grown in pots on benches. Of note were the private collections of Mr Shimizu in Kuga and Mr Hirose in Iwakuni. Both are collectors from the wild who are using their plants in their hybridizing programmes and both have large selections of rare hostas little seen in the West – a white-backed *H. pulchella* 'Urajiro', a white-flowered *H. gracillima*, and several wild variegated forms of the latter.

The most famous hybridizer in Japan for the past ten years has been Kenji Watanabe, the owner of the Gotemba Nursery, almost on the slopes of Mount Fuji. The mountain threw off its clouds as we arrived, allowing us a quick glimpse of its majesty before it disappeared for the rest of the day. Well-known for his *H. montana* selections, Watanabe-san greeted us warmly with his four sons and allowed us to roam through his three large greenhouses, in one of which he keeps his most treasured plants, all grown in hundreds of pots of various sizes in what appear to be extremely porous materials. Among the many interesting hostas we saw were an *H. longipes* called 'Tenryu Nishiki' (from the Tenryu area of Aichi Prefecture) and described as having large yellow/white variegated leaves (selling for Y6,000; approximately US $60), an *H. longipes* 'Gotemba Nishiki' (Y50,000/US $500) with round, deep yellow/white variegated leaves and labelled as 'rare', and an *H. montana* labelled 'Fujibotan', collected on the slopes of Fuji and described as having 'a light purple double flower bloom like a peony' (selling for the modest sum of Y80,000/US $800).

Having formerly paid little attention to a genus that flourishes in their own country, the Japanese now prize hostas (*Giboshi* in Japanese), especially variegated specimens, and they have recently even formed a Japan Hosta Society, some of whose members joined the American Hosta Society group at an informal meeting in the Shinjuku Gyoen, a large public garden in the middle of Tokyo. Mr Hirose delivered a short lecture on his programme of breeding for variegated hostas, after which members exchanged cards and discussed various hosta topics before adjourning to a tea house for cups of green tea.

The time was too short and the weather was occasionally uncooperative, but enough was seen to make any hosta-lover eager to see more native species in additional sites in Japan and to carry on the tradition begun by Englebert Kaempfer three centuries ago.

William C. Burto is Special Features Editor of the American Hosta Society's *Hosta Journal*. He lives in Cambridge, Massachusetts, where he has an extensive hosta collection.

12

HOSTAS IN NORTH AMERICA

Dr Warren I. Pollock

According to trade information, the genus *Hosta* is now the most favoured herbaceous perennial in the United States, overtaking *Hemerocallis* as the biggest seller in American nurseries. The advantages of *Hosta* are being increasingly recognized by home gardeners, the general nursery trade and landscape designers and contractors.

A prime reason for their popularity is that hostas can solve the problem of finding a perennial to grow in the shade. Hostas will tolerate shade; in fact, almost all of them need a degree of shade in the United States.

Hostas can grow in all but the semi-tropical and extremely frigid regions of North America, a vast geographic expanse extending from at least the US Department of Agriculture (USDA) Plant Hardiness Zone 7 in the South to Zone 2 in the North - the exact limit of their cold hardiness has not been determined. It seems that their only requirement is a period of dormancy during the winter months. Beautiful specimen clumps can be found in Birmingham, Alabama; Atlanta, Georgia; the Carolinas; Portland, Maine; Minneapolis, Minnesota; Salt Lake City, Utah; Portland, Oregon; and Toronto, Ontario. Though the season is short, hostas will grow even in Anchorage, Alaska.

Low-maintenance gardening is fashionable today, especially with busy young homemakers and senior citizens, and hostas are a relatively maintenance-free plant. They require no periodic dividing as is necessary for many other perennials such as daylilies (*Hemerocallis*) and irises. Slugs, snails and black vine weevils eat hosta leaves, but many people choose to ignore this disfigurement. Further, although hostas thrive best with copious watering and moderate fertilizing, these are not essential requirements for establishing clumps.

As hosta clumps become older and bigger, they become more attractive. Borders on variegated leaves become wider; depressions in leaves, such as dimples and seersuckering (puckering), become more prominent; and leaf colouring often becomes more pronounced and intense. In addition, their handsome leaves are an attractive feature all season.

In recent years there has been considerable activity in developing hybrids and finding sports of hostas in the US. This has resulted in the introduction of a large number of very attractive new cultivars with blue, gold, green and highly variegated leaves; leaf blade sizes as small as 2.5cm (1in) wide to huge dimensions of over 38cm (15in); leaf shapes ranging from long and lance-like to heart-shaped (cordate) or round; leaf textures from smooth to seersuckered; and leaves flat as a table top to wavy-edged to deeply cupped like a fruit bowl. For just about every gardening need, it is possible to find a hosta with suitable leaf colour, pattern, size and shape, as well as suitable dimensions and growth habit of the clump.

Tissue culture propagation (micropropagation) of hostas, pioneered in the US, has made available scores of species and cultivars, each in quantities of tens of thousands, very rapidly and fairly inexpensively. The time from the discovery of a worthwhile new variety to its introduction and sale in a 0.5 litre (1pt US) pot in a nursery can be as short as just two years. Many large American retail nurseries and garden centres now carry a selection of two to three dozen different hostas in container sizes from 0.5 litre (1pt US)

84

to 14 litres (3 gal US) – and the number of varieties being stocked each year is increasing.

Many Americans have pioneered the introduction of new cultivars. Some early ones are Rod Cummings, of the Bristol Nursery in Connecticut, who hybridized the green-leaved, fragrant, lavender-flowered 'Honeybells' of *H. plantaginea* parentage; and John Grullemans of the old Wayside Nursery in Ohio, whose 'Royal Standard', also a green-leaved hybrid of *H. plantaginea* but with beautiful, large, highly fragrant white flowers, was the first hosta to be patented (1965).

To these must be added Mrs Frances Williams, who in the mid-1930s discovered the hosta that bears her name, a gold-edged sport of the big seersuckered blue-leaved *H. sieboldiana* 'Elegans'. This event can be considered to be the keystone for the interest worldwide in new and colourful hostas for the garden.

In the last 25 or so years there have been many prominent hosta introducers, including: Gus Krossa, whose large upright 'Krossa Regal' with blue-grey leaves is considered a classic hosta; Robert Savory, the hybridizer of the very popular small green-leaved and gold-edged 'Golden Tiara'; Peter Ruh, whose distinctive 'Paul's Glory' with yellow leaves and blue-green border is rapidly gaining popularity; Mrs Mildred Seaver, noted for hybridizing many hostas, one being 'Sea Dream' with yellow leaves and a white margin; and Dr Ralph (Herb) Benedict, another prolific hybridizer, whose 'Crested Surf' has long lance-shaped leaves, green with a variable golden margin and distinct undulating edges.

Two people especially stand out: Alex Summers and Paul Aden. Alex Summers helped to found the American Hosta Society (AHS), served as its first president and was the first editor of the *AHS Bulletin*, now the *Hosta Journal*. Many of his imports from Japan, for example the large gold-margined *H. fluctuans* 'Variegated' and the small white-edged *H.* 'Ginko Craig', as well as many American-originated hostas such as the large gold-leaved *H.* 'August Moon', are now widely available and are regarded as classics.

Paul Aden has hybridized perhaps the largest number of outstanding hostas. He was among the first to see the advantages of tissue culture propagation, and has had most of his introductions propagated in large quantities by means of this technique. His very popular large-leaved hybrid 'Sum and Substance', medium-sized to large seersuckered and cupped blue-leaved 'Love Pat', large blue-leaved 'Blue Angel' and other exceptionally fine cultivars have made him the doyen of hosta introducers.

The name of W. George Schmid cannot be omitted. His book *The Genus Hosta*, published in 1991, has become a standard reference. In particular, he has helped to clarify the taxonomy of both *Hosta* species and cultivars.

The American Hosta Society was founded in 1968 and today has a membership of well over 2500. The *Hosta Journal* is published twice a year and the *Hosta Yearbook*, a recent publication, is issued annually. A several-day AHS National Convention is held each summer with tours of gardens, a cut-leaf exhibit show (*Hosta* may be the only genus which has a competitive show where leaves, not flowers, are the entries), special lectures, and an auction where new and rare varieties are contributed by members for sale.

Supporting the AHS – and now a very important part of it – are regional and local hosta societies. There is, for example, a Midwest Regional Hosta Society which includes the Minnesota, Michigan and Indianapolis Hosta Societies. The Mid-Atlantic Hosta Society includes the Delaware Valley Hosta Society with members mainly in the Philadelphia area; the Potomac Hosta Club with members mostly in the Washington, DC, area; and the Carolina Hosta Society. Formation of these local groups, some with over 200 members, has increased markedly in recent years; it seems every geographic area has a handful of interested hosta gardeners wanting to establish a local hosta society. The attractions are that gardens with specimen hostas in the local area can easily be visited, common cultural problems can be discussed, and new varieties can be purchased at the meetings.

Several regional hosta societies sponsor one-day conferences which draw over a hundred aficionados. In the Chicago area in January a Winter Scientific Meeting is held; in Ohio in March there is a Hosta College with dozens of courses; and in the Washington, DC, area a Hosta in Focus Festival in November features photographic exhibits, video presentations and slide lectures.

CULTIVATION OF HOSTAS

Gardening in the shade is not as easy as gardening in the sun. There are many degrees of shade, ranging from the side of a building that never receives any direct sunlight or under the dense, low covering of overlapping large tree leaves in a heavily wooded site to the open, filtered and dappled light coming through the high canopy of an up-limbed, thinly branched pine tree.

Also, Americans must take into consideration whether they live in the South or North. In the South, two hours of direct sun in the afternoon is more intense than in the North, so more shade is often required and morning sun is preferred over afternoon sun. Descriptions of hostas which say they require sun for a quarter or half of the day have little meaning unless they include information on the geographic region.

In general, hostas often grow bigger in the North than in the South, given the same cultural conditions. Further, blue-leaved hostas seem to be more blue in the North, while yellow-leaved hostas often appear more yellow in the South.

British growers have noted that hostas grow bigger and the flowers are lighter in colour in the US than in the UK. The blooms of 'Halcyon' are often white or near-white in the States and greyish-lavender in Britain. Then, blue-leaved hostas seem to be bluer in Britain, perhaps due to a hazy atmosphere. Because of the generally mild climate, hosta flowers stay in bloom for a longer period in Britain than in the US. Also, hostas with viridescent variegation tend to fade earlier in the US than those in British or European gardens, a prime example of this being *H.* 'Fortunei Albopicta', one of the most popular hostas in Britain but hardly ever encountered in gardens in the US.

Thus the amount and type of shade and the geographical area will affect the selection, placement and performance of hostas, something that is not sufficiently recognized by many gardeners and garden designers. In general, yellow- or gold-leaved hostas need some sun to develop their

The 'Frances Williams' room' in the Warren and Ali Pollock garden, Wilmington, Delaware.

brightest colouring. It is frequently stated that a yellow hosta will brighten up a dark spot. This is true, but they often don't do well in such locations, finding them too shady.

The blue colouring of some hosta leaves, called pruinose or glaucous – given by a waxy, silvery coating that develops in the spring – will last longer if the plants are grown in light shade. It will also last longer in the North (because of the cooler weather) than in the South.

In general, green-leaved hostas can take a fair amount of sunlight, although in too much direct sun leaf colouring will be dulled considerably. For any hosta, too much sun, combined with lack of water, will scorch the leaves, especially in July and August.

The more sun, the more profuse the flowering. It comes as a surprise to many gardeners that there are several hostas with outstanding fragrance. *H. plantaginea* and the double-flowered *H. p.* 'Aphrodite', considered by many to have the most beautiful hosta flower, need considerable sun (and also hot weather and plenty of water) to bloom well. Their flowers are pure white with long trumpets. On the other hand, *H.* 'Royal Standard', with smaller, white, fragrant flowers, blooms well in fairly shady sites in both the North and South.

For variegated-leaf hostas, placement will depend on the most dominant leaf colour, usually the centre colouring. *H.* 'Gold Standard', with a dark green border, needs sunlight in mid-season to have its chartreuse centre change to a handsome parchment gold. In a very shady site, it becomes just a yellowish-green; given too much sun, the centre turns first to a gold and then to a light creamy white or even a near white, a less attractive colour in my opinion than the parchment gold.

H. 'June', the popular British hosta with a blue-green border, should not be grown in a very shady location. It needs considerable sun in early season to develop its brightly coloured yellow centre, and good sunlight throughout the season to help retain it.

The green-edged *H.* 'On Stage' also needs bright sunlight to develop and retain its yellow

centre. In the South, for example Raleigh, North Carolina, this is morning sun. Further north, near Philadelphia, where I live, strong afternoon sun is required and almost all-day sun is better, provided it is kept well watered.

The axiom is: experiment in placing your hostas. If one doesn't do well in a certain location, move it to another, or replace it with a different variety. Do not be be too categorical about placing a specific hosta in a specific location.

One point to bear in mind is that if your shade is from trees, the amount of shade will become more dense over the years and your hostas will not be as luxuriant; they may even decrease in size each year. Another is that some trees have greedy surface roots and will compete with the hostas for water and nutrients. Hostas don't like such competition, so if possible, plant your hostas far enough away from trees to avoid this problem.

Another solution is to plant hostas in containers. We have grown and overwintered hostas in containers for many years. They require, of course, very frequent watering during the growing season, and potting up or repotting – all requiring considerable effort. The results, though, are very rewarding as the potted hostas can be placed anywhere: on a patio, walkway, or driveway; next to a pool; hanging from a wall; and under trees among plants in the ground. They can also be moved at any time during the growing season according to whim.

Overwintering can be a concern, depending on the geographical area and the facilities the gardener has available. Our plants are overwintered in our unheated garage. The containers are lined up on shelves along the back wall up to the ceiling; 150 pots take up only 1m (3¼ft) of the garage's depth.

Hundreds of first-class hostas can be recommended for planting in North America if given a

The *H. sieboldiana* Elegans Group. Left to right: top row, *H. sieboldiana* 'Elegans', *H.* 'Devon Giant' *H.* 'True Blue'; middle row, *H.* 'Trail's End', *H.* 'Bold Ruffles'; bottom row, *H.* 'Mira', *H.* 'Blue Seer', *H.* 'Blue Angel', *H.* 'Big Daddy'.

88

suitable location and sufficient water. The best of these are:

H. 'Allan P. McConnell' (makes a good small mound)

H. 'Antioch'

H. 'August Moon' (needs sun for best gold colouring; a classic)

H. 'Birchwood Parky's Gold'

H. 'Blue Angel' (faster growing and better flowers than *H. sieboldiana* 'Elegans')

H. 'Christmas Tree'

H. 'Diamond Tiara' (one of the Tiara Group; new, worth seeking)

H. 'Emerald Tiara' (another Tiara; new, worth seeking)

H. fluctuans 'Variegated' (gorgeous; classic)

H. 'Francee' (classic)

H. 'Frances Williams' (classic)

H. 'Ginko Craig' (classic)

H. 'Gold Standard' (excellent; classic)

H. 'Golden Tiara' (yellow margin turns chartreuse in mid-season; classic)

H. 'Halcyon' (beautiful blue leaves; classic)

H. 'Invincible' (shiny green leaves; fragrant flowers)

H. 'June' (beautiful variegation; new, worth seeking)

H. 'Krossa Regal' (classic)

H. lancifolia

H. 'Lemon Lime'

H. 'Little Aurora' (very similar to 'Golden Prayers')

H. 'Love Pat' (superb big blue-cupped leaves that are seersuckered)

H. 'Patriot' (stands out in the garden; new, worth seeking)

H. 'Paul's Glory' (distinctive; new, worth seeking)

H. 'Piedmont Gold' (classic)

H. plantaginea 'Aphrodite' (beautiful fragrant white blooms)

H. 'Regal Splendor' (handsome 'Krossa Regal' with yellow margins; new, worth seeking)

H. 'Royal Standard' (classic)

H. sieboldiana 'Elegans' (classic)

H. 'Shade Fanfare' (unusual variegation; classic)

H. 'So Sweet' (attractive; fragrant flowers)

H. 'Sun Power' (classic)

H. 'Sum and Substance' (grows very large, makes a bold statement; classic)

H. ventricosa

H. ventricosa 'Aureomarginata' (classic)

H. 'Wide Brim' (classic)

H. 'Zounds' (big yellow-cupped leaves that are highly seersuckered).

HOSTA COLLECTIONS IN THE US

At the Minnesota Landscape Arboretum near Minneapolis is the AHS National Hosta Display, featuring hundreds of varieties. Called the 'Hosta Glade', it is visited by a large number of people wanting to see mature, named varieties in an attractive setting.

Some other horticultural sites that feature hosta displays are: Dubuque Arboretum and Botanical Gardens in Iowa; Boerner Botanical Gardens in Hales Corner, Wisconsin; Herb and Dorothy Benedict Hosta Hillside at Hidden Lake Gardens in Tipton, Michigan, the Michigan State University Garden; Idea Garden at the world-famous Longwood Gardens in Kennett Square, Pennsylvania; and Pine Tree State Arboretum in August, Maine.

There are large collections of hostas in private home gardens, some having over 500 different species and cultivars. They are often on garden tours and open to the public. In the south and east, to name a few, are the gardens of Joe and Olive Langdon, Birmingham, Alabama; Robert Harris, Stone Mountain, Georgia; W. George Schmid, Tucker, Georgia, specializing in hosta species; Judy Springer, Great Falls, Virginia; Alex Summers, Bridgeville, Delaware; and Warren and Ali Pollock, Wilmington, Delaware.

The Midwest has an abundance of excellent hosta gardens. A few are: Van and Shirley Wade in Beltville, Ohio; Peter and Jean Ruh in Chesterland, Ohio; Richard and Jane Ward in Columbus, Ohio; James and Jill Wilkins in Jackson, Michigan; William Brinka and Basil Cross in Michigan City, Indiana; and Russell O'Harra in Des Moines, Iowa.

Hosta specialist nurseries, of which there are scores in the US, usually have a large number of specimen hostas, many of them not mentioned in their catalogues and lists.

HOSTAS IN GARDEN DESIGN

A common fault when planting hostas is to group the young plants too closely together. Within five years they will have reached their mature sizes and be crowding each other. Except for some hosta borders, allow enough room for each clump to be recognized and show its full beauty.

All too frequently, hosta enthusiasts in North America will grow nothing but hostas, usually as borders along paths winding back and forth in back gardens and sometimes even as single-variety edging in front gardens. (One of the plants most commonly used in this way is *H.* 'Undulata', which was one of the first hostas to be grown in the US.) Often the entire gardening area will be used for displaying a hosta collection, resulting in a 'monoculture ghetto' (an interesting term coined by Ann Lovejoy, the American gardening writer). The well-known English plantsman Christopher Lloyd observes that 'monocultures, though simple to grasp as a concept, are unnecessarily restrictive'.

To all but the most dedicated hosta collector, large collections of hostas can be a boring scene, albeit one with very colourful foliage. To British gardeners, many hosta gardens in the States are perhaps too colourful, too garish, but America is a sunnier and hotter country than the UK, and bright, bold colours seem to suit the climate and living conditions.

In recent years, however, there is a trend to include other plants in hosta gardens, in particular those with attractive foliage all season. Combining them with hostas can be very effective, providing a pleasing foil to the hostas' foliage. Ferns, especially *Athyrium nipponicum* 'Pictum' (Japanese painted fern), *Polygonatum odoratum* 'Variegatum' (striped Japanese Solomon's seal), *Tricyrtis* (toad lily), *Heuchera* (coral bells) and *Pulmonaria* (lungwort) are popular. Take care when planting Solomon's seal, toad lily

and most ferns: they grow to a large size, and can quickly overpower small hostas.

Tricyrtis hirta 'Albomarginata' has handsome variegated leaves that blend well with solid-colour hosta leaves, while the flowers of any tricyrtis are welcome vertical splashes of brightness in late summer and autumn. Beautiful new tricyrtis, heuchera and pulmonaria cultivars are coming on the market yearly. Hellebores are good companion plants also, and small clumps of *Tiarella* (foam flower), with green maple foliage and usually white spring flowers, give a pleasing effect.

However, the mixed border, as exemplified in British gardens where the best features and examples of different plant categories are combined in a judicious mixture, is not often seen in American gardens. A rare exception is the gardens of James and Jill Wilkins, in Jackson, Michigan, where conifers and deciduous shrubs are used in some of the hosta beds. Blue-needled conifers, a speciality of the Wilkinses, are combined very effectively with blue-leaved hosta clumps.

In our garden in Wilmington, Delaware, *Hydrangea quercifolia* 'Snow Queen', a cultivar that is a great improvement on the species, is used as a background for *Hosta sieboldiana* 'Elegans' clumps. The hydrangea has white upright flower trusses; the hosta, scapes with near-white flowers. They both bloom at the same time, usually July. Other hostas could be used instead of 'Elegans', *H.* 'Blue Angel' being an excellent candidate. It has whiter flowers and taller scapes than 'Elegans'.

Information on joining the American Hosta Society and its regional and local societies can be obtained from the AHS Membership Secretary, 7802 NE 63rd Street, Vancouver, WA 98662. Information on hosta specialist nurseries are to be found in the national and local societies' publications.

Dr Warren I. Pollock advises on hosta plantings in both private and public gardens, including the Scott Arboretum at Swarthmore College, Pennsylvania. He and his wife Ali enjoy landscaping their woodland garden at home in Wilmington, Delaware.

13

HOSTAS IN EUROPE

Dr Ullrich Fischer

When I look back to the 1960s, when I first became interested in hostas, it is noticeable just how few hostas were available, and those few had been around for more than 100 years. It has taken many years for the European gardening public to become aware of and familiar with the multitude of new hostas that have been raised in the US and elsewhere in the last 30 years.

There are several reasons why hostas are not used by German gardeners and garden designers as they are in Britain or in the US, the main one being that most German perennial nursery catalogues still list only the old varieties. However, *H.* 'Big Daddy', *H.* 'Big Mama', *H.* 'Blue Angel', *H.* 'Gold Standard', *H.* 'Golden Tiara', *H.* 'Halcyon', *H.* 'Krossa Regal', *H.* 'Wide Brim' and others are slowly becoming more widely available in nurseries and even some garden centres. They are mostly imported from Holland, where hostas are grown in field rows in full sun to make them increase more quickly.

A second reason could be that in the past plain green-leaved or green and white-variegated hostas were planted in dark, neglected places where nothing else would flourish. Novice gardeners still site their hostas thus, thinking that is how they should be planted. Of course the hostas do not flourish, and gardeners soon lose interest in them.

A third reason hostas are not much used in garden design may well be the lack of books in German dealing specifically with hostas. Fortunately, this situation has changed since 1993.

Up until now, only a very few specialist nurseries have been offering a wider range of the newer hosta introductions from the US or England, and importing plants from abroad is still quite expensive. Lectures and exhibitions of hostas at various flower shows have contributed to the increasing interest in hostas and to the education of the gardening public in recent years, as have articles in many German gardening magazines. The main places at which hostas have been shown to a wide public in Germany are the Federal Garden Shows, which are held every other year in different cities, and International Garden Shows, which are held only every 10 years. Staudengartnerei Heinz Klose, the specialist hosta and paeony nurseryman of Kassel, and myself have exhibited hostas at several shows.

At the International Garden Show at Munich in 1983, I invited Diana Grenfell to help stage my exhibit. This featured a display board showing the history and development of the Tardiana Group, with examples of the hostas described appearing in the planting. It was very noticeable that our exhibit was a cool oasis of green foliage in a marquee otherwise given over to a riot of brilliantly coloured floral exhibits, mostly fuchsias, and it consequently created a great deal of interest and comment.

The last big event was the International Garden Show at Stuttgart in 1993, where, together with a colleague, I won a Big Gold Medal and several other medals for a stand of 120m² (144sq yd) showing a display of more than 100 varieties of hostas. There were hostas in pots,

---

The Fortunei Albomarginata Group. Left to right: top row, *H.* 'Francee', *H.* 'Fortunei Albomarginata', *H.* 'North Hills'; bottom row, *H.* 'Patriot', *H.* 'Carol', *H.* 'Fortunei Gloriosa', *H.* 'Zager's White Edge'.

hostas as ground cover and big hosta clumps as focal points in a perennial border. I also put on an exhibit of different hosta species with brief descriptions of their botanical characteristics and tables showing where they come from in Asia, as well as charts showing how hostas are propagated.

There is still no hosta society in Germany, but there are plans in the near future to found a specialist hosta group within the German Hardy Plant Society, GDS. The Dutch already have their own National Hosta Society, the Nederlandsche Hosta Vereeniging, started by Airie van Vliet of Boskoop a few years ago. One result of this is that the Dutch nursery trade is now producing more hostas in more varieties every year.

Heinz Klose must be mentioned as a major pioneer of hostas in Germany. He began introducing the Tardianas and new varieties from America more than 20 years ago and is responsible for the so-called 'German Tardianas', which are either unnamed seedlings bought from Eric Smith or the results of his own breeding lines. The best of these is H. 'Blaue Venus' ('Blue Venus'), a small and very blue Tardiana, now in the Scottish National Reference Collection, and H. 'Irische See' which is now in some British gardens and the British National Collections. He also imported H. plantaginea 'Aphrodite' from China. His catalogue includes more than 180 hosta varieties of which more than 40 are of his own raising, including H. 'Kasseler Gold', a large, glossy, yellow-leaved seedling from the German-raised 'Semperaurea', which is one of the many hostas growing in the Perennial Trial Grounds of Weihenstephan University outside Munich.

Over the years, I too have managed to produce a few worthwhile hybrids. Among the best are H. 'Heideturm' (or 'Heathtower'), with smooth green leaves and a flower stem up to 2.1m (7ft), its flowers evenly disposed around the stem, 'Phoenix', with long, elegant, ash-grey foliage, and 'Lucy Hooker', a sport of a green seedling with good white flowers and a creamy-yellow rim. A few others look promising, but need a few seasons' more evaluation. One of my breeding goals is to produce hostas with better flower colour and form.

Another keen breeder, mostly of small hostas, is Dr Fritz Köhlein of Bavaria, well known for his writing of monographs on several plant genera. In 1993 he finished writing the first German hosta book. Through his contacts in Japan he obtained a few small unnamed hostas, and from these he started breeding small hybrids, one of the better-known being H. 'Goldene Woge' ('Golden Wave'), a small golden hosta with wavy edges. We can expect many exciting dwarf hostas from him in coming years.

If I were asked which varieties I like best at the moment, I would say H. 'Fragrant Bouquet' and its sport H. 'Guacamole', which is more vigorous. Both have large fragrant flowers and good variegated leaves. H. 'Great Expectations', with its bright leaf pattern, really can turn a non-believer into a hosta-lover. Then there are the highly variegated hybrids of the Lachmans like H. 'Emily Dickinson' and the strange H. 'Bridegroom' from Dr Herb Benedict of Michigan. These expensive varieties will come down in price, as will the other new hybrids which at the moment only a few collectors can afford.

In the US there is rising interest in hosta species and their forms. I think W. George Schmid first drew attention to the beauty of these wild plants, describing and illustrating most of them in his book The Genus Hosta. H. venusta 'Variegated' (now H. 'Masquerade') and H. 'Tokudama 'Aureonebulosa' are very popular in Germany today. I like all the forms of H. longipes and H. kikutii and also the two newly introduced species from Korea, H. laevigata and H. yingeri. With their spider-like flowers, these hostas are very interesting as breeding material. I believe that as more and more small and miniature hostas become available an increasing number of gardeners will plant hostas in their gardens, either in perennial borders or in shady rock gardens.

Dr Ullrich Fischer is a well-known and highly respected plantsman who concentrates his attentions upon shade-loving plants. He gardens in northern Germany and now has a nursery specializing in hostas.

14

HOSTAS IN AUSTRALASIA

Gordon Collier

In New Zealand, hostas have been grown for only a relatively short time. It is known that *H.* 'Lancifolia' was in our gardens before 1940 and this plant is still commonly seen. However, New Zealand's great distance from foreign nurseries made it difficult to obtain and transport stocks of new plants of any kind, the five-week sea voyage from the other side of the world being the limiting factor.

The great rhododendron gardens of England profoundly influenced the style of gardens here in the 1940s, '50s and '60s, and indeed trees and shrubs held sway for a further 20 years. These shrub gardens peaked in spring, with interest tending to wane over the following seasons; perennials were in disfavour, being regarded as labour-intensive. In the early 1950s Richmond E. Harrison, a great all-round horticulturalist and nurseryman of Palmerston North, imported a number of hostas from Alan Bloom of Bressingham Gardens. These included the familiar *H.* 'Thomas Hogg' (syn. *H.* 'Undulata Albomarginata'), *H.* 'Fortunei Aureomarginata', *H. ventricosa* and *H. sieboldiana* 'Glauca'. The latter turned out to be a superb plant and is now the standard blue hosta all over the country, though it is known today as *H. sieboldiana* 'Elegans' for want of accurate identification. *H. plantaginea* was also in gardens at this time.

When I returned to New Zealand after a working holiday in England in 1962 I brought with me a consignment of plants, mostly perennials from Perry's Hardy Plant Farm of Enfield. Of all these the hostas survived best the five-week voyage in the ship's vegetable locker, although they closely resembled sticks of celery on arrival. These hostas, considered the outstanding members of the genus at the time, included *H.* 'Fortunei Aurea', *H.* 'Fortunei Albopicta', *H.* 'Undulata

H. 'Fortunei Albomarginata' with *Dicksonia fibrosa* and *Matteuccia struthiopteris* at Titoki Point, Taihape, New Zealand.

Erromena' and *H.* 'Fortunei Albomarginata'. It is significant that these were the only ones easily obtainable from UK nurseries.

From this time on a small number of enthusiasts, including Dr R. Freeman, Jim Rumball, Felix Jury, the late Hugh Redgrove, Lloyd Philips, Pat Hall-Jones and myself, imported hostas; three of our sources were the nurseries of Peter Ruh in Cleveland, Ohio, and Roy Khlem in Chicago, and the Savill Gardens in England. Two notable plants that arrived during this period were *H.* 'Frances Williams' and *H. montana* 'Aureomarginata'. The former created a sensation among gardeners in New Zealand, being the first variegated hosta with real substance.

New Zealand gardeners were gradually influenced by visits to England and by their reading of horticultural books written by Graham Thomas, Christopher Lloyd, Beth Chatto and Alan Bloom. They came to realize the beauty and low maintenance requirements of foliage plants such as pulmonaria, bergenia and hosta. Latterly, interest in the 'cottage' style and in perennials in general has reached a high point and has made a large contribution to the popularity of gardening in this country. The few perennial nurseries of yesteryear have turned into many, supplying a great range of interesting perennials, and larger nurseries, realizing the commercial worth of hostas, have begun to import significant quantities from the USA as plants or as tissue culture plantlets in flasks. The combination of air travel and tissue culture has meant the newest forms can quickly be made available in large numbers. A third advantage has been that tissue cultured plants in flasks are not subject to quarantine procedures here. The best hostas are readily obtainable in New Zealand now and the genus is enjoying quiet popularity, though some of the mystique of collecting is no longer there.

H. 'Carol' flourishing in a shady position, complemented by a variegated astilbe.

A cool climate combined with good soil produces excellent growing conditions, though with high sunshine hours, hostas in New Zealand need more shade than is usual. Gardeners here use companion plants freely – astilbe, rodgersia, grasses and ferns – and keep the highly coloured

The ravishing *H.* 'On Stage' requires more sunshine than the majority of hostas.

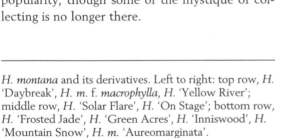

H. montana and its derivatives. Left to right: top row, *H.* 'Daybreak', *H. m.* f. *macrophylla*, *H.* 'Yellow River'; middle row, *H.* 'Solar Flare', *H.* 'On Stage'; bottom row, *H.* 'Frosted Jade', *H.* 'Green Acres', *H.* 'Inniswood', *H.* 'Mountain Snow', *H. m.* 'Aureomarginata'.

H. 'J. W. Matthews' – one of the most sought-after new hostas from New Zealand.

cultivars together in one part of their garden. Plain-leaved hostas, particularly blues, are the most popular.

There are a number of nurseries specializing in hostas, several offering up to 100 named forms, though there is only one specializing exclusively in them. From about 300 species and varieties currently grown, the following are among the most popular: *H.* 'Aspen Gold'; *H.* 'Big Daddy'; *H.* 'Blue Mammoth'; *H.* 'Camelot'; *H.* 'Francee'; *H.* 'Frances Williams'; *H.* 'Gold Standard'; *H.* 'Great Expectations'; *H.* 'Halcyon'; *H.* 'Krossa Regal'; *H.* 'On Stage'; *H. plantaginea*; *H. sieboldiana* 'Elegans'; *H.* 'Sum and Substance'.

HOSTAS IN AUSTRALIA
Robert Angus

Hostas were horticultural latecomers to Australia. Keen gardeners shared a few varieties, many imported as seed, until I started importing and swapping hostas in the 1980s. A small network of plant collectors then developed a collection of 60 varieties which has grown to over 200 today.

Many hostas grow effortlessly in Australia. *H.* 'Undulata' cultivars and the Fortunei Group flourish in the subtropics, and *H. plantaginea* grows as well in our coastal gardens as anywhere in the world. *H.* 'Kabitan', *H.* 'Fringe Benefit', *H.* 'Francee', *H.* 'Krossa Regal', *H.* 'Honeybells', *H.* 'Royal Standard' and *H.* 'Sugar and Cream' are reliable cultivars for foliage and flowers. Seed produces a good proportion of dependable garden plants that readily adjust to local conditions.

In the extreme summer heat of Australia, many hostas produce only one flush of leaves per year. They must be protected to prolong the vigour, and a moist, shady position with added humus and protection from hot winds, snails and slugs is essential.

The best hostas are seen in cooler mountain climates where winter chilling and a long, mild spring encourage and protect their initial soft growth. Mature clumps of the Tardiana and Tokudama Groups and the species and cultivars of *H. sieboldiana* and *H. ventricosa* make formidable contrasts in the gardens of the Blue Mountains, Dandenongs, Adelaide Hills and Tasmania.

Hostas are imported now in tissue culture, and a representative collection is readily available. The range will expand as importers multiply their stocks and the latest selections are marketed.

Gordon Collier is a horticultural writer and journalist, and the owner of one of the most beautiful gardens to be seen in New Zealand. He and his wife Annette run a nursery at Titoki Point, Taihape, where a large range of hostas are on sale.

15

A–Z OF HOSTAS
IN CULTIVATION

CLUMP SIZES

Dwarf	Less than 10cm (4in)
Miniature	13–23cm (5–9in)
Small	25–38cm (10-15in)
Medium	40–60cm (16–24in)
Large	64–91cm (25–36in)
Very large	Over 91cm (36in)

LEAF BLADE LENGTH

Tiny	Less than 2.5cm (1in)
Miniature	4–6.5cm (1½–2½in)
Small	7.5–15cm (3–6in)
Medium	16.5–25cm (6½–10in)
Large	27–35cm (10½–14in)
Very large	Over 36cm (14in)

The clump and leaf length sizes shown are for hostas grown in British gardens under good cultural conditions and are for mature plants – that is, plants which, starting from good-sized divisions, have been growing in the same place for five full seasons. Sizes in American and New Zealand gardens, and in some European gardens, will generally be larger, although the sizes of dwarf and miniature hostas will probably be similar in all cultural and climatic conditions. The first size given in the listing below refers to the clump size.

The name in brackets following the varietal or species name is that of the raiser or finder, or that of the person who named or registered the plant. The date is the date of naming or registration.

H. 'Abba Dabba Do' (Avent 1993) Medium to large: sport of 'Sun Power', from which it differs in having matt, leathery olive-green leaves, narrowly and irregularly margined yellow with some streaking back towards the midrib. Rare. Light shade.

H. 'Abby' (Ruh 1990) Small: an attractive sport of 'Gold Drop' with undulate, deep blue-green leaves and a muted, irregular yellow margin with some streaking towards the midrib. Notably tall flower scapes. Sterile. Vigorous but compact habit of growth. Light shade.

H. 'Abiqua Blue Crinkles' (Tokudama Group) (Walden-West) Small to medium: spread 45cm (18in), height 40cm (16in). Leaves small to medium, thick, cupped and intensely puckered, almost round, abruptly-tipped, glaucous dark blue-green. Flowers bell-shaped, palest lavender to nearly white, on straight, leafy 55cm (22in) scapes, mid-season. Vigorous. Relatively pest-resistant. Light to full shade.

H. 'Abiqua Drinking Gourd' (Tokudama Group) (Walden-West 1989) Small: spread about 35cm (14in), height 40cm (16in). Leaves small to medium, upright, conspicuously cupped and puckered, almost round, abruptly tipped, glaucous dark blue-green. Flowers bell-shaped, palest lavender to nearly

white on straight, leafy 55cm (22in) scapes, mid-season. More cupped than 'Love Pat'. Light to full shade.

H. 'Abiqua Moonbeam' (Walden-West 1987) Medium: sport of 'August Moon', from which it differs in having mid-green leaves with a chartreuse margin. The variegation is scarcely apparent on new leaves but gradually develops and is brightest and most attractive in some sun. *H.* 'Mayan Moon' appears the same, but the name was never published and therefore the correct name for 'Mayan Moon' is 'Abiqua Moonbeam'.

H. 'Abiqua Recluse' (Walden-West 1989) Large: spread about 76cm

98

H. 'Abiqua Moonbeam', a showy sport of *H.* 'August Moon'.

(30in), height 45cm (18in) tall. Leaves large, glossy, rather puckered, heart-shaped yellow. Flowers lavender, funnel-shaped, on leaning, leafy 85cm (34in) scapes, late. *H.* 'White Vision' × *H.* 'Sum and Substance'. Light shade to sun.

H. 'Akebono Fukurin' Probably an unacceptable name, according to the *Cultivated Plant Code.* Rare dwarf hosta suitable for a peat bed. A variegated form of *H. longissima* from Japan with miniature leaves with a narrow white margin. Plenty of moisture and light to full shade.

H. 'Alex Summers' (Santa Lucia 1989) Large: sport of 'Gold Regal', from which it differs in having leaves with an irregular green margin. 'Rascal' (Solberg 1991) is similar but has a chartreuse-green margin. Light shade to sun.

H. 'Allan P. McConnell' (Seaver 1980) Medium: spread about 45cm (18in), height 20cm (8in). Leaves small, oval when mature, flat, dark green with a narrow, clean near-white margin. Flowers bell-shaped, purple, on straight, bare 40cm (15in) scapes, mid-season. *H. nakaiana* hybrid with typical ridged scapes. A first-rate compact, ground-covering hosta. Light shade. Readily available.

H. 'Alvatine Taylor' (Minks 1990) Large: spread about 76cm (30in), height 45cm (18in). Leaves large, thick, oval, somewhat pointed, glossy blue-green with a regular, narrow, deep yellow margin. Flowers bell-shaped, palest lavender to nearly white on straight, bare 45cm (18in) scapes, mid-season. Stated to be a distinctive new look in hostas. Light shade.

H. 'Amanuma' (Maekawa 1960). Small: spread about 35cm (14in), height 20cm (8in). Leaves small, heart-shaped, flat, mid-green. Flowers small, bell-shaped, deep lavender on straight, bare, purple-dotted 40cm (16in) scapes, early to mid-season. Makes a small mound of wavy green leaves. Named by Dr Fumio Maekawa after his garden in Tokyo. *H. venusta* × *H. capitata*. Light shade. Readily available.

H. 'Antioch' (Antioch Group) (Tompkins/Ruh/Hofer 1979) Large: spread about 91cm (36in), height 50cm (20in). Leaves large, arching to the ground, oval, tapering to a point, with a wide, irregular, cream margin fading to white, with some celadon streaking back towards the midrib. Rich soil will produce more pronounced streaking. Flowers funnel-shaped, lavender, on leaning, leafy 80cm (32in) scapes, mid-season. Sterile. Differs from *H.* 'Fortunei Albomarginata' in its longer and more pointed leaves and wider variegation. Full shade. Readily available.

H. Antioch Group (Grenfell 1996) A cultivar-group here defined so as to include a number of cultivars with all the above similar characteristics. This includes, in addition to *H.* 'Antioch', *H.* 'Goldbrook', *H.* 'Hadspen Rainbow', *H.* 'Moerheim', *H.* 'Shogun' and *H.* 'Spinners'.

H. 'Aphrodite' (Maekawa 1940) Syn. *H.* 'Chingbanyuzan'. Sport of *H. plantaginea* having double flowers, the outer stamens being petaloid. It has been cultivated in China for at least 150 years but has only recently reached the West, where it has aroused a measure of excitement that may not be justified, the problem being that although it produces flower scapes the flower buds tend to abort. Only blooms well in a hot climate. Full sun.

H. 'Aqua Velva' (K. Vaughn 1983) Large: spread about 91cm (36in), height 70cm (28in). Leaves medium to large, oval, cupped and very puckered when mature, very glaucous blue-green. Flowers bell-shaped, lavender, on leaning, bare 60cm (24in) scapes, mid-season. Slightly fragrant. Reasonably slug-resistant. Light to full shade. Readily available.

H. 'Aspen Gold' (Golden Medallion Group) (Grapes/AHS 1986) Medium to large: spread about 91cm (36in), height 50cm (20in). Leaves medium-sized, nearly round, abruptly tipped, with a heart-shaped base, intensely cupped and puckered, chartreuse to yellow, tinged green. Flowers funnel-shaped, palest lavender to nearly white on straight, leafy 60cm (24in) scapes, mid-season. One of the first of the truly yellow-leaved, puckered hostas. Some sun.

H. 'August Moon' (Langfelder/ Summers 1968) Large: spread about 76cm (30in), height 50cm (20in). Leaves large, in spring oval to heart-shaped, slightly puckered, pale green at first becoming soft yellow with a slight glaucous bloom. Summer leaves longer, smoother and bright yellow. Flowers palest lavender to nearly white on straight bare 70cm (28in) scapes, mid-season. Vigorous and fast-growing. One of the easiest yellow-leaved hostas to grow, it colours better in sun. Some named sports are: *H.* 'Lunar Eclipse', *H.* 'September Sun', *H.* 'Abiqua Moonbeam'. Readily available.

H. 'Aurora Borealis' (Frances Williams Group) (Wayside 1986) Said to be larger and more vigorous than 'Frances Williams', with wider margins and more intense colouring. Arrived in the US from an English botanic garden in 1924. Eventually Mrs Williams obtained it and sent a piece to Mrs Thelma Rudolph in Aurora, Illinois, who named it for the town. Many, if not most, *H.* 'Frances Williams' in circulation are *H.* 'Aurora Borealis'. See *H.* 'Frances Williams'.

H. 'Beatrice' (Williams 1962) Small to medium: spread about 60cm (24in), height 45cm (18in). Leaves small to medium, oval, blade somewhat undulate, green or variously edged, striped, streaked, mottled or blotched white, cream or yellow. Flowers bell-shaped, lavender on straight, leafy 60cm (24in) scapes, mid-season. Presumed to be a sport or seedling of *H. sieboldii*. An unstable and unusual hosta, no two leaves ever looking the same. Its merit is that its offspring are usually streaked or variegated: it has been much used as a pod parent for streaked hybrids. Of little or no garden interest. Shade.

H. 'Bennie McRae' (Suggs 1989) Large: spread about 76cm (30in),

height 60cm (24in). Leaves large, oval to lance-shaped with undulate margins, glossy, mid-green. Flowers fragrant, funnel-shaped, lavender, on leaning, leafy 150cm (60in) scapes, mid to late. Rapid grower. Appears similar to *H.* 'Honeybells'. An open-pollinated *H. plantaginea* hybrid. Sun.

H. 'Betcher's Blue' (Tokudama Group) (Betcher/AHS 1986) Differs from *H.* 'Tokudama' in that the leaves are thick, deeply cupped and heavily puckered, longer and more pointed, resembling *H.* 'Tokudama Flavocircinalis' in shape. They are dark glaucous blue early in the year, becoming green later. Slow to increase, but should be better known. Light to full shade.

H. 'Betsy King' (AHS 1986) Medium: spread about 50cm (20in), height 35cm (14in). Leaves small to medium, upright, blunt-tipped, oval, flat, glossy dark green. Superb deep purple flowers on straight, bare 60cm (24in) scapes, late. Closely resembles *H.* 'Decorata' but is a hybrid of *H. sieboldii*. Light shade. Readily available.

H. 'Big Daddy' (Elegans Group) (Aden 1978) One of the best and most distinctive of this cultivar-group. Differs from *H. sieboldiana* in having nearly round and cupped leaves with an abrupt tip, veins sunken above with much furrowing and puckering between, chalky, dark glaucous-blue. Quite slow to establish. *H. sieboldiana* × *H.* 'Tokudama'. Light to full shade. Readily available.

H. 'Big Mama' (Elegans Group) (Aden 1978) Differs from *H. sieboldiana* 'Elegans' in its larger leaves of a less distinctive, flatter shape. Its leaf colour is greener than that of 'Big Daddy'. Light to full shade. Readily available.

H. 'Bill Brincka' (Brincka 1988) Large: appears identical to *H.*

100

'Opipara' as introduced by Lady Joyce Crossley to the UK. The need for a cultivar name in America arose because some H. 'Opipara' there was virused. H. 'Bill Brincka' was a name applied to a clone that was virus-free. Light to full shade.

H. 'Birchwood Parky's Gold' (Shaw/AHS1986) Large: spread about 75cm (36in), height 35cm (14in). Leaves small to medium, heart-shaped, undulate, the lobes lifted causing some cupping, at first greyish-yellow becoming clear light yellow with just a hint of green. Flowers bell-shaped, lavender, on straight, bare 95cm (38in) scapes, mid-season. Sterile. One of the classic yellows, increasing fast and making good solid clumps suitable for light woodland conditions. Light shade. Readily available.

H. 'Bizarre' (Kuk 1986) Small: tightly clump-forming seedling of H. 'Kabitan', from which it differs in having somewhat larger, chartreuse leaves with a white margin, and some puckering on mature leaves. Makes a lovely small hosta that increases rapidly and is superb in flower, the blooms being twice the size of the parent. Light to full shade.

H. 'Blaue Venus' (Tardiana Group) Medium: spread about 45cm (18in), height 35cm (14in). Leaves small to medium, thick, oval to heart-shaped glaucous blue-green. Flowers bell-shaped, pale lavender on straight, bare, glaucous 40cm (16in) scapes, mid-season. Reputed to be one of the bluest-leaved German Tardianas. Only well-known in European gardens. Light to full shade.

H. 'Blond Elf' (Aden) Medium: spread about 60cm (24in), height 20cm (8in). Leaves small, lance-shaped, pointed, the margin rippled, the veins closely spaced, of good texture, chartreuse to yellow. An abundance of funnel-shaped,

lavender flowers on straight, bare 45cm (18in) scapes, mid-season. Ideal for a rock garden. Useful for its tolerance to sun.

H. 'Blue Angel' (Elegans Group) (Aden 1986) Very large: larger and faster growing than most of the Elegans Group. The near heart-shaped, smooth, gently undulate, glaucous blue-grey leaves are pointed and held at right angles from the upright petiole with the leaf tips arching down. Near white flowers on 122cm (48in), bare scapes well above the leaf mound, mid to late. Sterile. Has a lush, tropical mien when well grown. Award of Garden Merit (RHS). Light to full shade. Readily available.

H. 'Blue Arrow' (Anderson 1982) Medium: spread about 45cm (18in), height 25cm (10in). Leaves medium, lance-shaped, flat, smooth, glaucous blue-green. Flowers bell-shaped, palest lavender to nearly white on straight, bare 45cm (18in) scapes, mid-season. In general effect similar to one of the smaller of the Tardiana Group and has most elegantly shaped leaves. Light to full shade.

H. 'Blue Blush' (Tardiana Group, TF 3 × 1) (E. Smith/BHHS 1988) Small: spread about 28cm (11in), height 16cm (6in). Leaves small, thick, cupped and puckered, heart-shaped to round, glaucous blue-green. Flowers bell-shaped, lavender on straight, bare 28cm (11in) scapes, mid-season. Light to full shade.

H. 'Blue Cadet' (Tokudama Group) (Aden 1974) Small: differs from H. 'Tokudama' in having smaller leaves and better purple flowers. A first-rate hosta. Dappled to full shade. Readily available.

H. 'Blue Danube' (Tardiana Group, TF 2 × 24) (E. Smith/BHHS 1988) Small: spread about 35cm (14in), height 20cm (8in). Leaves small,

heart-shaped, slightly puckered, glaucous dark blue-green. Flowers bell-shaped, lavender, on straight, bare 60cm (24in) scapes, mid-season. Light to full shade.

H. 'Blue Diamond' (Tardiana Group, TF 2 × 23) (E. Smith/BHHS 1988) Small to medium-sized: spread about 45cm (18in), height 30cm (12in). Leaves medium-sized, broadly diamond-shaped, smooth, flat, glaucous blue-green. Flowers bell-shaped, lavender on straight, leafy, occasionally branched 45cm (18in) scapes, mid-season. Light to full shade. Readily available.

H. 'Blue Dimples' (Tardiana Group, TF 2 × 8) (E. Smith/BHHS 1988) Medium: spread about 50cm (20in), height 30cm (12in). Leaves medium, thick, puckered, lightly undulate, near heart-shaped, pointed, glaucous blue-green. Flowers bell-shaped, purple-striped lavender on straight, bare 50cm (20in) scapes, mid-season. One of the best Tardianas for colour, substance and leaf texture. Often confused in the trade with H. 'Blue Wedgwood', which differs in its more wedge-shaped leaves. Light to full shade. Readily available.

H. 'Blue Ice' (Benedict 1987) Miniature: spread about 20cm (8in), height 10cm (4in). Leaves miniature, thick, outward-facing, cupped, puckered, round to heart-shaped, abruptly tipped, intensely glaucous blue-green on unfurling, becoming greener later. Flowers bell-shaped, lavender on straight, bare 25cm (10in) scapes, mid-season. A delightful little hosta resulting from the crossing of two of the smallest of the Tardiana Group, H. 'Dorset Blue' × H. 'Blue Moon'. Slow. Light to full shade.

H. 'Blue Mammoth' (Elegans Group) (Aden) Differs from H. sieboldiana 'Elegans' in its lighter chalky-blue colour and its less elegant shape. One of the largest 'blues'. Light to full shade. Readily available.

***H.* 'Blue Moon'** (Tardiana Group, TF 2 × 2) (E. Smith/BHHS 1976) Small: spread about 25cm (10in), height 20cm (8in). Leaves miniature to small, thick, somewhat cupped, puckered, abruptly tipped, round to heart-shaped, intense glaucous blue-green. Dense raceme of bell-shaped, pale lavender-grey to nearly white flowers on straight, bare 30cm (12in) scapes, mid-season. The smallest of the Tardianas. In commerce it has been confused with *H.* 'Dorset Blue', which has a similar leaf shape but is larger in all its parts. Light to full shade.

***H.* 'Blue Piecrust'** (Summers/AHS 1986) Very large: spread about 110cm (44in), height 80cm (32in). Leaves very large, elegant, heart-shaped with a pronounced piecrust margin, glaucous blue-green. Flowers funnel-shaped, palest lavender to nearly white on straight bare 105cm (42in) scapes, mid-season. One of the first hostas raised with a piecrust margin. A plant much prized by flower arrangers. Light to full shade. Readily available.

***H.* 'Blue Seer'** (Elegans Group) (Aden) Large: differs from *H. sieboldiana* 'Elegans' in its narrowly heart-shaped, very puckered, intensely chalky light blue-green leaves. Very floriferous. One of the most distinctive and attractive of the Elegans Group. Light to full shade.

***H.* 'Blue Shadows'** (Anderson 1980) Medium-sized: differs from *H.* 'Tokudama Aureonebulosa' in having more and deeper blue in the leaves. Light to full shade.

***H.* 'Blue Skies'** (Tardiana Group, TF 2 × 6) (E. Smith/BHHS 1988) Small: spread about 30cm (12in), height 23cm (9in). Leaves small, thick, smooth, heart-shaped, abruptly tipped, glaucous dark, steel blue-green. Flowers bell-shaped, palest lavender to nearly white on straight, bare, 40cm (16in) scapes, mid-season. One of the best of the Tardiana Group in flower, the flowers rather resembling hyacinths. Light to full shade. Readily available.

***H.* 'Blue Umbrellas'** (Elegans Group) (Aden 1978) Very large:

H. 'Blue Moon', the smallest of the Tardiana Group, with *Rhododendron haematodes* FCC Form.

102

differs from *H. sieboldiana* 'Elegans' in the convex curvature of the leaves, giving them a fancied resemblance to an umbrella, and in being less blue in colour. Veins widely spaced. Of stiff, upright habit. Leaves very thick and leathery. If you must grow a blue-leaved hosta in the sun this is the one to choose, but give it plenty of moisture. Prefers light shade. Readily available.

H. **'Blue Vision'** (Aden 1976) Medium to large: spread about 91cm (36in), height 80cm (32in). Leaves medium to large, thick, cupped and very puckered, round to heart-shaped, outstandingly glaucous, blue-green. Flowers bell-shaped, palest lavender to nearly white on straight, bare 91cm

(36in) scapes, mid-season. Light to full shade.

H. **'Blue Wedgwood'** (Tardiana Group, TF 2 × 9) (E. Smith/BHHS 1988) Medium: spread about 60cm (24in), height 35cm (14in). Leaves medium, thick, somewhat wedge-shaped, margins undulate, tapering to a point, intense glaucous blue-green. Flowers bell-shaped, palest lavender to near-white on straight, bare 40cm (16in) scapes, mid-season. Sometimes confused in the trade with *H.* 'Blue Dimples' as young plants are similar. Light to full shade. Readily available.

H. **'Bold Edger'** (K. Vaughn 1983) Medium: spread about 45cm (18in), height 50cm (20in). Leaves medium, oval to heart-shaped,

blade undulate, dark olive-green distinctly and regularly margined yellow to ivory. Flowers funnel-shaped, lavender, on straight, leafy 60cm (25in) scapes, mid-season. A densely-mounded clump. *H.* 'Frances Williams' hybrid. Light shade.

H. **'Bold Ribbons'** (Aden 1976) Medium: spread about 45cm (18in), height 40cm (16in). Leaves medium, elliptic, arching, olive-green with a distinct, irregular cream to white margin. Flowers funnel-shaped, purple on straight, bare 65cm (26in) scapes, mid-season. Stoloniferous habit and not suited to container-growing. Light to full shade. Readily available.

H. **'Bold Ruffles'** (Elegans Group) (Arett 1975) Very large: differs

H. 'Bright Lights', a larger and more vigorous selection from *H.* 'Tokudama Aureonebulosa'.

from *H. sieboldiana* 'Elegans' in that the leaf margins are distinctively rippled. Of stiff and upright habit. Not suitable for container-growing but a striking border plant. Light to full shade. Readily available.

H. 'Borwick Beauty' (George Smith Group) (MacBurnie/BHHS 1988) Similar to 'George Smith', but possibly the leaf is rounder.

H. 'Bressingham Blue' (Elegans Group) (Bloom 1984) Differs from *H. sieboldiana* 'Elegans' in its exceptional large, cupped and puckered almost round leaves of a superb glaucous blue. Light to full shade. Readily available.

H. 'Bridegroom' (Benedict/Gowen 1990) Small: spread 30cm (12in), height 25cm (10in). Leaves small, triangular, while the twisted tip curves upward, margin rippled, satiny, dark green. Flowers funnel-shaped, lavender on leafy, upright 45cm (18in) scapes, mid-season to late. *H.* 'Holly's Honey' selfed. Sterile. A most unusual hosta. Light to full shade.

H. 'Bright Lights' (Aden/Klehm) Small to medium: differs from 'Tokudama Aureonebulosa' in that the blue is mainly confined to the margin, while the centre is mainly yellow, and it is a more vigorous plant with larger leaves and less puckering. Light to full shade.

H. 'Brim Cup' (Aden 1986) Small: spread about 38cm (15in), height 30cm (12in). Leaves small, upright, stiff, cupped and seersuckered when mature, round to heart-shaped mid-green with a very wide, irregular creamy-yellow to white margin. Flowers bell-shaped, palest lavender to nearly white, disposed to one side, on straight, bare 45cm (18in) scapes, mid-season. Of moderate increase. Light shade.

H. 'Buckshaw Blue' (Tokudama Group) (E. Smith/AHS 1986)

Medium: spread about 60cm (24in), height 34cm (14in). Leaves medium, thick, heart-shaped, flat but upturned at the margins, veins narrowly spaced, intense glaucous blue-green. Flowers bell-shaped, palest lavender to near-white on straight, bare 35cm (14in) scapes, mid-season. Slow. A seedling found by Eric Smith at the Hillier Nurseries, Winchester, England and taken by him to Buckshaw Gardens, the Plantsmen Nursery, where some of the Tardiana Group were raised. *H. sieboldiana* × *H.* 'Tokudama'. One of the best 'blues'. Light to full shade. Readily available.

H. 'Calypso' (Lachman 1987) Small: spread about 35cm (14in), height 18cm (7in). Leaves medium, lance-shaped, flat, gracefully tipped, creamy-white with an attractive irregular chartreuse to bright green margin on very short petioles. Flowers funnel-shaped, outward-facing lavender on straight, bare 45cm (18in) scapes, mid-season. *H.* 'White Christmas' derivative. Full shade.

H. 'Camelot' (Tardiana Group, TF 2 × 27) (E. Smith/BHHS 1988) Medium: spread about 55cm (22in), height 38cm (15in). Leaves small, thick, flat, heart-shaped, glaucous blue-green. Flowers bell-shaped, palest lavender to nearly white on straight, bare 38cm (15in) scapes, mid-season. One of the bluest of the Tardianas. Light to full shade.

H. 'Candy Hearts' (Fisher 1971) Small to medium: spread about 70cm (28in), height 40cm (16in). Leaves small, somewhat cupped, heart-shaped, the lobes overlapping, glaucous grey-green. Flowers bell-shaped, palest lavender to nearly white on straight, bare 65cm (26in) scapes, mid season. *H. nakaiana* hybrid. Vigorous, very dense and compact hosta with good flowers. Good container specimen. Sports are *H.* 'Amber Maiden', *H.*

'Heartsong'. Light to full shade. Readily available.

H. capitata ([Koidzumi] Nakai 1930) Small to medium: spread about 45cm (18in), height 25cm (10in). Leaves miniature, heart-shaped, the margin very rippled, satiny mid-green above, shiny lighter green beneath, the petiole strongly red-dotted. Flowers purple with darker lines, bunched together at the top of the 50cm (20in) scape just above a single large, leafy bract, the scape ridged and intensely red- to purple-dotted, mid-season. Named for the way the flowers in bud are gathered together in a large purple 'head'. Closely related to *H. nakaiana* and now merged by some botanists. Light shade.

H. 'Carnival' (Lachman 1986) Large: spread about 91cm (36in), height 45cm (18in). Leaves large, thick, oval to heart-shaped, very puckered when mature, dark green with an irregular, wide bright yellow margin, with some streaking and mottling towards the midrib. Flowers funnel shaped, lavender on straight, leafy 91cm (36in) scapes, mid-season. *H.* 'Beatrice' seedling. Light to full shade.

H. 'Carol' (Fortunei Albomarginata Group) (Williams/AHS 1986) Differs from *H.* 'Fortunei Albomarginata' in its more oval blade shape and the noticeably glaucous bloom. An attractive hosta of subtle colouring. Late to emerge and slow to increase. Light to full shade.

H. 'Carousel' (Lachman 1989) Small: spread about 30cm (12in), height 23cm (9in). Leaves small, puckered, heart-shaped, dark green with an irregular yellow margin. Flowers funnel-shaped, lavender, on straight, bare 40cm (16in) scapes, mid-season. *H.* 'Reversed' hybrid. Full shade.

H. 'Carrie Ann' (Stone/Ruh 1988) Small: spread about 25cm (10in), height 10cm (4in). Leaves small, elliptic, slightly undulate, satiny olive-green above, shiny beneath, with a cream margin that fades to white, with some grey streaking back towards the midrib, the variegation extending down the wings of the petiole. Flowers funnel-shaped, pure white with green tips on straight, leafy 60cm (24in) scapes, the bracts variegated like the leaves, mid-season to late. Thrives on peaty soil. Full shade.

H. 'Celebration' (Aden 1978) Small to medium: spread about 35cm (14in), height 25cm (10in). Leaves small to medium, elliptic, creamy-white with an irregular dark green margin. Flowers funnel-shaped, deep lavender with purple stripes on straight, bare 45cm (18in) scapes, mid-season. Sterile. Generally similar to *H.* 'Gay Feather' but smaller in all its parts. Leaves emerge very early and are prone to frost damage. Melting out can be a problem so it needs careful placing in the border. Sometimes it will thrive in some sun, but generally shade is recommended. Readily available.

H. 'Change of Tradition' (Zilis 1985) Medium: spread about 60cm (24in), height 50cm (20in). Leaves medium, narrowly lance-shaped, veins deeply impressed and close together, glossy dark green with a very narrow clean white margin. Flowers funnel-shaped, pale lavender on straight, bare, 60cm (24in) scapes, late. A distinctive and refined new hosta, valuable for its late flowers. Excellent for mass planting or a good contrast with round-leaved hostas. A sport of *H.* 'Lancifolia'. Light to full shade.

H. 'Chantilly Lace' (Lachman 1988) Small: spread about 30cm (12in), height 25cm (10in). Leaves small, lance-shaped, ruffled, the tip twisted, satiny grey-green with a creamy-white margin, continuing down the petiole wings. Flowers

funnel-shaped, large, white on straight, leafy 30cm (12in) scapes, late. *H.* 'Halcyon' hybrid. Light to full shade.

H. 'Chartreuse Wiggles' (Aden 1976) Small: spread about 25cm (10in), height 20cm (8in). Leaves small, thin, narrowly lance-shaped, very undulate, chartreuse. Flowers bell-shaped, purple on straight, bare 45cm (18in) scapes, mid-season. Makes a flattish mound of conspicuously ripple-margined yellowish leaves. The good dark purple flowers are carried on unexpectedly tall, slender scapes. Stoloniferous in light soil. Not easy to grow. Full shade. Readily available.

H. 'Chelsea Ore' (Compton 1989) Sport of *H. plantaginea* 'Grandiflora', differing in having thin, shiny, chartreuse leaves with a very narrow dark green margin with some streaking back towards the midrib. Perhaps best grown as a conservatory plant in the UK. Originated at the Chelsea Physic Garden in the 1980s. Try semi-shade at the foot of a south wall. Rare.

H. 'Cherub' (Lachman 1989) Very small: spread about 23cm (9in), height 15cm (6in). Leaves miniature, slightly puckered, heart-shaped, bright light green with an irregular cream to white margin. Flowers funnel-shaped, lavender, on straight, bare 20cm (8in) scapes, mid-season. Light to full shade.

H. 'Chinese Sunrise' (Schaeffer/Summers/Ruh) Small to medium: spread about 60cm (24in), height 35cm (14in). Leaves medium, thin, glossy, narrowly lance-shaped, tapering to a point, chartreuse-yellow at first, fading to light green (viridescent), with an irregular, narrow, deep green margin. A profusion of bell-shaped, purple flowers, on leaning, very leafy 70cm (28in) scapes, late. One of the first hostas to emerge in the spring. *H. cathayana* form. Light to medium shade. Readily available.

H. 'Choko Nishiki'. See *H.* 'On Stage'.

H. 'Christmas Gold' (Golden Medallion Group) (C. Seaver) Medium: spread about 60cm (24in), height 45cm (18in). Leaves medium, cupped, very seersuckered, exceptionally round, lemon gold with attractive glaucous bloom, the undersides very glaucous light green. Flowers bell-shaped, palest lavender to nearly white on bare, glaucous 50cm (20in) scapes, mid-season. Bright purple seed capsules. Compact sport of *H.* 'Christmas Tree'. *H.* 'Sea Gold Dust' is similar but smaller. Will take full sun.

H. 'Christmas Tree' (K.Vaughn/M. Seaver 1982) Large: spread about 91cm (36in), height 50cm (20in). Leaves large, heart-shaped, the lobes lifted, deeply veined and deeply puckered, irregularly margined creamy white with some overlapping of the white on the green resulting in celadon green and grey streaking. Flowers bell-shaped, lavender on straight, leafy 45cm (18in) scapes, mid-season. Distinctive aubergine pods. Charming and showy. *H.* 'Frances Williams' hybrid, similar to *H.* 'Grand Master'. Light to full shade. Readily available.

H. 'Christmas Tree Gala' The name for the streaked form of *H.* 'Christmas Tree'. Rare and expensive because a large percentage of its seedlings are streaked and therefore in great demand by breeders. A collectors' plant. Full shade.

H. clausa (Nakai 1930) Small: spread about 70cm (24in), height 20cm (8in). Leaves medium, erect, spatulate to oval, the blade running into the petiole without clear distinction, satiny mid-green above, shiny beneath, the petiole increasingly red-dotted towards the base. Flowers dark lavender, not opening, on straight, bare 40cm (16in) scapes, early to mid-season. An

The long, tapering tip with its distinct twist sets *H.* 'Crispula' apart from other white-edged hostas.

interesting species on account of its stoloniferous habit, making excellent dense ground cover. Flowers not produced in sufficient quantity to be showy. Triploid. Not often found in the wild. Light shade.

H. clausa 'Normalis' (Maekawa 1938) Differs from the typical plant in being less stoloniferous and in that flowers open normally. Flowers are darkest lavender, large and among the showiest in the genus. Needs rich soil and plenty of moisture. May be under the name of just *H. clausa* in the US. *H.* 'Tapis Vert' is a selected form from France. Readily available.

H. 'Color Glory' (George Smith Group) (Aden 1980) Similar, or identical, to *H.* 'Borwick Beauty'.

H. 'Colossal' (Savory 1977) Very large: spread about 150cm (60in), height 91cm (36in). Leaves very large, oval with a heart-shaped base, the lobes lifted and pinched at the navel, the veins deeply impressed giving a furrowed appearance, matt, dull olive-green with a slight metallic sheen above, shiny, lighter green beneath; makes a huge mound of striking foliage. Flowers funnel-shaped, pale lavender, on straight, bare 91cm (36in) scapes, mid-season. *H. montana* hybrid. Light to full shade.

H. 'Cream Cheese' (Lachman 1991) Small: spread about 30cm (12in), height 15cm (6in). Leaves small, oval, slightly undulate, dark green with an irregular wide creamy-white margin. Attractive funnel-shaped, purple-striped lavender flowers on straight, distinctly leafy 35cm (14in) scapes, late. From streaked *H.* 'Crepe Suzette' selfed.

H. 'Crepe Suzette' (Lachman 1986) Small: spread about 30cm (12in), height 15cm (6in). Leaves small, round to oval, distinctively pointed, matt, mid-green with a wide and extremely irregular creamy-white margin. Some celadon streaking in the centre of the leaf blade, going down the flat, wide petiole which is decurrent to the blade. Attractive funnel-shaped, lavender-striped, purple flowers, on straight, distinctively leafy 30cm (12in) scapes, late. A very showy but slow-growing hosta. Light to full shade.

H. 'Crested Surf' (Benedict 1990) Miniature: spread about 20cm (8in), height 28cm (11in). Leaves small, spatulate, ruffle-margined, dark green with a very variable creamy-white margin, the undulation and variegation extending down the petiole. Flowers funnel-shaped, lavender, on leaning, leafy 30cm (12in) scapes, late. Attractive. *H.* 'Neat Splash' selfed. Light to full shade.

106

H. 'Crispula' (Maekawa 1940) Large: spread about 91cm (36in), height 45cm (18in). Leaves large, widely oval coming to a point, with a down-turned tip, the blade conspicuously undulate, deep green with a striking wide, irregular white margin, the white overlapping the green resulting in some celadon streaking back towards the midrib, dull above, shiny beneath on narrowly channelled petioles. Flowers funnel-shaped, pale lavender on straight, bare 91cm (36in) scapes, early. Sometimes confused with other white-margined hostas. Prone to viral infection. Full shade and shelter from wind. Very slow. Often offered, but sometimes causes disappointment when the plant turns out to be *H.* 'Undulata Albomarginata' (syn. *H.* 'Thomas Hogg').

H. 'Crown Jewel' (Walters Gardens 1984) Sport of *H.* 'Gold Drop', from which it differs in having chartreuse leaves with a white margin. Difficult. Light shade.

H. 'Crumples' (Grenfell & Grounds 1995) Medium: spread about 60cm (24in), height 35cm (14in). Leaves medium, heart-shaped, the lobes lifted and pinched at the navel, the blade cupped and conspicuously puckered and crumpled, light green above, paler and somewhat glaucous beneath, the petioles coarsely winged. Flowers bell-shaped, pale lavender on straight, bare 45cm (18in) scapes, early. Sterile. So named from the generally crumpled appearance of the leaves. Found in a row of *H. sieboldiana* 'Elegans' seedlings. Light to full shade.

H. 'Crusader' (Lachman 1989) Large: spread about 76cm (30in), height 40cm (16in). Leaves medium, thick to leathery, heart-shaped with a distinctive tip and pinched lobes, slightly puckered when mature, satiny dark green above, shiny below, with an irregu-

lar ivory margin. Flowers funnel-shaped, lavender on straight, bare 62cm (26in) scapes, mid-season. *H.* 'Halcyon' × *H.* 'Resonance'. Light to full shade.

H. 'Dawn' (syn. *H.* 'Sunset') (BHHS) Small, stoloniferous: spread about 30cm (12in), height 20cm (8in). Leaves dwarf, widely oval, bright yellow. Flowers funnel-shaped, rich purple with bluish anthers on straight, bare 30cm (12in) scapes, late. Has been confused with *H.* 'Hydon Sunset', though this hosta has distinctly heart-shaped leaves that gradually fade to green. Has sported *H.* 'Green With Envy'. Light to full shade. Readily available.

H. 'Daybreak' (Aden 1986) Very large: spread about 91cm (36in), height 60cm (24in). Leaves very large, somewhat shiny, wedge- to heart-shaped, margins lightly undulate, with a turned-down tip, emerging green becoming brassy yellow, on short petioles arching out at 45°. Flowers lavender on straight, bare 70cm (28in) scapes, mid to late. Very vigorous. Occasionally sets seed and supplies excellent yellow seedlings. Light shade. As near to gold as any so-called gold-coloured hosta leaf.

H. 'Decorata' (Bailey 1930) Large: spread about 76cm (30in), height 30cm (12in). Leaves medium, widely oval, matt mid green, crisply margined white, the variegation extending down broadly winged petioles. Narrow, bell-shaped purple flowers on 60cm (24in) leafy scapes, mid-season. Stoloniferous. Responds well to friable peaty soil but can be difficult. Light shade. Readily available.

H. 'Devon Blue' (Tardiana Group) (Bowden 1988) Large: spread about 100cm (40in), height 50cm (20in). Leaves medium, oval to heart-shaped, tapering to a point, glaucous blue-green. Flowers bell-

shaped, lavender, on 76cm (30in) scapes, mid-season. Acquired by Ann and Roger Bowden from unnamed Tardiana Group stock at the Plantsmen Nursery, Buckshaw Gardens. Light to full shade. Readily available.

H. 'Devon Giant' (Bowden 1995) Very large: spread 91cm (36in), height 91cm (36in). Leaves large, very thick, very cupped and puckered, almost round, glaucous dark blue-green. Flowers bell-shaped, pale lavender to near-white

_H._ 'Devon Green', one of the best green-leaved hostas for both leaf and flower.

on straight, bare, glaucous 94cm (37in) scapes, mid-season. A seedling of _H._ 'Hadspen Blue'.

_H._ 'Devon Green' (Tardiana Group) (Bowden 1988) Sport of _H._ 'Halcyon', from which it differs in having dark green, very shiny leaves and purple-dotted petioles. One of the best green-leaved hostas, and has a great future. _H._ 'Peridot' (Lydell) and _H._ 'Valerie's Vanity' are similar.

_H._ 'Dew Drop' (Walters Gardens 1988) Sport of _H._ 'Gold Drop', from which it differs in having cupped, dark green leaves with a narrow white margin. Often the first flush of leaves have the drawstring effect.

_H._ 'Diamond Tiara' (Tiara Group) (Zilis 1985) Differs from _H._ 'Golden Tiara' in having dark green leaves fairly regularly and crisply margined white. Vigorous and fast-growing. Good small hosta for edging. Full shade.

_H._ 'Dick Ward' (Hatfield 1991) Strikingly beautiful sport of _H._ 'Zounds', differing in having prominently veined chartreuse to brassy yellow, very puckered leaves with a broad, dark green margin. The colour becomes much paler if grown in any sun. Light shade to sun. Reputedly pest-resistant. _H._ 'Midwest Magic' is a similar sport.

H. 'Donahue Piecrust' (Donahue) Large, classic ruffled: spread about 76cm (30in), height 56cm (22in). Leaves large, oval to heart-shaped, tapering to a point, margins very rippled, blade furrowed, mid-green. Bell-shaped near-white flowers on leaning, leafy 86cm (34in) scapes, mid-season. One of the best hostas grown for its distinctive piecrust margins and much used as a parent for this characteristic. *H. montana* hybrid. Light to full shade.

H. 'Don Stevens' (M. Seaver 1990) Miniature: spread about 20cm (8in), height 15cm (6in). Leaves medium, heart-shaped, glossy, deep green with a yellowish-white margin. Juvenile plants have streaked variegation and a narrower leaf which settles down to becoming margined. Flowers purple on red-dotted scapes, mid-season. Light to full shade.

H. 'Dorothy Benedict' (Elegans Group) (Benedict 1983) Small: spread about 35cm (14in), height 23cm (9in). Leaves small, thick, cupped and puckered, glaucous blue with yellow streaking between the veins. A major breakthrough in hybridization as it was the first streaked hosta of *H. sieboldiana* lineage. Now a pod parent for a whole new line of streaked hostas. *H.* 'Frances Williams' selfed. Shade.

H. 'Dorset Blue' (Tardiana Group, TF 2 × 4) (E. Smith/Aden 1977) Small: spread about 30cm (12in), height 20cm (8in). Leaves small, thick, cupped, puckered round to heart-shaped, intense chalky light blue-green, this colour also on the flattish petioles. Flowers lavender-pink on straight, leafy 30cm (12in) scapes, mid-season. It holds its wonderful colour throughout the summer. Dappled to full shade.

H. 'Duchess' (Savory 1982) Small: spread about 30cm (12in), height 15cm (6in). Leaves small, heart-shaped, wavy, mid-green with a whitish-yellow margin. Flowers bell-shaped, purple on straight, leafy, 45cm (18in) scapes, mid-season. Lovely in a peat bed or rock garden. Full shade.

H. 'DuPage Delight' (George Smith Group) (Zilis) Similar to *H.* 'George Smith'. A sport of *H.* 'Frances Williams', not of *H. sieboldiana* 'Elegans'.

H. 'Elata' (Hylander 1954) Very large: spread about 100cm (40in), height 65cm (26in). Leaves very large, furrowed with sunken veins, oval tapering to a point, some forms having rippled margins, blade somewhat undulate, matt mid-green above, glaucous green below with prominent veins. Flowers widely spaced, funnel-shaped, lavender, on slightly leaning leafy 122cm (48in) scapes, early to mid-summer. Vigorous. Light to full shade. Nowadays usually only seen as mature clumps in long-established gardens.

H. 'El Capitan' (Lachman 1987) Large: spread about 100cm (40in), height 60cm (24in). Leaves medium, puckered, oval to heart-shaped, attractively pointed, margins rippled, glaucous sage-green above, glaucous below, with an irregular yellow margin, extending down the wide, flat petiole. Flowers bell-shaped lavender, on straight, bare 91cm (36in) scapes, early to mid-season. Increases rapidly. Somewhat pest-resistant. A promising new hosta. Light to full shade.

H. Elegans Group (Grenfell 1996) A cultivar-group here defined so as to include a number of named cultivars with characteristics similar to *H. sieboldiana* 'Elegans'. This includes *H.* 'Big Daddy', *H.* 'Big Mama', *H.* 'Blue Angel', *H.* 'Blue Mammoth', *H.* 'Blue Seer', *H.* 'Blue Umbrellas', *H.* 'Bold Ruffles', *H.* 'Gray Cole', *H.* 'Perry's True Blue', *H.* 'Trail's End', *H.* 'True Blue', *H.* 'Vicar's Mead'. Readily available.

H. 'Elfin Power' (Ruh 1987) Medium: spread about 45cm (18in), height 25cm (10in). Leaves medium, spoon-shaped, slightly cupped, mid-green with a white margin, the white overlapping the green resulting in some streaking back towards the midrib. Flowers funnel-shaped, lavender on straight, bare 66cm (26in) scapes, mid-season. Light shade.

H. 'Elisabeth' (Hensen 1983) Large: spread about 95cm (38in), height 66cm (26in). Leaves medium, with distinctly ruffled margins, oval, matt mid-green leaves. Flowers funnel-shaped, purple, on leaning, leafy 95cm (38in) purplish scapes, late. Found in Germany and named by Dr Hensen for his wife. Much grown in European gardens. Light shade.

H. 'Embroidery' (Aden) Medium: spread about 60cm (24in), height 45cm (18in). Leaves medium, heart-shaped, shiny, twisted, crimped, tucked and pinched, usually mid-green with a darker margin. Flowers bell-shaped lavender on straight, bare 40cm (16in) scapes, mid-season. A unique hosta that appears to have been shirred round the margin, the space between the two outer veins being deeply crimped. Rare and expensive. Light to full shade.

H. 'Emerald Tiara' (Tiara Group) (Walters Gardens 1988) Differs from 'Golden Tiara' in that it has gold leaves with a green margin. Dappled shade. In the US *H.* 'Emerald Scepter' has a paler centre and margin colouring and can suffer from melting out. Light to full shade.

H. 'Emily Dickinson' (Lachman 1987) Vigorous, erect, large: spread about 91cm (36in), height 50cm (20in). Leaves medium, oval, mid-green with a crisp cream margin. Flowers fragrant, funnel-shaped, deep lavender on straight,

The round, crumpled, silvery-blue leaves of *H*. 'Evelyn McCafferty', ultimately a very large hosta.

leafy 70cm (28in) scapes clustered in the middle of the clump, late. *H*. 'Neat Splash' × *H. plantaginea*. Light shade.

H. 'Evelyn McCafferty' (Elegans Group) (Lehmann 1975) Differs from *H. sieboldiana* 'Elegans' in its exceptionally round, cupped and puckered leaves, making it an outstanding specimen hosta.

H. 'Evening Magic' (Zilis 1988) Large: regular, narrowly-margined sport of *H*. 'Piedmont Gold'. First flush of leaves in spring often exhibits the drawstring effect. Not easy to grow. Light shade.

H. 'Fair Maiden' (Walters Gardens 1993) Sport of 'Amber Maiden', from which it differs in having dark green leaves with an irregular cream to almost white margin with some celadon streaking in the blade. Sterile. A handsome hosta which should have a great future. Light shade.

H. 'Fall Bouquet' (Aden 1986) Medium: spread about 45cm (18in), height 30cm (12in). Leaves medium, lance-shaped, dark green with a satiny surface, bluish-white below, the margins rippled, the petioles intensely red-dotted. Flowers funnel-shaped, lavender, on 40cm (16in) intensely red-dotted, straight, bare scapes, late to very late. Sterile. *H. longipes* var. *hypoglauca* form or hybrid. One of the best for red petioles and scapes and useful for its late flowers. Light shade.

H. 'Fascination' (Aden 1978) Medium: spread about 50cm (20in), height 45cm (18in). Leaves large, somewhat puckered, cream, streaked chartreuse, yellow, white and green, margined green. Flowers funnel-shaped, lavender, on straight, leafy 50cm (20in) scapes, mid-season. One of several streaked hostas whose main interest is that when used as a pod-parent a high proportion of the progeny produce streaked or variegated offspring. Sports to leaves entirely chartreuse called *H*. 'Golden Fascination'. Full shade.

H. 'Feather Boa' (O'Harra 1991) Small, semi-stoloniferous: spread about 30cm (12in), height 15cm (6in). Leaves small, narrowly oval, closely veined, chartreuse-yellow, somewhat viridescent. Profusion of bell-shaped, light lavender flowers, striped purple on straight, bare scapes, mid-season. Increases quickly. Light shade. Readily available.

H. 'Flamboyant' (Aden 1978) Medium: spread about 45cm (18in), height 30cm (12in). Leaves medium,

H. fluctuans 'Sagae' (syn. *H. fluctuans* 'Variegated'), one of the best plants in the genus.

heart-shaped, glossy, chartreuse streaked cream, yellow and green with an irregular creamy white margin. Flowers funnel-shaped, lavender on 50cm (20in) straight, leafy scapes; mid-season. One of the first streaked hostas, creating a sensation when it was introduced. However, as with most streaked hostas the streaking is unstable and migrates to the margin. Best divided every two or three years. *H.* 'Shade Fanfare' is the stable, marginally variegated form. Full shade.

H. 'Flower Power' (K. Vaughn 1987) Large: spread about 122cm (48in), height 76cm (30in). Leaves large, lance-shaped with slight ruffling, at first shiny, silvery-grey becoming medium green later. Flowers large, fragrant, funnel-shaped, pale lavender to white depending on climate, on straight, bare, 122cm (48in) scapes, mid-season. Sterile. Remarkable for its notably tall scapes. One of the earliest of the fragrant sorts to flower. Light shade to sun.

H. fluctuans 'Sagae' (Watanabe 1985) This is the correct name for the hosta that is commonly known in the West as *H. fluctuans* 'Variegated'. Very large: spread about 122cm (48in), height 91cm (36in). Leaves very large, very thick, held horizontal on upright petioles, broadly wedge-shaped, emerging twisted but becoming gently undulate, gracefully pointed, the lobes lifting making the blade boat-shaped, soft glaucous green with a bold cream to yellow

margin, with shades of celadon green in the transitional area, glaucous beneath. Flowers funnel-shaped, palest lavender suffused purple, on leaning, leafy 100cm (40in) scapes, mid-season. One of the most coveted of all hostas and one of the best garden plants in the genus, it was a legend in Japan long before it reached the West. Though slow to establish it makes a huge plant. Light to full shade. Readily available.

H. fluctuans 'Variegated' (AHS 1987) See *H. f.* 'Sagae'.

H. 'Fool's Gold' (Fortunei Group) (Grenfell & Grounds 1996) New cultivar name for what was formerly incorrectly named *H.* 'Fortunei Stenantha Variegated'. So named because its shadowy gold marginal variegation leads one to hope it will turn to brighter gold, though it never does. Differs from *H.* 'Fortunei' in the leaf shape, which is narrower and more pointed with two or three pronounced waves, the largest nearest the petiole, the others diminishing towards the tip, and in the leaf colouring, a paler green with a subtle yellow marginal variegation which begins at the widest part of the leaf and runs from there to the tip but is absent from the shoulders of the leaf, and from the petiole. The flower bracts are small as compared with other forms of 'Fortunei', and wither after flowering. Flowers funnel-shaped and very narrow, the lobes not expanding: the name stenantha comes from *stenos + anthos* meaning narrow flower. The subtlety of the variegation gives this hosta an elusive appeal. *H.* 'Fisher Cream Edge', also a sport of *H.* 'Fortunei Stenantha', has a creamy-white margin. Light to full shade.

H. 'Fortunei' (Baker 1876) It is now recognized that *H. fortunei* is not a true species, but rather an assemblage of sports and hybrids which arose from plants cultivated in Europe in the second half of the nineteenth century, possibly derived from plants imported from Japan by von Siebold and others. No *H.* 'Fortunei' has been found in the wild. Medium to large: spread about 60cm (24in), height 45cm (18in). Leaves oval to heart-shaped, the tip pointed, the surface matt to shiny, but always somewhat glaucous beneath. Flowers funnel-shaped, palest to deep lavender, produced on 91cm (36in) straight, leafy, usually glaucous scapes, relatively large, flat and broad: mid-season. Most forms are sterile but may produce occasional

capsules with aborted seeds. Small quantities of viable seed may be produced by careful hand pollination, but timing is of the essence.

H. Fortunei Group (Schmid 1991) A cultivar-group defined so as to include a number of named cultivars with all the above similar characteristics of *H.* 'Fortunei'.

H. 'Fortunei Albomarginata' (Zager 1941) Differs from *H.* 'Fortunei' in that the leaves are dark green and have a very irregular, ivory-white margin of varying width with some celadon green in the transition between the marginal white and the central green, the variegation continuing down the margins of the petiole. The variegation is somewhat unstable and occasional leaves may be as much as half white, while others may be scarcely variegated. Full shade essential.

H. Fortunei Albomarginata Group (Schmid 1991) A cultivar-group defined so as to include a number of named cultivars with all the above similar characteristics. This includes, in addition to *H.* 'Fortunei Albomarginata', *H.* 'Carol', *H.* 'Francee', *H.* 'Gloriosa', *H.* 'Minuteman', *H.* 'North Hills', *H.* 'Patriot', *H.* 'Zager's White Edge'. It does not include *H.* 'Antioch' and similar forms such as *H.* 'Spinners', *H.* 'Goldbrook', *H.* 'Shogun' and *H.* 'Moerheim', whose leaves are more tapered and less heart-shaped: these belong to the Antioch Group.

H. 'Fortunei Albopicta' (Miquel 1869) Differs from *H.* 'Fortunei' in that the leaves are clear, soft yellow with a narrow irregular dark green margin with some streaked overlapping of green and yellow between the centre and the margin, viridescent by flowering time but leaving just a colour shadow of the earlier variegation. The leafy bracts are variegated in the same way as the leaves. One of the showiest hostas in early summer, and one of the most popular. The original plant arose as a sport in von Siebold's garden in Leyden in 1840. Received the Award of Garden Merit (RHS). *H.* 'Elizabeth Campbell' is a sport with much wider green margins. Light to full shade. Readily available.

H. **'Fortunei Aokii'** (Siebold ex Bailey/AHS 1987) Differs from *H.* 'Fortunei Hyacinthina' in that the whole leaf is more puckered and less glaucous and the flower more pink than lavender. Introduced by the von Siebold nursery in 1879, it is difficult to distinguish from *H.* 'Fortunei Rugosa'. The name was originally spelt 'Aokii',

but is usually incorrectly listed as *H.* 'Fortunei Aoki'. *H.* 'Sundance' is a stable sport. Light shade. Readily available.

H. **'Fortunei Aurea'** (Hylander 1954) Differs from *H.* 'Fortunei' in that the leaves are rich, bright yellow early in the season, fading by mid-summer to medium dull green, somewhat glaucous beneath throughout. The yellow colouring is the result of an abnormality which in effect produces yellow instead of green chlorophyll. The original plant arose as a sport on a plant of *H.* 'Fortunei Albopicta' in von Siebold's garden in the 1860s. Full shade. Readily available.

H. **'Fortunei Aureomarginata'** (Wehrhahn 1931) Differs from *H.* 'Fortunei' in that the leaves are deep olive-green with a rich golden-yellow margin, the upper surface with a satiny sheen, the lower glaucous. The depth of the marginal colour fades to cream in strong light. The attractive flowers are produced in abundance and are followed by capsules whose seeds, however, are usually incapable of germinating. One of the most popular hostas, tolerant of a wide range of cultural conditions and grown around the world wherever hostas flourish. Excellent for general planting, flower arrangement and landscape use. Has been grown in

The dwarf form of *H.* 'Fortunei Aurea', still one of the best golds for spring effect.

H. 'Fragrant Gold' needs almost full sun for its leaf colour to develop fully.

the US as *H.* 'Gold Crown' and *H.* 'Golden Crown'. Light shade to sun. Readily available.

H. 'Fortunei Hyacinthina' (Hylander 1954) Differs from *H.* 'Fortunei' in that the leaves are more oval to heart-shaped than round heart-shaped, are distinctly silvery-grey in spring becoming glaucous blue-green to grey-green above, whitish beneath with a distinct white hyaline margin. Scapes glaucous grey-green with a purple cast and large, flat leafy bracts. The capsules, which produce mainly sterile seeds, are whitish-grey. The cultivar epithet refers to the flower colour, and this is generally considered to be the best of the Fortunei Group in flower. Its best known sport is *H.* 'Gold Standard'. Light shade. Readily available.

H. 'Fortunei Rugosa' (Hylander 1954) Differs from *H.* 'Fortunei'

in that the leaves are very pruinose in spring, becoming light greenish-blue and later bluish, always glaucous beneath, the whole leaf very puckered. The scape is shorter than in the other *H.* 'Fortunei' varieties, and the leafy bracts are large, stiff and long-lasting. It is so similar to *H.* 'Fortunei Aokii' that some authors believe the two plants to be one, and both of them are close to *H.* 'Fortunei Hyacinthina'. Light shade.

H. 'Fragrant Blue' (Aden 1988) Small: spread about 30cm (12in), height 20cm (8in). Leaves small, thick, very smooth, flat, heart-shaped, blue-green. Flowers funnel-shaped, lavender in bud, opening palest lavender to nearly white on straight, leafy 50cm (20in) scapes, mid-season. Only fragrant in hot climates. Light shade. Readily available.

H. 'Fragrant Bouquet' (Aden 1982) Large: spread about 65cm (26in), height 45cm (18in). Leaves large, heart-shaped, wavy, light green and chartreuse with an irregular yellowish-ivory margin. Flowers large, fragrant, radially arranged, funnel-shaped, palest lavender to white, mid-season, borne on straight scapes up to 91cm (36in) tall, with a single large variegated and twisted leafy bract just below the flowers. A superb hosta both in leaf and flower. A rapid increaser. *H.* 'Guacamole' is a sport. Light shade to full sun.

H. 'Fragrant Gold' (Aden 1982) Large: spread about 76cm (30in), height 45cm (18in). Leaves large, thick, stiff, puckered, the blade undulate, oval to heart-shaped, glaucous-bloomed, pale yellowish-green with a green line down the midrib, becoming more intensely yellow as the season advances.

114

Flowers lightly fragrant, funnel-shaped, lavender, on straight, bare 91cm (36in) scapes, mid-season. H. 'Sum and Substance' hybrid, whence comes the thickness of the leaves. Light shade to full sun. Readily available.

H. 'Francee' (Fortunei Albo-marginata Group) (Klopping/AHS 1986) Large: spread about 91cm (36in), height 60cm (24in). Leaves large, late to emerge, narrowly heart-shaped, flat, mid to dark olive-green with a narrow irregular clean white margin. Flowers funnel-shaped, lavender on leaning, leafy 100cm (40in) scapes, mid-season. One of the best of the white-margined hostas, looking good throughout the whole season. It is excellent in tubs. H. 'Patriot' is a sport. Light shade. Readily available.

H. 'Frances Williams' (Frances Williams Group) (Williams 1986) Large to very large: spread about 91cm (36in), height 60cm (24in). Leaves very large, thick, puckered, the outer leaves heart-shaped, the inner ones nearly round, glaucous deep blue-green with a wide, irregular creamy-beige to yellow margin. Flowers funnel-shaped, palest opalescent lavender to nearly white in dense heads on leafy 60cm (24in) scapes, the leafy bracts large and variegated like the leaves, the flowers only just over-topping the leaves, mid-season. One of the most popular hostas ever raised. A handsome garden plant, its only real failing being a tendency for the edges of the leaves to scorch by late summer, unless grown in full shade. It was discovered by Mrs Frances Williams as a variegated-margin sport in a field row of H. sieboldiana 'Elegans' at Bristol Nurseries, Connecticut in 1936. See H. 'Aurora Borealis'. Readily available.

H. Frances Williams Group (Trehane 1996). A cultivar-group here defined so as to include a number of named cultivars with all the above similar characteristics. The group includes, in addition to H. 'Frances Williams', H. 'Aurora Borealis', H. 'Eldorado', H. 'Golden Circles', H. 'Olive Bailey Langdon', H. 'Samurai'.

H. 'Freising' (Fortunei Group) (Klose 1982) Medium to large: spread about 91cm (36in), height 60cm (24in). Leaves medium, widely oval, blade flat, mid-green with a slight greyish overtone. Flowers white, funnel-shaped, on leaning, leafy 91cm (36in) scapes, mid-season. A compact hosta whose leaves are held distinctly upright. Slow to increase. Light shade.

H. 'Fringe Benefit' (Aden 1986) Large: spread about 91cm (36in), height 60cm (24in). Leaves large, puckered, heart-shaped, shallowly undulate at the margin, somewhat glaucous grey-green, darkest at the centre, becoming lighter with celadon streaking and an irregular light yellow to cream margin. Flowers bell-shaped to flaring, pale mauve with markedly protruding stamens on leaning, leafy, glaucous 105cm (42in) scapes, the leafy and flower bracts variegated like the leaves; mid-season. A relatively pest-resistant hosta that will grow in full sun in the UK if adequately moist at the root. Readily available.

H. 'Frosted Jade' (Maroushek 1978) Large, upright and arching: spread about 76cm (30in), height 76cm (30in). Leaves large to very large, oval with upturned and slightly rippled margins, sage green with celadon streaking towards the margins, the margins clean white. Flowers funnel-shaped, palest lavender to nearly white on upright to leaning leafy scapes, the leafy bracts well variegated, the flower bracts slightly so, mid-season. H. montana hybrid. Light to full shade. Readily available.

H. 'Gaiety' (Aden 1986) Medium: spread about 45cm (18in), height 23cm (9in). Leaves heart-shaped, yellowish-green becoming bright yellow with an irregular white margin and a green stripe down the midrib. Flowers funnel-shaped, white on 45cm (18in) straight, leafy scapes, mid-season. H. 'Gaiety' is the white-margined form of H. 'Good As Gold'. Light to full shade.

H. 'Gay Feather' (Benedict 1983) Medium, dense and semi-stoloniferous: spread about 45cm (18in), height 30cm (12in). Leaves small to medium, lance-shaped, some twisted at the tip, held upright, cream to white with a green margin. Flowers funnel-shaped, lavender on straight, leafy 60cm (24in) scapes. Sport of 'Yellow Splash' and of similar habit and vigour. Looks similar to 'Celebration', but is larger. Tends to melt out in the centre of the leaf unless grown in shade and shelter.

H. 'Geisha' (K. Vaughn 1983) Small, upright: spread about 30cm (12in), height 25cm (10in). Leaves small, ovate, slightly wavy, curving upwards with a twist, the tip curling under, glossy, chartreuse to yellow-streaked and speckled green, with wide mid-green margins. Flowers bell-shaped, on thin pedicels, lavender on straight, leafy, 35cm (14in) scapes, mid-season. The leafy bracts are variegated. Distinct in its poise, its leaf colouring and in the way the leaves twist. Slow. Light to full shade.

H. 'George Smith' (George Smith Group) (G. Smith 1983) Very large: spread about 122cm (48in), height 60cm (24in). Leaves very large, thick, puckered, heart-shaped, creamy-ivory to beige, with an irregular, wide glaucous deep blue-green margin, often with streaking in the transitional zone, the marginal colour continuing down the petiole, the blade pruinose below. Flowers bell-shaped, palest opalescent lavender to nearly white on straight, leafy, 70cm (28in) scapes, mid-season. Arose as a bud-sport in George Smith's garden at Heslington Manor, York. Full shade.

H. George Smith Group (Trehane 1996) A cultivar-group here defined so as to include a numbers of cultivars with all the above similar characteristics. The group includes *H.* 'Borwick Beauty', *H.* 'Color Glory', *H.* 'DuPage Delight', *H.* 'Great Expectations', *H.* 'Northern Sunray', *H.* 'Queen of Islip'. All are slow to establish, requiring at least five years to assume their full beauty. Full shade.

H. 'Ginko Craig' (Craig/Summers 1986) Small to medium: spread about 50cm (20in), height 45cm (18in). Mature leaves medium, matt mid-green with an irregular thin white margin with celadon streaking in the transitional zone. Juvenile leaves about 8cm (3in) by 2.5cm (1in) wide, with less celadon streaking, the petiole about 5cm (2in), while the adult leaves are about 15cm (6in) by 5cm (2in) wide, the petiole about 17cm (7in) long. Flowers funnel-shaped, deep lavender striped purple on straight, bare 45cm (18in) scapes, mid-season. Full shade. Readily available.

H. 'Gloriosa' (Fortunei Group) (Krossa/Summers/AHS1986) Large: spread about 76cm (30in), height 45cm (18in). Leaves eventually large, thin, spatulate, slightly concave, shiny dark olive green with a very narrow silvery-white hairline margin. Late to emerge. An abundance of funnel-shaped, lavender flowers, on leaning, leafy 91cm (36in) scapes, mid-season. A very distinctive hosta and not always easy. Slow to increase. Dappled to full shade.

H. 'Goldbrook' (Antioch Group) (S. Bond 1989) Differs from *H.*

'Antioch' in that it has smaller, narrower leaves.

H. 'Goldbrook Gold' (Golden Sunburst Group) (S. Bond 1989) Large: spread about 76cm (30in), height 58cm (23in). Leaves large, thick, cordate, bright yellow, viridescent, with a pruinose white back. Flowers sparse, bell-shaped on erect, bare 62cm (25in) scapes, mid-season. Said to be an improvement on *H.* 'Golden Sunburst' as it will take some sun and will not scorch at the margins. Slow.

H. 'Gold Drop' (Anderson 1977) Small: spread about 30cm (12in), height 15cm (6in). Leaves miniature, thick, heart-shaped, sharply pointed, flat, chartreuse. Flowers bell-shaped, pale lavender to nearly white on straight, bare 38cm (15in) scapes, mid-season. A putative hybrid between *H. venusta* and *H.* 'August Moon'. Needs sun to colour well. Sports are *H.* 'Abby', *H.* 'Pooh Bear', *H.* 'Crown Jewel', *H.* 'Dew Drop' and *H.* 'Lemon Drop'. Popular. Light shade to sun. Readily available.

H. 'Gold Edger' (Aden 1978) Large: spread about 70cm (28in), height 30cm (12in). Leaves small, thick, heart-shaped, the lobes raised, at first greenish-yellow becoming rich soft yellow: petioles long. Flowers abundant, bell-shaped, pale lavender to nearly white, on straight, bare 35cm (14in) scapes with some purple staining in the flower-bearing zone, mid-season. A good small hosta, increasing rapidly to make good ground cover. Often mistaken for *H.* 'Birchwood Parky's Gold', which has thinner leaves, longer petioles and is larger. Sports are *H.* 'Radiant Edger' and *H.* 'Pacific Blue Edger'. Light shade to sun. Readily available.

H. 'Gold Regal' (Aden 1974) Large, stately: spread about 100cm (40in), height 91cm (36in). Leaves large, oval, thick, with deeply

impressed veins, evenly chartreuse becoming greenish gold by mid-summer, somewhat puckered and heavily glaucous beneath. Flowers large, bell-shaped, ashen-mauve on straight, thick, bare, 76cm (30in) glaucous scapes, mid-season. Makes a dense clump of overlapping, rather erect leaves: flowers among the best in the genus. Needs time to establish. Sports are *H.* 'Alex Summers' and *H.* 'Rascal'. Needs a considerable amount of sun to develop the best yellow colour.

H. 'Gold Standard' (Fortunei Group) (Banyai 1976) Large: spread about 91cm (36in), height 50cm (20in). Leaves large, late to emerge, heart-shaped, flat, chartreuse-green at first becoming bright golden-yellow (parchment-gold), fading to beigy-parchment colour, with a deep green margin. Flowers funnel-shaped, lavender, on straight, bare, 106cm (42in) scapes, mid-season. One of the most popular of all hostas, but needs careful placing. In too much sun the centre of the leaf turns to a golden-yellow, then creamy-white or white and can burn; in too little they can remain green. Adequate moisture essential. Almost certainly a sport of *H.* 'Fortunei Hyacinthina'. Sports are *H.* 'Moonlight', *H.* 'Richland Gold', *H.* 'Striptease'. Readily available.

H. 'Golden Bullion' (Bennerup/ Ruh 1989) Medium to large: spread about 76cm (30in), height 36cm (15in). Leaves medium, thick, oval to heart-shaped, puckered, evenly chartreuse becoming yellow. Flowers bell-shaped, pale lavender, on straight, bare 50cm (20in) scapes, mid-season. A sport of *H.* 'Tokudama Flavocircinalis'. Leaves are longer, more pointed and less cupped than those of *H.* 'Golden Medallion'. Relatively pest-resistant. Dappled shade to sun.

H. 'Golden Medallion' (Golden Medallion Group) (AHS 1984)

H. 'Gold Standard', one of the most popular of all hostas.

Medium: spread about 60cm (24in), height 36cm (15in). Leaves medium, thick, heart-shaped to round, cupped, deeply puckered, greenish-yellow becoming golden-yellow. Flowers bell-shaped, palest lavender to nearly white, on straight, bare 45cm (18in) scapes, mid-season. A sport of *H.* 'Tokudama Aureonebulosa'. Leaves are strongly cupped and deeply puckered. Light shade to sun. Readily available.

H. **Golden Medallion Group** (Grenfell 1996) A cultivar-group here defined so as to include a number of yellow-leaved named

cultivars with all the above similar characteristics derived from *H.* 'Tokudama Aureonebulosa', including *H.* 'Abiqua Ariel', *H.* 'Aspen Gold', *H.* 'Midas Touch', *H.* 'Super Bowl'.

H. **'Golden Prayers'** (Aden 1976) Medium: spread about 50cm (20in), height 30cm (12in). Leaves small, held upright like hands in prayer, oval to heart-shaped, thick, bright yellow, paler beneath. Flowers bell-shaped, palest lavender to nearly white on straight, bare 45cm (18in) scapes, mid-season. One of the best small golds. The

plant in circulation as *H.* 'Golden Prayers' seems most likely to be *H.* 'Little Aurora' which is similar, therefore the sports (*H.* 'Delia' and *H.* 'Goldbrook Grace') should be attributed to *H.* 'Little Aurora'.

H. **'Golden Scepter'** (Tiara Group) (Savory 1983) Differs from *H.* 'Golden Tiara' in that the thin leaves are at first chartreuse becoming bright yellow.

H. **'Golden Sculpture'** (Golden Sunburst Group) (Anderson 1982) Differs from *H.* 'Golden Sunburst' in having a more vase-shaped mound. It needs a hot climate in which to succeed.

H. **'Golden Sunburst'** (Golden Sunburst Group) (AHS 1984) Large to very large: spread about 91cm (36in), height 45cm (18in). Leaves large to very large, thick, heart-shaped to nearly round, evenly chartreuse becoming bright yellow, puckered, the veins deeply impressed, glaucous beneath. Flowers bell-shaped, palest opalescent lavender to nearly white, on straight, bare, 51cm (20in) scapes, mid-season. The flowers just overtop the leaf mound, and the leaves are inclined to burn in sun. Readily available.

H. **Golden Sunburst Group** (Grenfell 1996) A cultivar-group here defined so as to include a number of yellow-leaved named cultivars with all the above similar characteristics when derived from *H. sieboldiana* 'Elegans' and its forms and cultivars, including *H.* 'Golden Sculpture', *H.* 'Kasseler Gold', *H.* 'Semperaurea', *H.* 'Zounds'.

H. **'Golden Tiara'** (Tiara Group) (Savory 1977) Medium: spread about 30cm (24in), height 38cm (15in). Leaves small, variable, the outer ones oval to heart-shaped, the inner ones heart-shaped to almost round, mid-green with a pattern of dark green, light green and celadon green streaks following the lines of the veins out towards the margin which is creamy yellow at first, chartreuse to yellow later, the petioles unusually long. Flowers bell-shaped, deep lavender striped purple with a white throat and protruding white anthers on 76cm (30in) straight, bare scapes, mid-season. One of the best small hostas, neat and compact in habit, showy in flower and of rapid increase. Sports are *H.* 'Diamond Tiara', *H.* 'Emerald Scepter', *H.* 'Golden Scepter', *H.* 'Grand Tiara', *H.* 'Jade Scepter', *H.* 'Platinum Tiara'. Dappled shade. Readily available.

H. gracillima (Maekawa 1936) Miniature: spread about 15cm (6in), height 2.5cm (1in). Leaves dwarf to miniature, elliptic, held rather upright, deep glossy green

above, lighter glossy green beneath, the petioles green but increasingly red-dotted towards the base. Flowers long-tubed and bell-shaped, deep lavender with purple striping inside, few on leaning, leafy 23cm (9in) scapes, late; the scapes red-dotted especially towards the base. One of the smallest hostas, often confused with *H. venusta* which however differs in having ridged, not smooth, flower scapes. *H.* 'Ko Mame' is a Japanese selection with very rippled leaves with creamy-white margins. Light to full shade.

H. 'Granary Gold' (Fortunei Group) (E. Smith/BHHS 1988) Large: spread about 91cm (36in), height 45cm (18in). Leaves large, oval to heart-shaped, the tip pointed, the surface matt, somewhat glaucous beneath, bright yellow at first fading attractively to greenish gold at

the top, pale parchment to ivory towards the tip. Flowers funnel-shaped, pale to deep lavender, on 91cm (36in) straight, leafy, usually glaucous scapes, the bracts relatively large, flat and broad: mid-season. *H.* 'Fortunei Albopicta Aurea' sport or hybrid, and greatly superior. Much used in flower arrangement. Light shade to sun.

H. 'Grand Master' (Aden 1986) Large: spread about 60cm (24in), height 40cm (16in). Leaves large, heart-shaped, blue-green with an irregular white margin, thick, deeply puckered. Flowers funnel-shaped, lavender, on straight, leafy 76cm (30in) scapes, abundantly produced, mid-season. Distinctive aubergine pods. Similar to *H.* 'Christmas Tree'. Light shade.

H. 'Grand Tiara' (Tiara Group) (A. Pollock 1991) Differs from *H.*

H. 'Granary Gold': the leaves pass through shades of gold to parchment and ivory white.

'Golden Tiara' in that the leaf is gold with a small green centre, rather than green with a gold edge. The gold margin is two to three times wider than in *H.* 'Golden Tiara'. Particularly attractive early in the season. Light to full shade.

H. **'Gray Cole'** (Elegans Group) (Kuk 1985) Reputed to differ from 'Elegans' in its larger, thicker, more cupped and puckered leaves and in that the flowers, of which there may be 54–60, held well above the leaf mound, are sometimes double, and that the scape may sometimes be branched.

H. **'Great Expectations'** (J. Bond/ Aden 1988) Differs from *H.* 'George Smith' in its more pointed, more twisted and folded leaf blades. It has good colour variegation on unfurling and the leaf centre is very light chartreuse to cream. Very slow and sometimes difficult to establish. Light shade.

H. **'Green Acres'** (Geissler 1970) Very large: spread about 130cm (50in), height 100cm (40in). Leaves

very large, deeply corrugated, oval to heart-shaped, tapering to a point, satiny, mid-green, as much as 33cm (13in) long. Flowers funnel-shaped, pale lavender to nearly white on straight, leafy 136cm (54in) scapes, early to mid-season. The large leaves seem almost to hang from the tall petioles. *H.* 'King Michael' and *H.* 'Mikado' are similar but possibly even larger. Light to full shade. Readily available.

H. **'Green Eyes'** (Benedict 1990) Miniature: spread about 20cm (8in), height 7.5cm (3in). Leaves miniature, narrowly lance-shaped, wavy, rippled margin, pronounced tip, chartreuse to cream with an irregular very narrow dark green margin and some streaking back towards the centre. Flowers flaring, lavender on straight, leafy 30cm (12in) scapes, mid-season. *H.* 'Kabitan' sport or hybrid, but smaller growing. Full shade.

H. **'Green Fountain'** (Aden 1979) Large: spread about 91cm (36in), height 60cm (24in). Leaves large, lanceolate, mid-green, shiny, wavy

at the margin, the blade running into the petiole, the petiole increasingly red-streaked towards the base. Flowers funnel-shaped, deep lavender, on 91cm (36in) leaning scapes that are conspicuously leafy just below the flowers and intensely red-streaked especially towards the base, mid-season to late. A distinctive hosta, the leaves cascading towards the ground from stiffly upright petioles: valuable for its showy late flowers. *H. kikutii* form or hybrid. Light shade to sun. Readily available.

H. **'Green Gold'** (Fortunei Group) (Mack/Savory/AHS 1986) Large: spread about 80cm (32in), height 50cm (20in). Leaves large, round to heart-shaped, olive-green with a wide irregular margin, at first creamy-yellow becoming creamy-white, the margin streaking back towards the leaf centre, the lobes uplifted, the blade somewhat cupped, the veins deeply impressed, the surface satiny and very puckered, glaucous beneath. Flowers funnel-shaped, lavender, on straight, leafy, 85cm (34in) scapes, mid-season. Sport of *H.* 'Fortunei Aureomarginata'. Light shade.

H. **'Green Sheen'** (Aden 1978) Very large: spread about 122cm (48in), height 80cm (32in). Leaves late to emerge in spring, very large, very thick, near heart-shaped (narrower when young), pinched at the navel, soft sage green with a waxy sheen above, glaucous beneath. Flowers bell-shaped, palest lavender to nearly white on straight, bare 150cm (60in) scapes, mid-season to late. The emerging shoots are conspicuously brown. Light shade to sun.

H. **'Green Wedge'** (Aden 1976) Densely mounded, large: spread about 76cm (30in), height 51cm (20in). Leaves large, heart- to wedge-shaped, cupped, dark green, paler beneath. Flowers palest lavender to nearly white on straight, bare

H. 'Grand Tiara', the most striking plant in the Tiara Group.

H. 'Hadspen Heron' has the narrowest leaves of any of the Tardiana Group.

122cm (48in) scapes, mid-season to late. A selfed seedling of *H. nigrescens* 'Elatior'. Light shade.

H. **'Green with Envy'** (Chrystal) Sport of *H.* 'Dawn', from which it differs in having green margins. Light to full shade.

H. **'Ground Master'** (Aden 1979) Medium, moderately stoloniferous: spread about 50cm (20in), height 30cm (12in). Leaves medium, thin, somewhat puckered when mature, narrowly oval, medium to dark green with an irregular creamy-yellow margin fading to white. Flowers funnel-shaped, deep lavender with purple stripes on the inside, the edges of the petals margined white, on straight, leafy 50cm (20in) scapes, mid-season to late. Slugs love it. Light shade to full shade. Readily available.

H. **'Guacamole'** (Solberg 1994) Vigorous sport of *H.* 'Fragrant Bouquet', from which it differs in having dark chartreuse margins. A good new one to look for. Light shade to sun.

H. **'Hadspen Blue'** (Tardiana Group, TF 2 × 7) (E. Smith/BHHS 1988) Medium: spread about 45cm (18in), height 25cm (10in). Leaves medium, heart-shaped, glaucous blue, thick, smooth. Flowers bell-shaped, lavender on straight, bare 40cm (16in) scapes, mid-season. Makes a neat, dense clump, and may be the bluest of the Tardiana Group. Light to full shade. Readily available.

H. **'Hadspen Hawk'** (Tardiana Group, TF 2 × 20) (E. Smith/BHHS 1988) Small, upright: spread about 30cm (12in), height 20cm (8in).

Leaves small, oval, on long petioles, glaucous blue-green, flat. Flowers bell-shaped, palest lavender to nearly white on straight, bare 40cm (16in) scapes, mid-season. Light to full shade.

H. **'Hadspen Heron'** (Tardiana Group TF 2 × 10) (E. Smith/Aden 1976) Small: spread about 30cm (15in), height 20cm (8in). Leaves thick, wavy, oval to lance-shaped, glaucous blue-green. Flowers bell-shaped, palest lavender to nearly white on straight, bare 35cm (14in) scapes, mid-season. It is unique among the Tardiana Group in that the leaves resemble those of the *H.* 'Tardiflora' parent but have the same intense blue colouring as the *H. sieboldiana* 'Elegans' parent. Makes a neat spreading clump. The leaves emerge early and may be liable to damage from late frosts. Light to full shade. Readily available.

H. 'Halcyon' (Tardiana Group, TF 1 × 7) (E. Smith/BHHS 1988) Large: spread about 100cm (40in), height 50cm (20in). Leaves medium, thick, smooth, lance-shaped to oval when young, heart-shaped when adult, glaucous blue-green. Leaves always narrower when newly propagated, especially true of micropropagated plants. Flowers bell-shaped, greyish-lavender to nearly white, densely borne on straight, bare 60cm (24in) scapes, mid-season. Generally considered the best and most beautiful of the Tardiana Group: one of the bluest, and most intensely blue in some shade. Received an Award of Garden Merit from the RHS. Sports are *H.* 'Devon Green', *H.* 'Goldbrook Glimmer', *H.* 'June', *H.* 'Peridot', *H.* 'Valerie's Vanity'. Readily available.

H. 'Happiness' (Tardiana Group, TF 1 × 5) (E. Smith/BHHS 1988) Medium: spread about 50cm (20in), height 30cm (12in). Leaves medium, thick, flat, heart-shaped, glaucuous blue-green. Flowers funnel-shaped, deep lavender, on straight, leafy 45cm (18in) scapes, mid-season. Has more deeply coloured flowers than most Tardianas, on relatively taller scapes. Light to full shade.

H. 'Happy Hearts' (Fisher 1973) Medium. Attractively heart-shaped, glaucous grey-green, somewhat puckered medium to large leaves, veins conspicuously impressed and fairly widely spaced. Flowers lavender-pink on bare, 60cm (24in) scapes, late. Vigorous and fast-growing. Makes a good container plant. Light to full shade. Readily available.

H. 'Harmony' (Tardiana Group, TF 2 × 3) (E. Smith/Aden 1976) Small: spread about 30cm (12in), height 20cm (8in). Leaves small

to medium, heart-shaped, glaucous blue-green, thick. Flowers bell-shaped, purple with a deeper purple stripe, on straight, leafy 30cm (12in) scapes, mid-season. One of the smaller of the Tardianas, making a neat, compact blue mound. Light to full shade.

H. 'Harvest Glow' (Walters Gardens 1988) Medium: spread about 50cm (20in), height 40cm (16in). Leaves large, thick, somewhat cupped and puckered, heart-shaped, shiny, lemony-chartreuse becoming rich, deep yellow. Flowers bell-shaped, pale lavender to nearly white on straight, bare 60cm (24in) scapes, mid-season. An all-gold sport of *H.* 'Moon Glow'. Light shade to sun.

H. 'Heartsong' (Walters Gardens 1984) Sport of *H.* 'Candy Hearts', from which it differs in its mid-green leaves with an irregular, narrow creamy-white margin with some celadon streaking back towards the midrib. Funnel-shaped lavender flowers on straight, leafy 70cm (28in) scapes, the bracts narrow and variegated. Light to full shade.

H. 'Helen Doriot' (Elegans Group) (Reath 1982) Very large: Similar to *H. sieboldiana* 'Elegans'. *H.* 'Frances Williams' × *H. sieboldiana* 'Elegans'. Light to full shade.

H. 'Holly's Honey' (AHS 1986) Very large: spread about 100cm (40in), height 58cm (23in). Leaves large, thin, glossy, dark green, ruffled margins, heart-shaped, with widely spaced veins. Urn-shaped purple flowers on leafy 83cm (33in) scapes, mid- to late season. Much used as a breeding parent by the Lachmans and other hybridizers, *H.* 'Bridegroom' for example. An 'improved' *H. ventricosa*. Light to full shade as it can burn at the edges.

H. 'Honeybells' (Cummings/AHS 1986) Very large: spread about 122cm (48in), height 60cm (24in).

Leaves large, lax, widely oval, blade undulate, light green, turning a dull, yellowish-green in sun, glossy above, somewhat shiny beneath. Flowers lightly fragrant, bell-shaped, white, streaked lavender, on straight, leafy 150cm (60in) scapes, mid-season. A remarkably vigorous hosta, multiplying rapidly. Light shade to sun. Received an Award of Garden Merit from the RHS. Sports are *H.* 'Sugar and Cream', *H.* 'Sweet Standard'. The latter differs in that the leaves are irregularly splashed and speckled white; needs good cultivation and to be divided every three or four years otherwise the variegation migrates to the margin, leaving one with *H.* 'Sugar and Cream'. Light shade to sun. Readily available.

H. 'Honeysong' (Summers) Medium: spread about 45cm (18in), height 30cm (12in). Leaves medium, round to heart-shaped, matt dark green with a cream margin, becoming puckered with age. Flowers bell-shaped, palest lavender to nearly white, on straight, bare, 50cm (20in) scapes, mid-season. It forms a beautiful mound of arching foliage (unexpected in view of its *H.* 'Tokudama' lineage). Light to full shade.

H. 'Hydon Sunset' (BHHS 1988) Small: spread 20cm (8in), height 10cm (4in). Leaves miniature, heart-shaped, matt, chartreuse to yellow gradually turning green, blade slightly undulate. Flowers bell-shaped, deep purple, on narrow, straight, bare, 35cm (14in) scapes, mid-season. Full shade.

H. hypoleuca (Murata 1962) Large: spread about 60cm (24in), height 30cm (12in). Leaves very large, heart-shaped or oval to heart-shaped, slightly glaucous olive-green above, white pruinose beneath, the margin slightly wavy, the petioles broadly channelled near the blade, folded and closed towards the base, light green,

H. 'Invincible' occasionally produces double flowers.

'Maekawa' (Aden 1988). Light shade to sun.

H. **'Inaho'** (Japan) Small: spread about 30cm (12in), height 15cm (6in). Leaves medium, oval, pointed, dull yellow streaked green, the petioles yellow edged green, the underside red-dotted especially towards the base. Flowers funnel-shaped, lavender-striped purple on straight, leafy, red-dotted, 35cm (14in) scapes, mid-season, the scapes bearing small, leafy bracts all along its length. Virtually sterile. Probably *H. sieboldii* selection, sometimes incorrectly called *H. tardiva* 'Aureostriata'. Light to full shade.

H. **'Inniswood'** (Inniswood Metro Gardens 1993) Very large: spread about 122cm (48in), height 60cm (24in). Leaves large, heart-shaped, puckered, chartreuse becoming rich yellow with a narrow, deep green margin. Flowers funnel-shaped, lavender, on straight, bare 76cm (30in) scapes, mid-season. Of *H.* 'Tokudama' lineage, being a sport of *H.* 'Sun Glow'. Not much variegation apparent as the leaves unfurl, but they colour well by mid-summer. Light shade.

H. **'Invincible'** (Aden 1986) Densely mounded, large: spread about 100cm (40in), height 38cm (15in). Leaves medium to large, thick, wedge-shaped, very undulate, tapering to a long point, olive green above, shiny beneath, the petioles lightly red-dotted. An abundance of fragrant, funnel-shaped, occasionally double (hose in hose) lavender flowers on leaning leafy 50cm (20in) scapes, stained red where the leafy bracts are attached and immediately above the bracts. Late. One of the best of the newer hostas, reasonably slug- and snail-proof. Light shade to sun. Of *H. plantaginea* lineage. Readily available.

H. **'Iona'** (Fortunei Group) (Lavender/Chappell BHHS 1988) Large: typical *H.* 'Fortunei' with

intensely purple-streaked towards the base. Flowers bell-shaped, palest mauve to milky-white on leaning, leafy 35cm (14in) scapes purple streaked towards the base, mid-season, but in flower only briefly. Grown for its intensely white-backed leaves; in Japan sometimes grown in an elevated position, the better to show the

undersides. In the wild this hosta grows in full sun on volcanic cliffs and the white is an adaptation to protect the back of the leaves from the sun's heat reflected off the rocks, a feature also found in other rock-dwelling hostas. A form reported to have extra large, glaucous blue-green leaves with undulate margins is named *H.*

glaucous grey-green leaves with an irregular white margin with a large area of overlap resulting in grey streaking and small streaks of celadon green. A delightful hosta of subtle leaf colouring and good in flower. Some seed capsules. Lovely in a container. Light to full shade.

H. 'Irische See' (Tardiana Group) (Klose) Small to medium: spread about 60cm (24in), height 18cm (7in). Leaves small to medium, thick, oval, abruptly tipped, blade flat, closely veined, glaucous light bluish-green on purple-dotted petioles. Flowers bell-shaped, pale lavender on straight, bare 25cm (10in) scapes, mid-summer. The capsules are light glaucous green. Light to full shade. Best known in European gardens.

H. 'Iron Gate Glamour' (Sellers 1981) A sport of 'Iron Gate Supreme', differing from it in having stable, irregular cream margins. A superb garden plant and deserves to be better known. Light shade.

H. 'Iron Gate Supreme' (Sellers 1980) Large: spread about 91cm (36in), height 60cm (24in). Leaves large, undulate, heart-shaped, deep green with attractive, multi-coloured, unstable streaking. Flowers fragrant, funnel-shaped, pale lavender on 91cm (36in) straight, bare scapes, mid-season. H. plantaginea × H. 'Tokudama Aureonebulosa'. Light shade.

H. 'Jade Scepter' (Tiara Group) (Zilis/T & Z Nursery 1988) Differs from H. 'Golden Tiara' in that the leaves are evenly mid-green.

H. 'Janet' (Fortunei Group) (O'Harra 1981) Medium: spread 61cm (24in), height 38cm (15in). Leaves medium to large, somewhat puckered, oval to heart-shaped, emerging chartreuse with a narrow, irregular dark green margin, but turns parchment white (albescent) by mid-summer. Flowers funnel-

shaped, lavender, on straight, bare 60cm (24in) scapes, mid-season. A beautiful hosta when well grown, but hard to please. Lacks vigour, slow to increase and prone to revert to all-green leaves. Light shade.

H. 'Julie Morss' (Morss 1983) Medium: spread about 50cm (20in), height 30cm (12in). Leaves medium, oval to heart-shaped, somewhat convex, puckered at maturity, the tip turning under, light yellow with a very irregular glaucous blue margin, streaking back towards the midrib. Late to emerge. Flowers bell-shaped, lavender to pale lavender on straight, bare glaucous 45cm (18in) scapes, mid-season. Beautiful given suitable conditions. H. 'Frances Williams' seedling. Light to full shade.

H. 'June' (Tardiana Group) (Neo Plants 1991) Sport of H. 'Halcyon', from which it differs in that the leaves are yellow with an irregular blue-green margin, the margin overlapping the centre resulting in blue-green and celadon streaking into the centre of the leaf. Leaves can darken to chartreuse in mid-season. Requires some sun to develop the yellow colour in spring. One of the best of the new British hostas, and a first-rate garden plant. Lovely grown in a dark blue glazed pot. H. 'Early Times', with glaucous yellow leaves, is a sport. Readily available.

H. 'Just So' (Aden 1986) Small: spread about 38cm (15in), height 15cm (6in). A sport of H. 'Little Aurora', with leaves oval to heart-shaped, chartreuse to golden-yellow with a narrow, deep green margin with occasional green streaks reaching into the centre, puckered. Flowers funnel-shaped, lavender to pale lavender, on straight, leafy 30cm (12in) scapes, mid-season. The leaf centre and margin colours make a striking contrast. H. 'Shere Khan' is a sport. Shade.

H. 'Kabitan' (Maekawa/AHS 1987) Small, somewhat stoloniferous: spread about 25cm (10in), height 20cm (8in). Leaves small, lance-shaped, tapering to a fine point, bright yellow with a narrow dark green margin, the margins rippled and flowing into the petiole without clear distinction, the petiole variegated as the blade. Flowers funnel-shaped, purple with deep purple stripes inside, borne on straight, leafy 25cm (10in) scapes, mid-season. An eye-catching hosta when well grown, but not always easy, requiring a moist position open to morning sun but well shaded for the rest of the day. The dark flowers are a great bonus and show up especially well against the foliage. Sport or selection of H. sieboldii. Light to full shade, but once established can tolerate some sun. H. 'Sea Sprite' is very similar but usually suffers from virus infection. Readily available.

H. 'Kasseler Gold' (Golden Sunburst Group) (Klose) Large to very large: differs from H. 'Golden Sunburst' in having thinner, shiny, less puckered leaves. Named after the town of Kassel in Germany where the Klose nursery is based. Better known in Europe than elsewhere. A selected seedling from H. 'Semperaurea'.

H. kikutii (Maekawa 1937) Medium: spread about 45cm (18in), height 30cm (12in). Leaves medium, ovate to lanceolate, shiny mid- to dark green above, shiny light green beneath, borne on strong upright petioles, the petiole and leaf together making an upward and outward arch, the leaf tip recurving. Flowers bell-shaped, white or slightly stained lavender, on stiff, horizontal pedicels, the 60cm (24in) scapes conspicuously leaning, leafy. A variable species, in its best forms making a fountain-like mound of bright green leaves. Emerges early and the thin leaves can be damaged by late frosts.

Reputed to be more prone to adult vine weevil damage than other hostas. Light shade.

H. k. 'Albo-stricta' Differs from *H. kikutii* in its pure white flowers. Still awaits an acceptable name.

H. k. 'Caput-avis' (Maekawa 1950) Differs from the species in being somewhat smaller, and in the fancied resemblance of the flowerhead while in bud to the head of the Japanese Kutari crane. *H. k.* 'Caput-Avis' has nearly black scapes, almost horizontal, with very large, showy bracts. The flowers are produced in a tight bunch at the top instead of being spread out along the scape. Light shade.

H. k. 'Green Form' A selected green form.

H. k. 'Hokkaido' A selected green form.

H. k. 'Joy Bulford' A very dwarf selection.

H. k. 'Kifukurin' An invalid name according to the *Cultivated Plant Code* Article 17.11. See *H.* 'Shelleys'.

H. k. 'Leuconota' (W. G. Schmid 1991) Differs from the species in that the leaves are about half the size and much narrower and the leaves and petiole emerge with a pruinose white coating, the upper surface of the leaf fading to green by flowering time. Incorrectly called *H. k.* 'Pruinose'.

H. k. 'Polyneuron' (Fujita 1976) Differs from the species in that the veins on the leaves are closely spaced. Light shade.

H. 'Kinbotan' (Japan) A dubious name for a very narrowly cream-margined form of *H. venusta*. Extremely rare in the West. Probably best grown in a pot until well established. Light shade.

H. 'King Michael' (Krossa/ Summers 1992) Very large: spread about 150cm (60in), height 100cm (40in). Leaves very large, heart-shaped, mid-green, deeply corrugated. Flowers funnel-shaped, palest lavender to nearly white on straight, leafy 122cm (48in) scapes, mid-season. Makes a huge mound of almost hanging green leaves. Similar to *H.* 'Green Acres'. Light to full shade.

H. 'Knockout' (Aden 1986) Large: spread about 76cm (30in), height 45cm (18in). Leaves medium, dark green with an irregular creamy margin, with some overlapping resulting in grey-green streaking. Flowers funnel-shaped, pale lavender on straight, bare 30cm (12in) scapes, mid-season. (The plant described is the one in commerce, not as described on the AHS Registration Form). A most desirable and eye-catching hosta. Light to full shade.

H. 'Koriyama' (Horst ex Schmid 1991) Small: spread about 30cm (12in), height 20cm (8in). Leaves medium, oval, undulate, dark green, slightly celadon streaked, with regular and very distinct yellow margins. Flower funnel-shaped, purple-striped lavender, on straight, leafy 35cm (14in) scapes, mid-season. *H.* 'Koba' is similar but smaller. Both are probably forms of *H. sieboldii*. Light to full shade.

H. 'Krossa Regal' AGM (Krossa 1980) Very large: spread about 91cm (36in), height 76cm (30in). Leaves very large, widely lance-shaped, grey-blue, pruinose, the blade gently undulate, on tall, erect petioles, the petiole and leaf forming an upright arch. Flowers funnel-shaped, lavender on erect, zig-zag, 140cm (56in) scapes. Outstanding in leaf and flower. Young plants are vase-shaped but with age become more spreading. A classic hosta. Has received an Award of

Garden Merit from the RHS. *H.* 'Regal Splendor' is a sport. Light to full shade. Readily available.

H. 'Lady Isobel Barnett' (Grenfell & Grounds 1996) Sport of *H.* 'Sum and Substance', differing in having thick, glossy green leaves with an irregular creamy-yellow margin.

H. laevigata (Schmid 1991) Small: spread about 30cm (12in), height 10cm (4in). Leaves small, erect to spreading, narrowly lanceolate, light green with wavy margins, very thick. Flowers large, palest lavender or white suffused purple, the tube narrow suddenly flaring into narrow, spreading and recurving petals, on straight, erect, leafy scapes up to 91cm (36in) tall, mid-season. A remarkable new hosta which has only recently reached the West, opening up the possibility of new breeding lines. Its very thick leaves (probably a phenomenon due to its coastal habitat) may lead to a new line of lanceolate-leaved cultivars, replacing the thin-leaved sorts bred from *H. sieboldii*, while the large spidery flowers offer the prospect of new floral forms.

H. 'Lakeside Black Satin' (Chastain 1993) Medium: spread about 55cm (22in), height 23cm (9in). Leaves large, broadly oval with a heart-shaped base, margin slightly rippled, lustrous darkest green, sometimes appearing almost black. Flowers bell-shaped, deep purple with white stripes on 66cm (26in) scapes, mid-season. *H. ventricosa* hybrid, outstanding for its nearly black leaves. Light to full shade.

H. 'Lakeside Symphony' (Chastain 1988) Sport of *H.* 'Piedmont Gold', differing in having somewhat twisted, chartreuse to cream-coloured leaves with an irregular, muted lime-green margin with some overlapping of the cream and the lime green resulting in some streaking back towards the midrib. Light shade.

124

H. 'Lancifolia' (Engler [in Engler & Prantl] 1888) Medium: spread about 60cm (24in), height 30cm (12in). Leaves medium, oval to lance-shaped, the tip pointed, shiny mid-green above, glossy lighter green beneath, the margin slightly wavy, the blade running into the petiole, the petiole increasingly red-dotted towards the base. Flowers bell-shaped, intense purple-violet, on lax, leaning, leafy 45cm (18in) scapes, mid- to late. Considered to be sterile. *H. cathayana* is generally similar in appearance but differs in being fertile, so if a purported plant of *H.* 'Lancifolia' produces seed it may be *H. cathayana*. Formerly regarded as a species, and much confused with several other hosta species and varieties. Live plants were sent to Holland by von Siebold in 1829, and this was reputedly the first hosta to reach America. A useful ground cover plant which, if left undisturbed, will form large colonies. Always popular because of its shiny dark leaves and dark, showy flowers in late summer. Sometimes bears extraordinarily large, leafy bracts just below the flowers. The flowers can be attacked by blackfly. Light shade.

H. 'Leather Sheen' (Zilis/Lohman 1988) Large: spread about 76cm (30in), height 35cm (14in). Leaves medium, very thick, long, pointed, very glossy dark spinach green on upright, red-dotted petioles, making a dense, flat mound. Flowers bell-shaped, pale lavender on straight, red-dotted, leafy 76cm (30in) scapes, mid-season. The narrow bracts are near the raceme. *H.* 'Sum and Substance' × *H. venusta*. Light shade to sun.

H. 'Lemon Lime' (Savory 1988) Small to medium: spread about 45cm (18in), height 30cm (12in). Leaves small, lance-shaped, bright chartreuse yellow, flat. Flowers bell-shaped, lavender striped purple on straight, bare 45cm (18in) scapes, mid-season. Sports are *H.* 'Lemon Delight' (green with yellow margin) and *H.* 'Twist of Lime' (yellow with green margin). Shade. Readily available.

H. 'Leola Fraim' (Lachman 1986) Large: spread about 91cm (36in), height 45cm (18in). Leaves medium to large, heart-shaped, dark green with a wide, white margin that is usually widest near the tip, the leaves generally cupped and puckered. Flowers funnel-shaped, lavender on straight, bare 60cm (24in) scapes, mid-season. *H.* 'Swoosh' (streaked) is pollen parent. Increases well. Light shade.

H. 'Lime Krinkles' (Golden Medallion Group) (Soules 1988) Large: spread about 91cm (36in), height 45cm (18in). Leaves medium, cupped, very puckered, blade undulate, nearly round, chartreuse-yellow fading to lime-green. Flowers bell-shaped, nearly white on straight, leafy 60cm (24in) scapes, mid-season. *H.* 'Tokudama' seedling. Light shade to sun.

H. 'Little Aurora' (Golden Medallion Group) (Aden 1978) Small: spread about 30cm (12in), height 20cm (8in). Leaves small, thick, heart-shaped, at first chartreuse becoming golden-yellow, cupped and puckered. Flowers bell-shaped, palest lavender to nearly white on straight, bare 30cm (12in) scapes, mid-season. Most of the hostas circulating as *H.* 'Golden Prayers' are now thought to be *H.* 'Little Aurora'. The smallest *H.* 'Tokudama' hybrid so far, and delightful. Sports are *H.* 'Just So' and *H.* 'Vanilla Cream'. Light shade to sun. Readily available.

H. 'Little Blue' (Englerth 1976) Medium: spread about 45cm (18in), height 30cm (12in). Leaves thin, small, oval to heart-shaped, medium green. Flowers bell-shaped, purple on straight, bare 76cm (30in) scapes, mid-season. An *H.*

ventricosa selection, but neither really little nor blue. Light to full shade. Readily available.

H. 'Little Wonder' (Lachman 1989) Small: spread about 30cm (12in), height 15cm (6in). Leaves small, flat or lightly undulate, oval to heart-shaped, dark green with an irregular creamy-white to white margin, with some streaking to the centre and some overlapping producing grey streaks on reddish petioles. Flowers funnel-shaped, purple borne at right angles to the straight, bare 30cm (12in) reddish scape, mid-season. Increases rapidly. Outstanding. Light to full shade.

H. longipes ([Franchet & Savatier] Matsumura 1894) Small: spread about 30cm (12in), height 20cm (8in). Leaves medium, heart-shaped, glaucous or shiny green, flat, usually nearly closed at the navel, the petioles deeply channelled, winged in the upper half, dotted dark red especially near the base. Flowers bell-shaped, pale mauve to milky-white on 30cm (12in) scapes, the scapes round, red-dotted especially near the base, oblique or even horizontal. Mid-season. Seldom grown but a fascinating and very variable hosta, with many named forms. Known in Japan as the rock hosta, the specific epithet referring to its long 'feet' (roots), it being normally epiphytic or petrophytic in the wild, though in cultivation it can be grown as other hostas. *H. longipes* f. *hypoglauca* is being used by Roy Herold and other hybridizers in the US to inject red dotting into petiole and leaf colour, as in *H.* 'Brandywine'.

H. longissima (Honda 1937) Small: spread about 23cm (9in), height 15cm (6in). Leaves small, thick, erect, very narrow, lance-shaped or even linear to lance-shaped, shiny dark green above, glossy paler green beneath, wavy at the margin, tapering to a fine tip. Flowers funnel-shaped, pale reddish-mauve with purple veins and purple anthers, produced sparsely on straight, conspicuously leafy 45cm (18in) scapes, mid-season. Known in Japan as the swamp hosta since it grows in swampy grasslands and wet places, often exposed to full sun in the spring, but later shaded by taller-growing grasses. In such habitats the narrow leaves make it difficult to spot among the true grasses. The flower scapes are freely produced as if to compensate for the paucity of flowers on each scape. In gardens it prefers wetter ground than most hostas. Sometimes confused with narrow-leaved forms of *H. sieboldii* which differ in having thinner leaves and yellow anthers. *H. l.* 'Akebono' is a dwarf form with a yellow central variegation.

H. **'Love Pat'** (Tokudama Group) (Aden 1978) Medium to large:

spread about 60cm (24in), height 60cm (24in). Leaves medium to large, thick, very cupped and deeply puckered, heart-shaped to nearly round, intensely glaucous blue. Flowers bell-shaped, palest lavender to nearly white on straight, bare, 62cm (25in) scapes, mid-season. In effect a larger, improved *H.* 'Tokudama' of more upright habit, faster-growing and with even bluer leaves. Well worth growing and should become a classic hosta. Received an Award of Garden Merit from the RHS. Light to full shade. Readily available.

H. **'Lucy Vitols'** (Seaver 1989) Small to medium: spread about 40cm (16in), height 25cm (10in). Leaves medium, thick, cupped and puckered, nearly round, widely spaced prominent green veins, yellow or yellowish-green with an

irregular blue-green margin with some streaking into the centre. Flowers excellent, funnel-shaped, pale lavender, irregularly spaced on straight, leafy 45cm (18in) scapes, mid-season. Vigorous. Pest-resistant. Still rare. Light to full shade.

H. **'Lunar Eclipse'** (Zilis 1985) Sport of *H.* 'August Moon' differing in having a white margin to the leaves. The first flush of leaves usually have the drawstring effect. It is best in a warm to hot climate. Light shade to full sun.

H. **'Manhattan'** (Brincka-Petryszyn 1994) Large: spread about 81cm (32in), height 91cm (36in). Leaves very large, thick, cupped, puckered, margin rippled, blade undulate, heart-shaped, glossy light green becoming darker with blue overlay. Flowers tubular on straight, bare,

H. 'Love Pat' with *Rudbeckia* 'Goldsturm' at Longwood Gardens, Kennett Square, Pennsylvania.

126

H. 'Mildred Seaver', dramatically variegated and ultimately large-growing.

blue-green to purple 91cm (36in) scapes, late. Light to full shade.

H. 'Marilyn' (Zilis 1990) Large: spread about 76cm (30in), height 30cm (12in). Leaves medium, ovate to lance-shaped, margins wavy, unfurling yellow-gold becoming yellow. Flowers bell-shaped, pale lavender on 60cm (24in) scapes. Leaves early, may be damaged by late frost. Light shade to sun.

H. 'Mary Marie Ann' (Englerth 1982) Small: spread about 30cm (12in), height 20cm (8in). Leaves small, oval to lance-shaped, creamy-white or light chartreuse fading to mid-green with a broad green margin pencilled in white, the margin wavy, the blade sometimes twisting. Flowers funnel-shaped, lavender on straight, bare 36cm (15in) scapes, mid-season. Needs some strong sun to develop its attractive colouring. Found in a row of *H.* 'Aokii'.

H. 'Masquerade' (Grenfell & Grounds 1996) New name for what was formerly known as *H. venusta* 'Variegated', an invalid name. So named because it has been masquerading as a *venusta*. Miniature, somewhat stoloniferous: spread about 15cm (6in), height 10cm (4in). Leaves lance-shaped, white at first with a green margin and some streaking back towards the centre, sometimes becoming palest green. Flowers funnel-shaped, lavender striped purple inside, anthers purple, on straight, leafy 30cm (12in) scapes, mid-season. Almost certainly a hybrid

H. 'Midas Touch' (Golden Medallion Group) (Aden 1978) Large: spread about 76cm (30in), height 91cm (36in). Leaves medium, cupped and deeply puckered, heart-shaped, rich golden-yellow with a bronzy-metallic cast. Flowers bell-shaped, palest lavender to nearly white on straight, bare 76cm (30in) scapes, mid-season to late. An outstanding gold that will take almost full sun in the UK.

H. 'Mildred Seaver' (K. Vaughn 1981) Large: spread about 76cm (30in), height 36cm (15in). Leaves medium to large, heart-shaped, mid-green with a broad creamy white margin, puckered. Flowers funnel-shaped, lavender on straight, very pronounced leafy 60cm (24in) scapes, bracts heart-shaped, narrowly variegated, mid-season. *H.* 'Frances Williams' crossed with a *H.* 'Beatrice' seedling. Vigorous and eye-catching.

H. 'Minnie Klopping' (Klopping 1968/IRA 1975) Small: spread about 35cm (14in), height 20cm (8in). Leaves small, heart-shaped on long petioles, medium green with a greyish caste. Flowers bell-shaped, purple, on straight, leafy 50cm (20in) scapes, mid-season. Makes a neat, dense mound of overlapping leaves and produces abundant good flowers. Increases rapidly. Usually cited as an *H.* 'Fortunei' derivative but more likely to come from *H. nakaiana.*

H. minor (Nakai 1911) Miniature, stoloniferous: spread 20cm (8in), height 13cm (5in). Leaves small, oval to heart-shaped, margins undulate, yellowish-green with a metallic sheen, light green and shiny on undersides. Flowers funnel-shaped, re-blooming, light violet, on straight, ridged, leafy 35cm (14in) scapes, mid-season. Light shade.

H. 'Minuteman' (Machen 1994) Sport of 'Patriot', from which it differs in having blue-green leaves

with a wide, white margin, being more cupped and having more substance.

H. 'Moerheim' (Antioch Group) Similar to 'Antioch'. Raised at the Dutch Royal Nurseries.

H. montana (Maekawa 1940) Very large: spread about 100cm (40in), height 60cm (24in). Leaves very large, upright and arching, variable from oval to nearly heart-shaped coming to a point, the tip turned under, the veins deeply impressed causing a furrowed effect, the surface flat, the margins flat to rippled, with a dull sheen or quite glossy, deep green. Flowers funnel-shaped, white or suffused lavender, on straight, leafy scapes, early to mid-season. A native of woodland and forest margins in Japan where it is probably the commonest hosta, and therefore very variable. Forms have been found with distinct leaf shapes, with central and marginal variegations in white or yellow, as well as streaking, spotting and clouding, and there are forms with double flowers and with branched scapes. Many of these are cultivated in Japan but only a few have reached the West. A Mount Fuji or highland form emerges later in the spring, often by a month. Light to full shade. Readily available.

H. m. 'Aureomarginata' (AHS 1987) Differs in its leaves being narrower especially when young and slightly wavy, the lobes lifted, with broad golden-yellow margins, the yellow overlapping the green and producing celadon streaking. Usually the first hosta to emerge and very prone to damage by frost. If damaged leaves are removed the next flush will often escape the frosts. *H.* 'Mountain Snow' is a sport. Full shade. Readily available.

H. m. f. macrophylla (Schmid 1991) Differs in its exceptional size, the leaf mound sometimes exceeding 150cm (60in) wide,

between *H. sieboldii* and *H. venusta* (*fide* Schmid). Dramatically variegated little hosta but can revert. Best in a pot until it is a mature plant. Full shade. Readily available.

H. 'Maui Buttercups' (W. Vaughn 1991) Vigorous, small, compact: spread about 35cm (14in), height 25cm (10in). Leaves thick, cupped and deeply puckered, nearly round, rich, vivid yellow. Flowers bell-shaped and flared, lavender, on 45cm (18in) scapes, mid-season. Like a smaller version of *H.* 'Aspen Gold'. *H.* 'Frances Williams' × *H.* 'August Moon'. Light shade.

128

80cm (32in) tall, with leaves 45cm (18in) long and 30cm (12in) wide, and in its earlier flowering, the scapes having flowering bracts that roll in on themselves. Previously incorrectly known as *H. montana* f. *praeflorens*, a name which properly refers to a different form of *H. montana* which is not in cultivation.

H. 'Moon Glow' (Anderson 1977) Large: spread about 76cm (30in), height 50cm (20in). Leaves large, heart-shaped, cupped, bright chartreuse-yellow with a white margin. Flowers funnel-shaped, lavender on straight, leafy 60cm (24in) scapes, mid-season. A seedling of *H.* 'August Moon', differing from the rather similar *H.* 'Moonlight' in its shinier and more cupped leaves, and in its smaller stature. It can suffer from the drawstring effect. Needs shade for at least half the day.

H. 'Moonlight' (Fortunei Group) (Banyai 1977) Sport of *H.* 'Gold Standard', differing in that the leaves are at first mid-green turning bright yellow and finally parchment colour with a narrow white margin. A most beautiful hosta, but needs good cultivation and careful placing to avoid scorching in too much sun or failing to colour properly in too much shade.

H. 'Moon River' (Lachman 1991) Medium: spread about 40cm (16in), height 27cm (11in). Leaves dwarf, thick, somewhat puckered, heart-shaped glaucous dark blue-green with an irregular cream margin and some streaking going back towards the midrib. Flowers funnel-shaped, lavender on straight, bare, 40cm (16in) scapes in late summer. Sterile. *H.* 'Crepe Suzette' × *H.* 'Blue Moon'. A promising new hosta. Light to full shade.

H. 'Moon Waves' (Plater-Zyberk/Solberg 1994) Medium: spread about 60cm (24in), height 35cm (14in). Leaves medium, thick, lance-shaped with a rounded base, mid-yellow, dull both above and beneath, the veins prominent, the blade wavy, the margin very rippled. Flowers bell-shaped, palest lavender to nearly white on straight, bare 76cm (30in) scapes. Hybrid of *H.* 'August Moon' but distinct on account of its lance-shaped and extraordinarily wavy and rippled leaves. Probably sterile. Light shade to sun.

H. 'Mountain Snow' (T & Z/Mark Zilis 1988) Very large: sport of *H. montana* 'Aureomarginata' with mid-green leaves having an irregular white margin and considerable overlapping of the white on the green resulting in grey streaking, occasionally reaching the midrib. Flowers nearly white. Sprouts later in the spring than its parent. Slow-growing but eventually as much as 150cm (60in) across. Shade.

H. nakaiana (Maekawa 1935) Small: spread about 23cm (9in), height 13cm (5in). Leaves small, oval to narrowly heart-shaped, dull matt mid-green above, shiny beneath, with a thin white hyaline margin. Flowers bell-shaped, lavender, anthers white, on straight, leafy 50cm (20in) scapes, mid-season. Forms a dense mound and produces an abundance of flowers bunched together at the tops of the scapes, which are ridged at the sides. Closely related to *H. venusta* but larger.

H. 'Nakaimo' (AHS 1986) Large: spread about 76cm (30in), height 60cm (24in). Leaves large, heart-shaped, sharply pointed, the point down-turned flat, dull mid-green above, shiny beneath. Flowers bell-shaped, pale pinkish-purple on straight, leafy 60cm (24in) scapes, mid-season. Though raised in Tokyo and imported to America before 1939, this is still rated one of the best hostas for flower, unmistakable both in bud and blossom on account of its ball-shaped buds and densely packed heads.

H. 'Nancy Lindsay' (Fortunei Group) (BHHS 1988) Differs from *H.* 'Fortunei Hyacinthina', of which it is a form, in its smaller, narrower leaves and in the leaves being mottled with a yellow mosaic in spring, gradually turning green as summer advances. Late to emerge. An eye-catching variety. *H.* 'Windsor Gold' is similar but has larger, broader leaves. Light to full shade.

H. 'Neat and Tidy' (Simpers 1980) Large: spread about 80cm (32in), height 60cm (24in). Leaves large, anything but neat and tidy, thick, convex, slightly twisted, irregularly heart-shaped, glaucous blue-green. Flowers bell-shaped, palest lavender or nearly white on straight, leafy 91cm (36in) scapes, mid-season to late. Light to full shade.

H. 'Neat Splash' (Aden 1978) Medium, stoloniferous: spread about 60cm (24in), height 30cm (12in). Leaves medium-sized, oval to lance-shaped, running into the petiole, dark green with a wide, irregular bright yellow becoming creamy-yellow margin, the margin overlapping the green centre, resulting in considerable yellow, cream and grey streaking back towards the midrib. Flowers funnel-shaped, lavender, on straight, bare 70cm (28in) scapes. Showy both in leaf and flower. The variegation is unstable and tends to migrate to the margins unless the plant is divided every three or four years. Much used for breeding hostas with streaked variegation. Not for container growing. Shade.

H. 'Neat Splash Rim' (AHS 1986) The stable form of *H.* 'Neat Splash' in which the variegation has migrated to the margins. Readily available.

H. 'Night Before Christmas' (Machen 1994) Sport of *H.* 'White Christmas', from which it differs in having larger, white leaves with a wide green margin, the leaf rather pointed and twisted, the plant rather upright. Light to full shade.

H. nigrescens (Maekawa 1937) Large: spread about 70cm (28in), height 65cm (26in). Leaves large, oval to roundly heart-shaped, cupped, puckered, the lobes lifted and almost closed at the navel, ashy grey-green, the petiole tall, up to 50cm (20in), distinctly upright and merging with the midrib to hold the blade rather upright, making a tall clump. Flowers bell-shaped, palest lavender to near-white, on straight, leafy 150cm (60in) scapes, mid-season to late. Known in Japan as the black hosta; the specific epithet means blackish, referring to the almost black but pruinose emerging buds in the spring. Remarkable for the leaf colour and the very tall, often zigzag scapes which can exceptionally reach 180cm (72in). Light to full shade. Readily available.

H. n. f. elatior Differs from the species in its light green not pruinose leaves, and in being notably larger in all its parts, the scape straight, the flowers also larger. Rare. Light to full shade. *H.* 'Green Wedge' (Aden) is a selected clone. Both of these, and *H. nigrescens*, make large, striking specimens.

H. 'Nonsuch' (Grenfell & Grounds 1996) Very large: spread about 150cm (60in), height 79cm (31in). Leaves very large, oval to heart-shaped, 40cm (16in) long, 25cm (10in) wide, grey, white pruinose beneath, the blade somewhat cupped and furrowed, veins deeply impressed, the margins boldly wavy. Petioles 52cm (21in). Flowers funnel-shaped, large, light lavender, mostly pendent, up to 85 per scape, the scapes leafy, leaning, at first upright, then arching outwards, downwards then upwards in a horizontal S-shape. Generally similar to *H.* 'Snowden', but showier and with much better flowers. Seedling of an unnamed *H. montana* selection.

H. 'North Hills' (Fortunei Group) (Summers/AHS 1986) Large: spread about 91cm (36in), height 50cm (20in). Leaves large, oval to heart-shaped, flat, puckered, medium green with an irregular narrow white margin which can assume yellow and then pale green tints. Flowers funnel-shaped, lavender on leaning, leafy 100cm (40in) scapes, mid-season. Sterile. Full shade. Readily available.

H. 'Northern Exposure' (Falstead) Differs from *H.* 'Frances Williams' in having yellow margins which fade to white, and differs from *H.* 'Northern Halo' in having a flat leaf blade. Full shade.

H. 'Northern Halo' (Walters Gardens 1984) Differs from *H.* 'Frances Williams' in having white margins, the leaf blade intensely puckered and crumpled, and in its generally smaller stature. Forms in commerce range from leaf blades flat to having the drawstring effect. The drawstring form is *H.* 'Exotic Frances Williams'. Full shade.

H. 'On Stage' (Aden 1986) Reputed to be identical to *H.* 'Choko Nishiki'. Medium: spread about 60cm (24in), height 35cm (14in). Leaves large, puckered, heart-shaped to wedge-shaped, rich golden-yellow with an irregular green and celadon margin, the green and celadon streaking into the centre, dull above, shiny beneath, the blade not clearly differentiated from the petiole. The yellow colour darkens during the season, especially if grown in shade. Flowers funnel-shaped, lavender on straight, bare 60cm (24in) scapes, mid-season. One of the most outstanding of all hostas but difficult to propagate and slow to build up into a sizeable plant. *H. montana* sport, emerging much later in the spring. Light shade to sun.

H. 'Opipara' (F. Maekawa 1937) Medium, somewhat stoloniferous: spread about 50cm (20in), height

35cm (14in). Leaves medium to large, oval or elliptical coming to a pointed tip, wavy at the margin, the blade running into the broad winged petiole without clear differentiation, shiny dark green with a broad, irregular yellow margin, the margin fading to nearly white in strong light. Flowers funnel-shaped, lavender striped purple inside on leaning, leafy 76cm (30in) scapes, mid-season. The stoloniferous roots and flowers suggest close affinity with *H. sieboldii*. It is outstanding when grown in full shade as the subtle tones in the celadon streaking become apparent and the margin is chartreuse green, a lovely contrast with the glossy dark green leaves. Introduced to Britain from Japan 1985 and independently into America, possibly more than once. Some early stock in America suffered viral infection but this stock has now mostly been ousted by *H.* 'Bill Brincka', which appears identical with the plant grown in Britain but may differ in its greater vigour. Not suitable for containers.

H. 'Osprey' (Tardiana Group, TF 2 × 14) (BHHS 1988) Medium hosta, leaf mound about 45cm (18in) wide, 30cm (12in) tall. Leaves medium, thick, heart-shaped, glaucous deep blue-green. Flowers palest lavender to nearly white, densely borne on straight, bare 35cm (14in) scapes, mid-season. Reported to have white flowers in the US. Light to full shade.

H. 'Pacific Blue Edger' (Heims) Sport of *H.* 'Gold Edger', from which it differs in having glaucous blue-green leaves. One of the best small blues, producing an abundance of good flowers, for which the blue leaves make a perfect foil. Some scapes have an extra branch. Increases rapidly. Light to full shade.

H. 'Patrician' (Skrocki/Avent 1993) Small: spread about 36cm (15in), height 20cm (8in). Leaves small,

H. 'Patriot', probably the best white-edged hosta ever raised.

rounded, wavy, mid-green with a wide, regular, bright yellow margin. Flowers funnel-shaped, dark lavender on straight, leafy 30cm (12in) scapes, late. Delightful small hosta especially valuable for its abundant late flowers. Named for a Packard motor car. Light to full shade.

H. 'Patriot' (Machen 1991) Sport of *H.* 'Francee', from which it differs in having violet sprouting shoots, a very much wider, white

margin, the variegation overlapping the green and resulting in some celadon and grey streaking back towards the centre. A great advance on *H.* 'Francee', and probably the most striking white-edged hosta so far. It stands out in the garden. Light to full shade.

H. 'Paul's Glory' (Ruh/Hofer 1987) Reported to be a sport (but may be a seedling) of *H.* 'Perry's True Blue', from which it differs in having

leaves that are yellow becoming creamy-white in the centre, lasting throughout the season, with an irregular, broad blue-green margin. Does not burn or melt out. One of the most eye-catching of hostas. Light shade to some sun.

H. 'Peace' (Aden 1987) Small: spread about 25cm (10in), height 13cm (5in). Leaves small, heart-shaped, puckered, glaucous blue-green with a variable chartreuse to

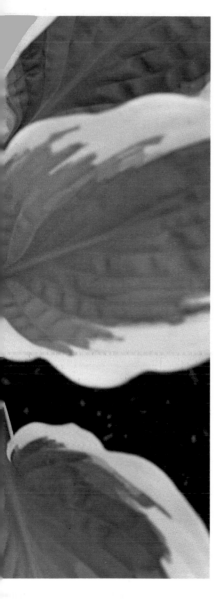

flat, on long petioles, grey-green, glaucous beneath. Profusion of funnel-shaped, light lavender to nearly white flowers on straight, bare, 76cm (30in) scapes, mid-season. Vigorous and multiplies fast, making dense mounds. Lovely as an individual or massed. Very responsive to its growing situation; in open ground the leaves become much bigger, in pots it remains a fine, neat, small-leaved plant. *H.* 'Veronica Lake' is a sport. Light to full shade. Readily available.

H. **'Peedee Elfin Bells'** (Syre-Herz 1987) Large: spread about 50cm (30in), height 25cm (10in). Leaves small, dark green with a satiny sheen, the margins sometimes wavy, the tips sometimes twisted. Flowers bell-shaped, reddish-purple on straight, leafy 55cm (22in) scapes, mid-season. *H. ventricosa* seedling, open pollinated. Light to full shade.

H. **'Peedee Gold Flash'** (Syre-Herz 1987) Medium: spread about 45cm (18in), height 25cm (10in). Leaves small, lance-shaped, flattish, yellow becoming green with a narrow green margin. Flowers funnel-shaped, lavender with purple stripes on straight, leafy, 30cm (12in) scapes, mid-season. Hybrid of *H.* 'Kabitan', differing little.

H. **'Perry's True Blue'** (Elegans Group) (Hofer/Ruh 1981) Very large: spread about 91cm (36in), height 55cm (22in). Leaves very large, thick, heart-shaped, puckered and somewhat cupped, glaucous blue-green. Flowers bell-shaped, palest lavender to nearly white on straight, bare 76cm (30in) scapes, mid-season. Sometimes confused with *H.* 'True Blue', a different plant. A slow-growing *H. sieboldiana* hybrid with leaves of a good colour and substance. Light shade.

H. **'Phoenix'** (Fischer) Very large: spread about 91cm (36in), height 66cm (26in). Leaves large, late to emerge from narrow, delicately pointed, dark brown shoots, 28cm (11in) long, 13cm (5in) wide, lance-shaped, gracefully pointed, wavy, the veins deeply impressed, the lobes lifted, the blade and petiole running together in a continuous upward and outward arch, glaucous grey-green, intensely white pruinose beneath and down the back of the petiole, the very base of the petiole intensely red-dotted. Flowers bell-shaped, pale lavender, on straight, leafy, pruinose 122cm (48in) scapes, the leafy bracts conspicuously large, their petioles flushed purplish-red where they join the scape. Parentage unknown. Leaves are unexpectedly narrow for such a large hosta. Makes an elegant, open clump. Light shade.

H. **'Phyllis Campbell'** (Fortunei Group) (BHHS 1988) Eric Smith thought this was a sport of *H.* 'Fortunei Albopicta', but it seems to more closely resemble *H.* 'Fortunei Hyacinthina'. Medium to large: leaves creamy-ivory, overlaid with fine, dark cross-veins, giving a 'netted' appearance with irregular glaucous dark-green margins. It fades to a dull, patchy green at flowering time. Similar, or identical, to *H.* 'Gene Summers' and *H.* 'Sharmon'. Light to full shade.

H. **'Piedmont Gold'** (Piedmont 1974) Very large: spread about 100cm (40in), height 50cm (20in). Leaves very large, thick, oval to heart-shaped, blade shallowly undulate, prominently veined, puckered, glaucous-bloomed, soft golden yellow, pale beneath. Flowers funnel-shaped, palest lavender to nearly white on straight, bare 76cm (30in) scapes, mid-season. A classic yellow-leaved hosta, best in light shade. Sometimes confused with *H.* 'Sun Power', which needs more shade. Sports are *H.* 'Evening Magic' and *H.* 'Lakeside Symphony'.

H. **'Pineapple Poll'** (E. Smith/BHHS 1988) Medium: spread about 45cm

cream margin, the white overlapping the centre resulting in some grey streaking. Flowers bell-shaped, lavender on straight, bare 30cm (12in) scapes, mid-season. Enchanting small hosta, the leaf and flower colours working well together. Light to full shade.

H. **'Pearl Lake'** (Piedmont Gardens 1982) Small to medium: spread about 60cm (24in), height 45cm (18in). Leaves small, heart-shaped,

132

(18in), height 45cm (18in). Leaves medium, conspicuously undulate, gracefully tapering to a point, dull glaucous grey-green above, whitish beneath, the blade running into the petiole, the petiole shallowly U-shaped and slightly winged, mauve-dotted near the base but more intensely red-dotted behind. Flowers pale lavender, on glaucous, 50cm (20in) scapes, very leafy just below the flowers, mid- to late. A most unusual hosta, making open mounds of very narrow upright or arching leaves, the scapes carrying large tufts of leafy bracts just below the flowers suggesting a fancied resemblance to the top of a pineapple. *H. sieboldiana* × *H.* 'Lancifolia'. Light to full shade.

H. 'Pizzazz' (Aden 1986) Medium: spread about 45cm (18in), height 30cm (12in). Leaves medium, oval to heart-shaped, cupped and puckered with a rippled margin, frosted blue-green with deeper green and paler grey streaks with an irregular cream margin streaking back into the leaf centre, matt above, pale glaucous beneath. Flowers bell-shaped, palest lavender to nearly white clustered near the tip, on straight, leafy 45cm (18in) scapes, mid-season. Light to full shade.

H. plantaginea ([Monnet de Lamarck] Ascherson 1863) Large: spread about 91cm (36in), height 45cm (18in). Leaves large, heart-shaped, veins deeply impressed and widely spaced, very slightly puckered, blade lightly undulate, light to mid-green, glossy above, paler green and shiny beneath.

H. 'Piedmont Gold', a classic yellow-leaved hosta which does best in light shade.

Flowers very large, very fragrant, pure white, the tube exceedingly long, up to 13cm (5in), on straight, leafy 76cm (30in) scapes, late to very late. An outstanding and exotic hosta, known in the West as the August lily or Paris hosta because of its popularity in Paris soon after its introduction. The flowers open in late afternoon or evening and have a fragrance comparable to an Asiatic lily. A native of China, it has a more southerly distribution than any other hosta and this is reflected in

its cultural needs. It can scarcely be induced to flower outside in Britain further north than London, and even in the most southerly counties cannot be relied on to flower every year, even at the foot of a south wall. It is perhaps better grown, as Gertrude Jekyll recommended, in large tubs, either in a conservatory or stood out in summer, preferably near a path or seat where its fragrance can be enjoyed. It generally flourishes better in some parts of continental Europe and America, where summers are hotter. A number of variants are in existence. *H. p.* 'Grandiflora' has larger, longer flowers but is inferior in foliage, having narrower leaf blades with a lax habit, appearing rather limp and giving the mound an untidy appearance; however, it has even larger flowers. This is the form of *H. plantaginea* which was given an Award of Merit by the RHS in 1948 and is incorrectly known as *H. p.* 'Japonica' in the US. *H.* 'Chelsea Ore' is a sport.

H. p. 'Japonica' (Maekawa 1938) was introduced to Japan from China and was grown there and in Korea for a very long time before it came to the West. In 1830 von Siebold took plants from Japan and planted them in his *jardin d'acclimatization* in Buitenzorg, Java, from where they were sent on to him at Leyden in 1841. Plants from this original Siebold introduction are still growing at Trompenberg Arboretum in Holland. This hosta is probably not *H. p.* 'Grandiflora' as discussed by Schmid (1991). The leaves are dark green, more round than heart-shaped. It flowers in the shade at Trompenberg, which other forms of *H. plantaginea* do not.

H. p. 'Stenantha' (Maekawa 1940) has more narrowly funnel-shaped flowers and slender lobes. It has no particular garden merit. *H. p.* 'Aphrodite' has double flowers (see *H.* 'Aphrodite') and *H. p.* 'Venus' has double-double flowers.

H. 'Platinum Tiara' (Tiara Group) (Walters Gardens 1987) Differs from *H.* 'Golden Tiara' in having yellow green leaves with white margins.

H. 'Pooh Bear' (Falstead 1988) Sport of *H.* 'Gold Drop', from which it differs in having leaves that are yellow with a narrow, irregular, indistinct, green margin. Slow. Light shade to sun.

H. 'Popo' (O'Harra 1993) Small: spread about 25cm (10in), height 15cm (6in). Leaves miniature, cupped, heart-shaped, glaucous blue-green. Flowers palest lavender heavily striped purple inside, the striping showing through to the outside, the flowers mostly gathered near the top of the straight, leafy 30cm (12in) scape, mid-season. One of the smallest of all the blue-green hostas, and looking rather like a miniature Tardiana but with relatively taller flower scapes. Light shade.

H. pulchella (Fujita 1976) Miniature, moderately stoloniferous: spread about 20cm (8in), height 10cm (4in). Leaves dwarf, moderately thick, oval to heart-shaped, waxy, polished dark green above, lighter green beneath. Flowers funnel-shaped, the tube white, the lobes purple, on straight, leafy 20cm (10in) scapes, mid-season. Ideal for a rock garden or peat bed. Light to full shade.

H. pulchella 'Kifukurin' (Japan) An unacceptable name according to the *Cultivated Plant Code*, Article 17.11. Sport of *H. pulchella*, its leaves having pale yellow margins. An attractive new hosta. Probably best started off in a pot. Light to full shade.

H. 'Purple Lady Finger' (Savory 1982) Medium: spread about 50cm (20in), height 35cm (14in). Leaves medium, erect, narrowly lance-shaped, flat, dark green.

134

Flowers funnel-shaped, bright purple remaining closed at the mouth, on straight, bare 50cm (20in) scapes, mid-season. Perhaps more curious than beautiful, but makes a good ground cover in some gardens. Seedling of *H. longissima*. Light to full shade and moist soil.

H. pycnophylla (Maekawa 1976) Small to medium: spread about 45cm (18in), height 25cm (10in). Leaves medium, oval to heart-shaped, tapering to a point, flat with a piecrust margin, rather limp, matt, light blue-green above becoming more shiny as the season advances, intensely white pruinose beneath, the petioles strongly red-streaked especially towards the base. Flowers bell-shaped, purple to dark purple held perpendicularly on scapes that lean out obliquely from the leaf mound becoming horizontal where the flowers are carried. A rare and lovely species, needing skilful cultivation. Used in breeding for its piecrust margins. Light to full shade.

H. 'Queen Josephine' (Kuk 1991) Medium: spread about 45cm (18in), height 30cm (12in). Spring leaves oval to heart-shaped, glossy dark green with an irregular wide cream margin fading to nearly white, with a little streaking towards the midrib, summer leaves oval to lanceolate. Flowers funnel-shaped, lavender on straight, leafy 60cm (24in) scapes, mid-season to late. A very striking hosta. Sport of *H.* 'Josephine'. Light to full shade.

H. 'Queen of Islip' (George Smith Group) (Goffery 1990) Similar, or possibly identical, to *H.* 'George Smith', *H.* 'Borwick Beauty' and *H.* 'Color Glory'. Rare.

H. 'Radiance' (Anderson 1980) Large: spread about 76cm (30in), height 60cm (24in). Leaves large. heart-shaped, puckered, evenly yellow fading to mid-green (viridescent) later in the season. Flowers

funnel-shaped, pale lavender on straight, bare 91cm (36in) scapes, mid-season. Parentage not recorded but looks like a yellow-leaved *H.* 'Fortunei'. Light shade.

H. 'Radiant Edger' (Zilis 1990) Sport of *H.* 'Gold Edger', differing in having rich green leaves with a wide, irregular, bright golden-yellow margin. Slower growing than *H.* 'Gold Edger' but has the same excellent mound-forming habit. Light shade to sun.

H. 'Raleigh Remembrance' (Zilis 1991) Medium to large: spread about 91cm (36in), height 60cm (24in). Leaves large, very glossy, oval to heart-shaped, chartreuse to yellow. Flowers bell-shaped lavender, on 76cm (30in) scapes, mid-season. *H.* 'Sum and Substance' × *H. plantaginea*. Not always easy to grow well. Sun.

H. 'Raspberry Sorbet' (Zilis) Small: spread about 30cm (12in), height 15cm (6in). Leaves miniature to small, thick, widely lance-shaped, pointed tip, undulate margins, glossy, olive-green, on narrowly channelled petioles which are flecked or spotted dark purplish-red reaching up into the base of both sides of the leaf, the undersides very shiny and much lighter green. Flowers funnel-shaped, purple-striped lavender, on slender flecked purplish-red straight, leafy 25cm (10in) scapes. Light shade to sun.

H. rectifolia (Nakai 1930) Medium: spread about 45cm (18in), height 35cm (14in). Leaves medium, oval, slightly concave, matt, dark green above, glossy and lighter green on the undersides. Flowers narrow-tubed then widely flaring, deep purple striped violet, on upright, sterile-bracted, light-green 87cm (35in) scapes in late summer. Light to full shade. Readily available. *H. r.* 'Aureomarginata' (an invalid name according to the *Cultivated*

Plant Code) is an extremely striking marginally variegated form not yet grown in British or European gardens. *H. r.* 'Chionea', a spatulate-leaved, white-margined form, appears identical to what is mistakenly circulating in Europe as *H. rectifolia* 'Nakai'.

H. 'Red Neck Heaven' (Avent 1995) Small to medium: spread about 45cm (18in), height 30cm (12in). Leaves small to medium, lance-shaped, the veins deeply impressed, mid-green with a satiny sheen above, waxy white beneath, the petioles red-streaked along their entire length, becoming almost solidly red at the base, the streaking extending beyond the lobes into the midrib of the leaf. Flowers bell-shaped, pendent, lavender or nearly white on stiff red-streaked scapes that arch upwards and outwards and then curve down and up again. Seedling from *H. kikutii* 'Caput-avis'. Tolerates full sun. Curious because of the way the leaning scapes produce all the flowers like a fringe round the edge of the leaf mound.

H. 'Reefed Sails' (C. Seaver 1994) Small: spread about 23cm (9in), height 45cm (18in). Of upright habit. Leaves small, lance-shaped, tapered at the base, undulating, glossy dark green with very rippled cream margins. Petioles red-dotted at the base, cream-margined. Flowers tubular, lavender striped purple, with straight, bare, solid maroon scapes in late summer. Light shade.

H. 'Regal Rhubarb' (Sellers 1983) Medium: spread about 60cm (24in), height 76cm (30in). Leaves large, oval, flat, mid-green, petioles very thick to chunky, streaked vinous reddish-purple, the streaking so dense at the base as to appear a solid colour but fading towards the leaf blade. Flowers funnel-shaped, purple, on straight, bare 150cm (60in) scapes, mid-season.

Purple seed capsules. Probably *H. rectifolia* hybrid, grown for the colouring of its petioles which resemble sticks of rhubarb. Light to full shade.

H. **'Regal Splendor'** (Walters Gardens 1987) Sport of *H.* 'Krossa Regal', differing in that the leaves have a creamy-white to creamy-yellow margin with some overlapping of the marginal colour on the centre resulting in some streaking. The margin increases with maturity. Handsome. Light shade.

H. **'Resonance'** (Aden 1976) Medium, somewhat stoloniferous: spread about 45cm (18in), height 20cm (8in). Leaves medium, thin, oval to lance-shaped, undulate, mid-green with an irregular yellow to ivory margin. Flowers funnel-shaped, deep purple, on straight, bare 50cm (20in) scapes, mid-season to late. A good ground-covering hosta but not suitable for containers. Light to full shade. When young can be mistaken for *H.* 'Ground Master'. Readily available.

H. **'Reversed'** (Aden 1978) (An unacceptable name under Article 17.11 of the *Cultivated Plant Code*). Large: spread about 91cm (36in), height 50cm (20in). Leaves medium to large, puckered, oval to heart-shaped, tapering to a point, cream to nearly white with an irregular blue-green margin. Flowers funnel-shaped, lavender, on straight, ivory, leafy 76cm (30in) scapes, mid-season. When well grown a most striking hosta, but not always easy, and sometimes very slow. While it needs good light to colour well, the centre of the leaf may melt out in too much sun. It may need moving several times in order to find suitable growing conditions. The leaves can revert to green if not divided every few years. Generally partial shade.

H. **'Richland Gold'** (Fortunei Group) (Wade 1987) Sport of 'Gold Standard', from which it differs in having plain yellow leaves which turn parchment as they age. A lovely golden-yellow-leaved hosta but needing just as much care in placing as its parent.

H. **'Robert Frost'** (Lachman 1988) Very large: spread about 105cm (42in), height 60cm (24in). Leaves very large, heart-shaped, flat, glaucous mid-green with a wide, very irregular yellowish-white margin with streaking back towards the midrib. Flowers bell-shaped, palest lavender or nearly white on straight, bare 91cm (36in) scapes, mid-season. *H.* 'Banana Sundae' × *H.* 'Frances Williams'. Light to full shade.

H. *rohdeifolia* (Maekawa 1937) Small: spread about 38cm (15in), height 35cm (14in). Leaves small, erect, lance-shaped, flat, green with a thin, irregular yellowish to ivory margin, the blade running into the wide, winged petiole without clear distinction. Flowers lily-shaped, lavender with purple stripes on straight, bare 60cm (24in) scapes, mid-season to late. The specific epithet refers to the similarity of the leaves to those of the Japanese woodlander, *Rohdea japonica*. It forms a mound of upright leaves with extraordinarily tall flower scapes, and has many similarities with *H. sieboldii*, including the anther colour. The hosta formerly known as *H.* 'Helonioides Albopicta' may also belong here, though it has purple anthers. Light to full shade.

H. **'Rough Waters' (Tokudama Group)** (Armstrong 1969) Differs in having more dimpled, greyer leaves. It is more suitable than some of the bluer-leaved Tokudamas in a woodland or less formal planting. Light to full shade.

H. **'Royal Standard'** (Grulleman/Wayside/AHS 1986) Large: spread about 91cm (36in), height 45cm (18in). Leaves large, narrowly heart-shaped, puckered when mature, bright, light green, somewhat glossy above, shiny beneath. Flowers funnel-shaped, white from lilac-tinted buds, fragrant, occasionally semi-double, on straight, leafy, 60cm (24in) scapes, mid-season to late. The best fragrant white for general planting, the flower scapes freely produced, the flowers held well above the foliage. Best planted where the flowers and the fragrance, which is strongest in the evenings, can be appreciated. *H.* 'Hoosier Harmony', a sport with green-margined, yellow leaves, shows great promise. Full sun if there is enough moisture. Readily available.

H. **'Royal Super'** (Walters Gardens) Medium: spread about 60cm (24in), height 45cm (18in). Leaves medium, glossy, thick, light green with an irregular narrow greenish-yellow to nearly white margin with some streaking towards the midrib. Flowers white, fragrant, the first few flowers on each scape semi-double with petaloid stamens. The scapes are shorter than on *H.* 'Royal Standard'. Interesting both for its quiet variegation and its unusual flowers. Tissue culture sport from *H.* 'Royal Standard'. Needs sun to flower well.

H. **'Royalty'** (Anderson 1982) Small: spread about 35cm (14in), height 25cm (10in). Leaves dwarf, upright, blade flat, heart-shaped, chartreuse to yellow. Flowers bell-shaped, purple, on straight, bare 35cm (14in) scapes. Flower heads fasciated (compacted tightly and uniformly). *H. capitata* hybrid. Light to full shade.

H. *rupifraga* (Nakai 1930) Small: spread about 30cm (12in), height 20cm (8in). Leaves small, thick to almost succulent, broadly heart-shaped, dark green with a satiny sheen above, glossy beneath, the petiole red-streaked especially towards the base. Flowers bell-shaped, purple with deeper stripes

136

on arching bare 30cm (12in) scapes, late. A rare and delightful hosta, growing in the wild in a tiny area on the rim of a volcano at 762m (2,500ft). Leaves emerge in sun but are later shaded by grasses. Well adapted to growing on screes, though it flourishes when grown much as other hostas. Reasonably slug- and snail-resistant. Light shade to some sun. *H.* 'Hydon Twilight' (Grenfell & Grounds 1986) is a free-flowering selection.

H. **'Ryans Big One' (Elegans Group)** (Englerth 1982) Differs from *H. sieboldiana* 'Elegans' in that it makes a huge, dense hosta, increasing rapidly, and in that it holds its flowers high above the leaf mound on straight scapes up to 122cm (48in) tall.

H. **'Sagae'** (Japan) See *H. fluctuans* 'Sagae'.

H. **'Saishu Jima'** (Japan) Sport or selection of *H. sieboldii*, from which it differs in having small, dark, glossy green leaves with very rippled margins, the leaves being held almost horizontal. Makes an interesting texture when used as a carpet.

H. **'Samurai'** (Frances Williams Group) (Aden) Similar or identical to *H.* 'Frances Williams'.

H. **'Sea Dream'** (M. Seaver 1984) Large: spread about 76cm (30in), height 30cm (12in). Leaves large, heart-shaped, somewhat puckered, at first light green quickly becoming yellow with a clean, wide white margin. Flowers bell-shaped, lavender on straight, bare 45cm (18in) scapes, late. Makes a rather loose leaf mound but is one of the best white-edged yellows. *H.* 'Neat Splash' hybrid. Full shade.

H. **'Sea Drift'** (M. Seaver 1978) Large: spread about 76cm (30in), height 55cm (22in). Leaves large, thick, oval, with a piecrust edge,

The rippled yellow leaves of *H.* 'Sea Gold Star'.

deeply veined, shiny deep green. Flowers funnel-shaped, lavender striped purple on straight, bare 91cm (36in) scapes, late. Slow to establish. An attractive hosta useful for flower arrangement. It is

relatively slug-proof and tolerant of quite a lot of sun.

H. **'Sea Gold Star'** (M. Seaver 1984) Large hosta, spread about 76cm (30in), height 38cm (15in).

Leaves large, round to heart-shaped, puckered, the margins somewhat undulate, at first chartreuse becoming evenly bright golden-yellow. Attractive, star-shaped, palest lavender to nearly white flowers on straight, bare 45cm (18in) scapes, mid-season. *H.* 'Wagon Wheels' seedling. Light shade.

H. **'Sea Lotus Leaf'** (M. Seaver 1985) Large, vigorous: spread about 91cm (36in), height 50cm (20in). Leaves large, conspicuously upturned, puckered, almost round, widely veined, glossy blue-green presented in a vase-shaped mound. Flowers bell-shaped, palest lavender to nearly white on bare, leaning 60cm (24in) scapes, mid-season. *H.* 'Wagon Wheels' hybrid. Light to full shade.

H. **'Sea Mist'** (M. Seaver) Large, spread about 50cm (30in), height 45cm (18in). Leaves medium, nearly round to heart-shaped, cupped and puckered, yellow to chartreuse with an irregular, wide, subtle, muted light green margin. Flowers funnel-shaped, pale lavender. Needs careful cultivation and slug protection. Light shade.

H. **'Sea Monster'** (M. Seaver 1978) Very large: spread about 105cm (42in), height 70cm (28in). Leaves very large, heart-shaped, cupped and distinctly puckered, glaucous grey-green. Flowers palest lavender to nearly white on straight, bare 76cm (30in) scapes, mid-season. Light shade.

H. **'Sea Octopus'** (M. Seaver 1981) Small: spread about 35cm (14in), height 20cm (8in). Leaves small, lance-shaped with very wavy margins, the blade running into the petiole, matt mid-green above, shiny beneath. Flowers funnel-shaped, deep lavender with purple stripes on straight, bare 76cm (30in) scapes, the scapes red-streaked especially near the base,

late to very late. An elegant late-flowering hosta, the scapes extraordinarily tall compared with the leaf mound. Clump must be divided every few years to retain the rippled margins. Light shade. Readily available.

H. **'Sea Thunder'** (M. Seaver) Medium: spread 60cm (24in), height 30cm (12in). Leaves small to medium, upright, oval, tapering to a point, blade flat, white with an irregular, wide mid-green margin which goes down the length of the petiole. Flowers funnel shaped, lavender, on straight, bare 62cm (25in) scapes in mid-summer. Full shade.

H. **'Sea Yellow Sunrise'** (M. Seaver) Medium: spread 50cm (20in), height 40cm (16in). Leaves medium, oval, blade flat, golden-yellow becoming green. Flowers funnel-shaped, lavender, on bare, straight 60cm (24in) scapes, mid-season. The stable form of *H.* 'Sea Sunrise', which has green leaves, irregularly streaked chartreuse, yellow and white. Light shade.

H. **'See Saw'** (Summers 1986) Sport of *H.* 'Undulata Erromena', from which it differs in its narrow, concave, almost oval to lance-shaped leaves, olive-green and satiny above, shiny, lighter green beneath, with an irregular, narrow, white margin and some white streaking back towards the centre. The leaf margin seems too small for the centre of the leaf, causing crumpling and puckering (the drawstring effect). Not a good plant in all gardens. Light to full shade.

H. **'September Sun'** (Solberg 1985) Sport of *H.* 'August Moon', whose yellow leaves have a mid-green margin which is barely apparent on first unfurling, coming darker green by the end of the summer.

H. **'Serena'** (Tardiana Group) (Grenfell & Grounds 1996) A recently

named Tardiana hybrid, given to Roger Hunt at Hadspen House and named for his wife. Medium: spread about 52cm (20in), height 30cm (12in). Leaves small, thick, smooth to lightly puckered, cupped, nearly round, abruptly tipped, lobes pinched or overlapping, intensely chalky light blue-green on narrow channelled glaucous green petioles. Flowers bell-shaped, pale lavender-grey, on straight, bare 35cm (14in) scapes in mid-summer. Possibly one of the best of the recently named Tardianas. Light to full shade.

H. **'Serendipity'** (Tokudama Group) (Aden 1978) Small: spread about 28cm (11in), height 35cm (14in). Leaves small to medium, thick, puckered, round to heart-shaped, blue-green with a waxy-blue sheen early in the season. Flowers deep lavender, bell-shaped, on straight, bare, 38cm (15in) scapes in mid-summer. Light to full shade.

H. **'Shade Fanfare'** (Aden 1986) The stable, marginally variegated form of *H.* 'Flamboyant', the leaf being light green to almost chartreuse with a wide cream to white margin with very little overlapping. Generally agreed to be one of the best variegated hostas, the subtle colouring affording relief from hostas with too garish colouring. Equally lovely in a container. Light to full shade. Readily available.

H. **'Sharmon'** (Fortunei Group) (Donahue 1972) Probable sport of *H.* 'Fortunei Hyacinthina', similar, or identical, to *H.* 'Phyllis Campbell'. Light to full shade.

H. **'Shelleys'** (Hodgkin/Brickell 1988) Has been distributed under the invalid name *H. kikutii* 'Kifukurin'. Medium: spread about 60cm (24in), height 30cm (12in). Leaves medium, oval to lance-shaped, the veins close together, deeply impressed, the blade undulate, matt mid-green above, shiny beneath, with a narrow yellow margin, the

H. 'Shelleys', collected in Japan by Elliott Hodgkin and named for his garden.

yellow continuing down the petiole wings. Flowers typical *H. kikutii.* Light shade to some sun.

H. 'Sherborne Profusion' (Tardiana Group, TF 2 × 21) (E. Smith/ BHHS 1988) Small: spread about 30cm (12in), height 20cm (8in). Leaves small, heart-shaped, glaucous blue-green. Flowers bell-shaped, lavender with purple markings on

straight, bare 20cm (8in) scapes, late. Produces multiscapes. Light to full shade.

H. 'Sherborne Swift' (Tardiana Group, TF 2 × 26) (E. Smith BHHS 1988) Small: spread about 30cm (12in), height 20cm (8in). Leaves small, thick, oval to lance-shaped, glaucous grey-blue. Dense racemes of bell-shaped, lavender to near

white flowers on straight, leafy 36cm (15in) scapes, mid season. Light to full shade.

H. 'Shere Khan' (Zumbar) Miniature: tightly-mounded sport of *H.* 'Just So', said to have oval to heart-shaped leaves of tawny-yellow with a feathered narrow white margin and some white streaking into the centre. Named for the tiger

conspicuously red-streaked. Flowers borne two or three together on each scape, funnel-shaped, lavender with darker streaking within, the anthers protruding and strongly recurved, on straight, leafy, slender 23cm (9in) scapes, the scape and bracts red-dotted, mid-season. *H. venusta* hybrid. One of the very best small hostas for sink gardens or peat beds. Light shade, some sun. Widely available.

H. **'Shogun'** (Antioch Group) (Aden) Very similar to *H.* 'Antioch'.

H. sieboldiana ([Hooker] Engler 1888) Very large: spread about 91cm (36in), height 60cm (24in). Leaves very large, thick, generally heart-shaped though varying from almost oval to almost round, generally glaucous grey-green above but sometimes green, generally glaucous or pruinose beneath, wavy and puckered, exceptionally as large as 45cm (18in) long and 35cm (14in) wide. Flowers bell-shaped, palest lavender to nearly white on straight, leafy scapes about the same height as the leaf mound, early to mid-season. Although it is now a hosta with a sufficiently clear

identity, a number of very different plants have been grown under this name over the years, some of which may still be in circulation. *H. sieboldiana* as described here and as grown in Western gardens is in fact a selected form conforming to Western ideals of what *H. sieboldiana* should look like. No such plant has ever been found in the wild in Japan. *H. sieboldiana* grows best in a sheltered, semi-shaded position with ample moisture at its roots and responds well to generous feeding. When well suited it will make a magnificent specimen, but may take 15 years to achieve maturity. It is not always satisfactory under trees as the somewhat cupped leaves are inclined to collect their debris. It looks excellent grown beside paving and in courtyards or used in open glades with ferns, astilbes, grasses and candelabra primulas.

H. s. **'Elegans'** (Elegans Group) (Hylander 1954) Huge, sumptuous hosta, differing from typical *H. sieboldiana* in its intensely glaucous silvery-blue leaves, which are strongly cupped and deeply puckered, and in the flowers which are

H. 'Shining Tot' spreads vigorously despite its tiny leaves.

in Kipling's *Jungle Book*. Light to full shade.

H. **'Shining Tot'** (Aden 1982) Miniature: spread about 15cm (6in), height 5cm (2in). Leaves dwarf, heart-shaped, mid- to dark green, glossy above, shiny beneath, flat or often wavy, the lobes sometimes lifted and touching, the petioles very short, flattish and

palest, opalescent lavender or near-white, scarcely overtoppping the leaf mound. Originally thought to be a botanical variety, *H. sieboldiana* var. *elegans* of Hylander (1954) is now considered a cultivar (*H. s.* 'Elegans'). It is identified with *H. s.* 'Robusta', a hybrid between *H. sieboldiana* and probably *H.* 'Fortunei' raised in Germany by Arends in or before 1905, although the link has never been definitely proven and it is now uncertain which if any of the several clones now in circulation may be Arends' plant. Schmid (1991) records that there are more than 100 clones that broadly fit the *H. sieboldiana*/*H. s.* 'Elegans' description.

H. s. 'Frances Williams' See *H.* 'Frances Williams'.

H. sieboldii ([Paxton] Ingram 1967) Small: spread about 25cm (10in), height 20cm (8in). Leaves small, lance-shaped, the blade running into the petiole, wavy, the margin slightly or strongly rippled, dull dark green above, lighter glossier green beneath, the petiole generally very long, lightly red-dotted at the base. Flowers lily-shaped with a narrow tube, deep lavender with dark purple stripes, on straight leafy 50cm (20in) scapes, mid-season. Often confused with other narrow-leaved species but distinct on account of its yellow anthers, those of confusing species usually being purple. One of the commonest and most widespread hostas in the wild in Japan, and therefore very variable. Wild plants are almost invariably green-leaved,

H. sieboldii and its derivatives. Left to right: top row, *H.* 'Ginko Craig', *H.* 'Subcrocea', *H. s.* 'Paxton's Original', *H.* 'Feather Boa', *H.* 'Haku Chu Han'; bottom row, *H.* 'Kabitan', *H.* 'Mt Kirishima', *H. sieboldii, H.* 'Louisa', *H.* 'Weihenstephan'.

and it was the white-margined form that was the first to reach the West, where it therefore became regarded as the name-bearing type of the species, being published by Paxton in 1838 (see *H. s.* 'Paxton's Original' below). In the wild this species is generally found growing in lowland moors and meadows, where it is fully exposed to the sun and the weather. The only shade it receives is that cast by the grasses and other perennial vegetation among which it lives. At flowering time the leaves are usually completely hidden by this vegetation, only the flowers being visible. In cultivation it generally needs a damper situation than other hostas, and will also stand more sun than many. *H.* 'Haku Chu Han' is a sport. See under *H.* 'Silver Kabitan'.

H. s. 'Paxton's Original' (Trehane 1994) Formerly known in gardens as *H. sieboldii*, and also incorrectly as *H.* 'Albomarginata', this form does not sustain itself in the wild. Differs from the above only in its white-margined leaves. A delightful garden plant, generally a good doer, slowly spreading into extensive clumps, the dark flowers on their tall scapes contrasting beautifully with the white-edged leaves. Light to full shade. Readily available.

H. s. 'Alba' (W. Robinson 1893) White-flowered sports or forms of *H. sieboldii* have arisen from time to time both in the wild and in cultivation and the name probably embraces several cultivars that differ only in minor details. The plant long grown as *H. minor* 'Alba', with somewhat rounder leaves than the type and a loosely stoloniferous habit, is thought to be a white-flowered sport that arose in von Siebold's garden in 1868. The true *H. minor* 'Alba' has ridged, not smooth, flower scapes and differently shaped leaves. Sports are *H.* 'Snowflakes', with noticeably puckered leaves, and *H.* 'Bianca'. *H.* 'Weihenstephan' is a hybrid with larger flowers, as is *H.*

'Mount Royal'. *H.* 'Louisa' is a hybrid with both white flowers and white margins to the leaves, but not easy to grow. Light to full shade. Readily available.

H. 'Silver Lance' (Savory 1982) Small, densely mounded: spread about 30cm (12in), height 20cm (8in). Leaves small, lance-shaped, arching, glossy mid- to dark green with an irregular, narrow white margin. Flowers recurved, funnel-shaped, deep lavender with purple stripes on straight, bare 45cm (18in) scapes, in late summer. Differs from *H. sieboldii* in its darker leaves, the cleaner differentiation between blade and petiole, the petiole being narrower and more refined, and in the petiole being red-dotted especially towards the base, as is the flower scape. Light to full shade.

H. 'Silver Kabitan' (Schmid 1991) Sport or form of *H. sieboldii*, differing in having the leaves white with a well-defined dark green margin. In summer the white becomes greenish with green streaks or spots. Having leaves that are so largely white, this cultivar needs careful siting in moist ground where it can receive sun in the early morning but shade for the rest of the day. It is not easy to cultivate. *H.* 'Haku Chu Han' is a similar clone.

H. 'Silvery Slugproof' (Tardiana Group) (Grenfell & Grounds 1996) A recently named Tardiana. Large: spread about 100cm (40in), height 40cm (16in). Leaves medium, thick, narrowly heart-shaped, blade slightly undulate, glaucous silvery blue-grey, paler and pruinose beneath, the petiole 30cm (12in) or more, glaucous blue-grey becoming green and red-streaked towards the base. Flowers bell-shaped, palest lavender to near-white, gathered together near the top of straight, leafy, 55cm (22in) scapes, the scapes glaucous, suffused with purple towards the flowers, purple-streaked towards

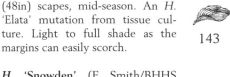

the base. A second or third generation Tardiana seedling so named
because over the years it has proved
itself to be one of the most slug-
resistant hostas in our garden even
when other hostas have been badly
damaged. Light to full shade.

H. **'Sitting Pretty'** (Aden 1987)
Miniature: spread about 20cm (8in),
height 10cm (4in). Leaves small
to medium, lance-shaped, blade
flat, creamy-yellow with an irregular two-tone green margin. Flowers
funnel-shaped, lavender striped
purple, on straight, leafy 30cm
(12in) scapes. Light to full shade.

H. **'Snow Cap'** (Aden 1980) Large:
spread about 91cm (36in), height
60cm (24in). Leaves medium,
thick, puckered, the lobes a little
lifted causing some cupping, but
convex towards the tip, heart-
shaped, glaucous blue-green above,
paler beneath, with a wide irregular
creamy-white margin, the creamy
white overlapping the blue-green
causing some mottling in inter-
mediate shades of grey. Flowers
funnel-shaped, palest lavender to
nearly white on straight, bare
91cm (36in) scapes, mid-season. An
unusual hosta in its combination of
blue-green and cream leaves, the
leaves beautifully shaped. Slow
growing. Similar to *H.* 'Knockout'.
Does best in some sun and seems
not to scorch.

H. **'Snow Crust'** (T & Z /Mark Zilis
1985) Very large: spread about
137cm (54in), height 70cm (28in).
Leaves large, heart-shaped, flat,
mid-green with a uniform white
margin. Flowers funnel-shaped,
lavender on straight, bare 122cm

H. 'Silvery Slugproof' in the Blue
Hosta Walk at Apple Court, with
H. 'Summer Fragrance' (back left),
H. sieboldiana 'Elegans' (behind
right) and *H.* 'Undulata' (left
foreground).

(48in) scapes, mid-season. An *H.*
'Elata' mutation from tissue culture. Light to full shade as the
margins can easily scorch.

H. **'Snowden'** (E. Smith/BHHS
1988) Very large: spread about
132cm (52in), height 80cm (32in).
Leaves very large, narrowly heart-
shaped, the lobes almost meeting
at the navel, glaucous grey-green
above, paler glaucous grey beneath.
Flowers funnel-shaped, white,
tinged greenish-lavender, white in
the US, on straight, bare 95cm
(38in) scapes, early to mid-season.
It resembles a 'Fortunei' but grows
to the size of an *H. sieboldiana*.
Slow to establish but eventually
makes a magnificent, stately, arching specimen. *H. sieboldiana* × *H.*
'Fortunei Aurea'. Occasionally sets
seed. Excellent in a large tub if
profusely watered. Light to full
shade. Readily available. Named for
the mountain in Wales, but incorrectly spelt.

H. **'Solar Flare'** (US Plant Patent
7046) Raised by Ross in 1981. Very
large: spread about 130cm (52in),
height 70cm (28in). Leaves very
large, thick, heart-shaped, pointed,
flat, puckered, glossy bright yellow fading to chartreuse towards
the edges, the widely spaced
veins green. Flowers funnel-shaped,
palest lavender on straight, bare
85cm (34in) scapes, mid-season.
Probably the largest-growing yellow-leaved hosta. Can make a
magnificent specimen. Of *H. montana* origin.

H. **'So Sweet'** (Aden 1986)
Medium: spread about 55cm (22in),
height 35cm (14in). Leaves medium, oval, the lobes raised and
almost touching, the navel pinched,
the upper surface glossy, the lower
shiny somewhat puckered, mid-
green with a wide creamy-white
margin, the petioles very long,
the variegation extending down the
wings of the petiole. Flowers
fragrant, funnel-shaped, opening

white from mauve buds, borne on straight, leafy 55cm (22in) scapes, mid- to late. A vase-shaped, upright clump. Seedling of *H.* 'Fragrant Bouquet'. Flowers best in rather more sun than most hostas. Readily available.

H. 'Sparkling Burgundy' (Savory 1982) Medium: spread about 50cm (20in), height 30cm (12in). Leaves medium, thick, puckered, glossy dark olive-green. Flowers funnel-shaped, purple on distinctive dark reddish-purple purple-dotted, straight, bare 60cm (24in) scapes, mid- to late season. Distinctive burgundy seed pods. Has recently become much sought-after. Light shade to sun.

H. 'Spilt Milk' (M. Seaver) Medium: spread about 60cm (24in), height 35cm (14in). Leaves medium, very thick, nearly round to heart-shaped, very cupped and puckered, glaucous dark blue-green irregularly but lightly brushed with streaky, narrow white and grey markings, the margin often darker green. Flowers bell-shaped, palest lavender to nearly white on straight, bare 45cm (18in) scapes, mid-season. A most unusual variegation, striking rather than lovely. Incredibly slow to multiply so still rare. An *H.* 'Tokudama' selection. Light to full shade.

H. 'Spinners' (Antioch Group) (E. Smith/BHHS 1988) Differs from *H.* 'Antioch' in its slightly narrower leaves. Readily available.

H. 'Spritzer' (Aden 1986) Medium, forming an upright and arching mound: spread about 45cm (18in), height 45cm (18in). Leaves medium to large, lance-shaped tapering to a fine point, blade undulate, the upper surface satiny, the lower glossy, golden-yellow, becoming almost white at the centre with a mid- to dark green margin with a little streaking towards the centre, the petioles red-dotted especially

towards the base. Flowers gathered towards the top of the scape among large leafy bracts, palest lavender with darker streaks on straight, leafy 76cm (30in) scapes, mid-season to late, the scapes purple-streaked especially towards the top and base, becoming solid purple towards the base. A most elegant hosta, both in its form and variegation; viridescent. Seedling of *H.* 'Green Fountain'. Lovely in a terracotta chimney pot. Light to full shade. Readily available.

H. 'Stiletto' (Aden 1987) Small, stoloniferous: spread about 30cm (12in), height 15cm (6in). Leaves small, lance-shaped, flat, the margins rippled, satiny above, shiny beneath, mid-green with a clean narrow white margin. Flowers lily-shaped, flared, rich lavender purple with purple stripes and white edges to the petals on straight, leafy 60cm (24in) scapes, mid-season to late. A most attractive variegated little hosta, the very showy flowers held high above the leaf mound. Increases rapidly. Light to full shade.

H. 'Striptease' (Fortunei Group) (Thompson 1991) Striking sport of *H.* 'Gold Standard', differing in that the leaves are chartreuse with wide, dark green margins often with a very narrow to flecked white line at the junction of the two colours. Sterile. Shade.

H. 'Sugar and Cream' (Zilis 1984) Sport of *H.* 'Honeybells', differing in that the mid-green leaves are surrounded by a wide, irregular white margin with grey streaks extending back towards the midrib. Fragrant. As vigorous as *H.* 'Honeybells', and certainly more decorative. Light shade to sun. Increases rapidly. Readily available.

H. 'Sultana' (Zumbar 1988) Sport of *H.* 'Little Aurora', differing in having wavy, mid-green leaves with a striking chartreuse to yellow

margin and some streaking back towards the centre. Nearly sterile. Slow-growing. Very decorative. Fairly sun-tolerant.

H. 'Sum and Substance' (Aden 1980) Very large, impressive: spread about 150cm (60in), height 76cm (30in). Leaves very large, very thick, oval to heart-shaped, the lobes prominent and lifted, usually closed at the navel, the blade flat but corrugated, smooth on young plants but somewhat puckered on mature plants, shiny above, mealy white beneath, chartreuse to greenish yellow, sometimes old gold, the petiole closed for most of its length and red-streaked towards the base. Flowers bell-shaped, palest lavender to nearly white, on leaning, leafy scapes, mid-season to late, sometimes re-blooming. A huge hosta requiring plenty of space and moisture. It is not usually troubled much by slugs or snails. The colour varies from lime green or chartreuse in the shade to a quite strong yellow in sun. Sun-tolerant even in the southern states of America. Sports are *H.* 'Lady Isobel Barnett' and *H.* 'Sum Total'. Has been the most popular hosta in the American Hosta Society's Popularity Poll. Readily available.

H. 'Summer Fragrance' (K. Vaughn 1983) Very large: spread about 100cm (40in), height 60cm (24in). Leaves large, oval, satiny above, shiny beneath, mid-green with an irregular cream to white margin with some grey streaking back towards the centre, the variegation extending down the wings of the petioles, the navel pinched and almost closed. Flowers fragrant, large, bell-shaped, rich lavender-purple on straight, bare 150cm (60in) scapes, mid-season to late. Makes a large, very dense clump and like most *H. plantaginea* offspring is happy in more sun than most hostas. Long seed capsules. Readily available.

H. **'Summer Music'** (Klehm NR) Large: spread about 60cm (24in), height 36cm (15in). Leaves large, blade broadly undulate, oval to heart-shaped, tapering to a point, ivory with irregular, wide chartreuse to yellow margins. Flowers light lavender on upright, attractively leafy ivory 50cm (20in) scapes in mid-season. Full shade.

H. **'Sundance'** (Fortunei Group) (Walters Gardens 1984) Sport of *H.* 'Fortunei Aokii', differing in that the matt, dark green leaves have a narrow margin, cream fading to white. Does not do well in all gardens. Bears a strong resemblance to *H.* 'Gloriosa'. Light to full shade.

H. **'Sun Power'** (Aden 1986) Large: spread about 91cm (36in), height 60cm (24in). Leaves large, oval to heart-shaped tapering to a point, the blade attractively undulate, the veins close together, the upper surface chartreuse becoming bright golden-yellow in sun but remaining chartreuse in shade, the lower surface pruinose. Flowers funnel-shaped, lavender on leaning, leafy 91cm (36in) scapes, mid-season to late. One of the first good yellow-leaved hostas, and still one of the best. Somewhat thin-leaved and tends to burn in too much sun, in spite of its name. *H.* 'Abba Dabba Do' is a sport. Light shade or morning sun only. Readily available.

H. **'Super Bowl'** (Golden Medallion Group) (Aden) Medium: spread about 55cm (22in), height 45cm (18in). Leaves medium, deeply cupped and puckered, heart-shaped, abruptly tipped, yellow. Flowers bell-shaped, palest lavender to nearly white, on straight, bare 60cm (24in) scapes mid-season. *H.* 'Tokudama' hybrid. Light shade to sun.

H. **'Sweetie'** (Aden 1988) Large: spread about 76cm (30in), height 50cm (20in). Leaves medium to large, oval to heart-shaped, blade attractively undulate, the lobes lifted, pinched at the navel, the tip turned under, satiny above, shiny beneath, bright chartreuse with a wide, creamy-ivory margin with some streaking back towards the midrib. Flowers very fragrant, funnel-shaped, palest lavender to nearly white on straight, leafy 80cm (32in) scapes in late summer. The leafy bracts are variegated and exceptionally large. A hybrid of *H.* 'Fragrant Bouquet'. A spectacular hosta which should be better known. Vigorous. Light shade to full sun.

H. **'Sweet Standard'** (Zilis 1984) Sport of *H.* 'Honeybells', differing in having leaves that are streaked creamy-white and white. Needs good cultivation as the leaves can be rather limp, and it should be divided regularly every two or three years as otherwise the variegation tends to migrate to the margin, in which case it becomes *H.* 'Sugar and Cream', the margined form of *H.* 'Honeybells'. Vigorous and rapidly increasing. Light shade to sun.

H. **'Sweet Susan'** (Williams 1986) Large: spread about 76cm (30in), height 45cm (18in). Leaves large, heart-shaped, flat, mid-green. Flowers funnel-shaped, fragrant, purple, edged white on leaning, leafy 80cm (32in) scapes. One of the earliest introduced fragrant hybrids and still much valued because it re-blooms in a hot summer. *H. plantaginea* × *H. sieboldii*. Light shade to sun.

H. **'Tall Boy'** (Montreal/Savill/J. Bond 1983) Large: spread about 76cm (30in), height 60cm (24in). Leaves large, oval to heart-shaped, blade flat, rather coarse, mid-green, satiny above, shiny beneath. Flowers funnel-shaped, purple on straight, leafy 91cm (36in) scapes, mid-season. Grown for its very tall scapes of showy flowers. Best grown at the back of a border where the leaves are hidden by more interesting foliage. An *H.* 'Rectifolia' hybrid. Sent to Sir Eric Savill by Gulf Stream Nurseries of Virginia, US in 1961 as *Funkia japonica* and later named by him. Light shade. Readily available.

H. **'Tall Twister'** (Minks 1973) Small: spread about 30cm (12in), height 30cm (12in). Leaves small, upright, blade conspicuously undulate, mid-green. Flower funnel-shaped, purple striped lavender, on 30cm (12in) straight, bare scapes. *H.* 'The Twister' is similar. Light to full shade.

H. **Tardiana Group** (Grenfell & Grounds 1996) A cultivar-group here designated to cover a range of hybrids raised by Eric Smith in the 1960s and 1970s, all originating from a chance cross made between a late flower on a young plant of *H. sieboldiana* 'Elegans' (normally flowering in mid-summer) and an early flower on 'Tardiflora' (normally flowering in September or October). The progeny of this first cross (denoted as TF1s) generally combine the blueness of the first parent with the dwarfness of the second, and that is their real merit. Many of this first generation were crossed with each other to produce a second generation (TF2s). However, no descriptions of any individual selections within the group were published and over the years the identities of many of these became obfuscated. To resolve this problem the nomenclature committee of the BHHS, with secondments from and in association with the AHS, are studying the various plants being sold under the various names and from them are selecting Standard Specimens for each of the Tardiana Group. These will be on permanent record in the herbarium of the Royal Horticultural Society's garden at Wisley in England. One interesting sidelight that emerged during the search for Standard Specimens was that many of the hostas in circulation as belonging to the Tardiana Group were in fact hybrids of *H. nakaiana*, though how this confusion came about and whether it dates back to the raiser is not known.

The 12 Tardiana Group hostas that were originally named by Eric Smith and Alex Summers, plus a few others that have emerged more recently, are possibly the only ones really worth naming, though considerable time and trouble has been spent on naming all the others, both in Britain and the United States. The 12 are *H.* 'Blue Diamond', *H.* 'Blue Dimples', *H.* 'Blue Moon', *H.* 'Blue Skies', *H.* 'Blue Wedgwood', *H.* 'Dorset Blue', *H.* 'Hadspen Blue', *H.* 'Hadspen Hawk', *H.* 'Hadspen Heron', *H.* 'Halcyon', *H.* 'Happiness', and *H.* 'Harmony'. Others of great merit are *H.* 'Blue Blush', *H.* 'Camelot', *H.* 'Devon Blue', *H.* 'Irische See', *H.* 'Osprey', *H.* 'Serena', and *H.* 'Sherborne Swift'.

H. **'Tardiflora'** (Leichtlin ex Irving 1903) Small to medium: spread about 45cm (18in), height 25cm (10in). Leaves small, thick, lance-shaped, blade flat, satiny mid- to dark green above, shiny, lighter green beneath, the blade running into the petiole, the petiole red-dotted especially towards the base. Flowers funnel-shaped, purple, held horizontally on straight, leafy, intensely red-dotted, 30cm (12in) scapes, late to very late. A classic hosta which is valued not only for its late flowering but also for its dark, upright leaves which are reasonably slug- and snail-resistant. It looks lovely with liriopes, dwarf asters, *Saxifraga fortunei*, especially the red-leaved forms, colchicums and other gems of the autumn. It is not always successful in the colder parts of Great Britain; there is a suspicion that this hosta may not be completely frost-hardy. It can be prone to virus infection. Light shade. Readily available.

H. **Tiara Group** (Pollock 1986) Previously known as the Tiara Series, a group of neat, compact *H. nakaiana* hybrids, the first originated by Robert Savory in the mid-1970s. Savory deliberately subjected some 750 *H. nakaiana* seedlings to a mixture of hormones and vitamins in the hope of obtaining a higher proportion of sports than could be expected to arise under normal circumstances. A sport of one of these seedlings was named *H.* 'Golden Tiara'. Others have arisen as sports: these are *H.* 'Diamond Tiara', *H.* 'Emerald Scepter', *H.* 'Emerald Tiara', *H.* 'Golden Scepter', *H.* 'Grand Tiara', *H.* 'Jade Scepter', *H.* 'Platinum Tiara' and *H.* 'Royal Tiara' (the latter is not easy to grow).

H. ***tibae*** (Maekawa 1984) Medium: spread about 60cm (24in), height 25cm (10in). Leaves medium, narrowly oval to lance-shaped, tapering to a long thin tip, blade somewhat undulate, glossy mid-green above, shiny lighter green beneath. Flowers bell-shaped, deep lavender borne on branched candelabra-like scapes, each scape with as many as eight branches, the whole inflorescence bearing as many as 80 flowers, late. A remarkable hosta, scarcely known in the West, which may, as hosta breeders' interests turn more to flowers than foliage, lead to a race of multi-scaped hostas. Rare. Known as the Nagasaki hosta as it was collected in the Nagasaki district of Japan by von Siebold. Light shade.

H. **'Tiny Tears'** (Savory 1977) Miniature: spread about 15cm (6in), height 5cm (2in). Leaves dwarf, thick, oval, pointed, dark glossy green above, shiny beneath, the blade running into the petiole, the petiole lightly red-dotted. Flowers bell-shaped, light lavender with darker stripes borne two or three together at the tops of straight, bare, red-dotted 25cm (10in) scapes, mid-season. Makes

dense mounds of dark glossy leaves. *H. venusta* derivative.

H. **'Tokudama'** (Maekawa 1940) Medium: spread about 60cm (24in), height 30cm (12in). Leaves medium, thick, strongly cupped, deeply puckered, nearly round, abruptly tipped, intensely glaucous dark blue above, paler glaucous blue beneath. Flowers bell-shaped, never opening fully, palest lavender to nearly white on straight, bare 45cm (18in) scapes, mid-season. One of the most beautiful of all hostas and still the benchmark by which other blues are measured. Not satisfactory under trees as the deeply cupped leaves tend to collect debris. Slow to increase. A number of lovely forms have been introduced, including *H.* 'Abiqua Blue Crinkles', *H.* 'Abiqua Drinking Gourd', *H.* 'Betcher's Blue', *H.* 'Love Pat' and *H.* 'Moscow Blue'. Light to full shade.

H. **Tokudama Group** (Grenfell 1996) A cultivar-group here defined so as to include a number of named cultivars with all the above characteristics.

H. **'Tokudama Aureonebulosa'** (Maekawa 1940) Differs from *H.* 'Tokudama' in that the centre of the leaf is clouded and mottled various shades of chartreuse or yellow. Many different selections are in existence, varying in the degree or intensity of the yellow clouding. *H.* 'Blue Shadows' is one such with more blue in the leaves. *H.* 'Tokudama Flavoplanata' (Maekawa 1940) is an extreme form with smaller, almost clear yellow leaves with a thin blue-green margin. *H.* 'Bright Lights' (*qv*) is more vigorous, with larger leaves and less puckering, and with the blue and yellow components separated out, most of the blue being in the margin while most of the yellow is in the centre. Slow to increase. Light to full shade.

H. 'Tokudama Flavocircinalis' (Maekawa 1940) Differs from 'Tokudama' in its more oval and pointed, less heart-shaped leaves, and in their variable and irregular rich yellow margin, which may or may not streak back towards the leaf centre. Quite slow to increase. Sometimes mistaken for a young plant of *H.* 'Frances Williams'. Rare. Light to full shade.

H. 'Trail's End' (Elegans Group) (Ruh 1978) Very large: similar to *H. sieboldiana* 'Elegans'. Light to full shade.

H. 'True Blue' (Elegans Group) (Aden 1978) Very large. Differs from *H. sieboldiana* 'Elegans' in its more intensely blue leaves which arch downwards on sloping petioles, making a distinctive clump. Light to full shade.

H. 'Twist of Lime' (Banyai/Solberg 1991) An attractive sport from 'Lemon Lime'. Leaves chartreuse-yellow with irregular dark green margins. Full shade.

H. 'Undulata' (Thunberg 1797) Medium: spread about 45cm (18in), height 35cm (14in). Leaves medium, thin, varying from broadly oval to almost lance-shaped, extremely undulate, the tip twisting often through 180°, the blade running into the petiole, without clear differentiation, the petiole broadly winged, the leaves white with a two-tone green margin, the green overlapping the white and resulting in light green, chartreuse and cream streaking, the variegation continuing without interruption from the blade into the petiole. Flowers funnel-shaped, lavender on 91cm (36in) straight, very leafy, ivory scapes, early to mid-season. Nearly sterile. This is an essentially unstable hosta, the variegation varying not only over the years but also within each year, the first flush of leaves being at first almost entirely white to ivory with an irregular green margin, the second flush having leaves which are more streaked and mottled with green. However, over the years plants will gradually become less and less variegated, the white centre becoming merely a white central stripe (at which stage it is called *H.* 'Undulata Univittata' and finally becoming entirely green when it is known as *H.* 'Undulata Erromena', these named forms being merely transitional stages in the process of reversion to the all-green form). The undulating and twisting of the leaf blade in the highly variegated forms is due to the margin of the leaf growing faster than the variegated centre: as the leaves become gradually less variegated they also become less undulate and less twisted. In order to maintain any of these forms without further deterioration of the variegation the clumps should be divided about every three years. At their best they are among the most beautiful of hostas for spring and early summer foliage. Received an Award of Garden Merit from the RHS. They are prone to pest damage. Full shade. Readily available.

H. 'Undulata Albomarginata' (AHS 1987) Large: spread about 91cm (36in), height 45cm (18in). Leaves medium to large, oval, flat or slightly undulate towards the tip, mid- to dark green above with a slight sheen, shiny, lighter green beneath, with an irregular white margin, the white overlapping the green resulting in some grey streaking towards the centre of the leaf, the blade not clearly distinct from the petiole, the variegation continuing down the wings of the petiole. Flowers funnel-shaped, lavender on straight, conspicuously leafy 91cm (36in) scapes, early to mid-season. Sterile. Also incorrectly, but very often, known as *H.* 'Thomas Hogg'. One of the commonest white-margined hostas, it is valuable for inexpensive mass planting. It is sometimes confused with *H.* 'Crispula', from which it differs in its broader, flat petioles, the flatter leaf blade and further by the extremely large leafy scapes. Light to full shade. Readily available.

H. 'Undulata Erromena' (Stearn 1932) Medium: spread about 60cm (24in), height 50cm (20in) tall. Leaves large, oval to heart-shaped, slightly undulate, dark green above, paler and shiny green beneath. Flowers funnel-shaped, lavender on straight, leafy 91cm (36in) scapes, early to mid-season. *H.* 'See Saw' is a sport.

H. 'Vanilla Cream' (Golden Medallion Group) (Aden 1986) Differs in having much smaller leaves that are at first light lemon green becoming yellow and finally cream, on a leafy, reddish scape. A sport of *H.* 'Little Aurora'. Light shade to sun.

H. ventricosa ([Salisbury] Stearn 1931) Large: spread about 91cm (36in), height 50cm (20in). Leaves large, heart-shaped, twisted towards the tip, veins widely spaced, the lobes lifted and the margins rippled, mid to glossy, dark spinach green above, paler, lighter green beneath, the petioles lightly red-streaked only at the extreme base. Flowers urn-shaped, rich bluish-purple on straight, leafy 91cm (36in) scapes. The only hosta known to come absolutely true from seed because the seeds are produced without fertilization by a process called pseudogamous apomixis. It can however be used as a pollen parent. One of the best hostas for flower and one of the best green-leaved hostas, having well-shaped leaves and a characteristic poise of its own. The leaves are however somewhat thin and inclined to scorch at the edges. Full shade. Readily available.

H. v. 'Aureomaculata' (Miquel 1869) Differs from *H. ventricosa* in being somewhat smaller in all its parts and in the leaves being bright

148

yellow with a deep green margin streaking back to the centre with some celadon streaking in the overlapping area, the colouring fading as the season advances (viridescent), but never disappearing completely. Arose as a sport in von Siebold's garden before 1856 and is still rare because of its slowness to increase. Full shade.

***H. v.* 'Variegata'** (Regel 1876) (syn. *H. v.* 'Aureomarginata' in the US). Differs from *H. ventricosa* in that the leaves have a wide, irregular creamy-ivory margin with some ivory and grey streaking back towards the centre. Discovered in a row of *H. ventricosa* in a Dutch nursery before 1968 and still considered to be one of the best variegated hostas. Full shade. Readily available.

H. venusta (Maekawa 1935) Dwarf, somewhat stoloniferous: spread about 10cm (4in), height 7.5cm (3in). Leaves miniature, variable, but usually oval to heart-shaped, the blade somewhat undulate, dark satiny green above, shiny, lighter green beneath. Flowers bell-shaped, deep lavender with purple-dotted anthers, gathered together at the tops of straight, bare 20cm (8in) scapes, mid-season, the scapes sometimes red or purple-dotted, and always with distinct lamellar ridges. The smallest hosta species, a native of Korea. A few forms have been named. *H.* 'Red Dwarf' (Grenfell & Grounds 1995) is a selection whose flowers have very long (2cm/¾in) red tubes on slender 28cm (11in) scapes which are intensely red-dotted at the base. *H.* 'Suzuki Thumbnail' is an excellent very dwarf selection. Variegated forms are known to exist, but few have reached the West. For *H. venusta* 'Variegated' see *H.* 'Masquerade'. *H. v.* 'Kinbotan' is a tiny form with cream-margined leaves.

***H.* 'Vera Verde'** (Aden/Klehm 1990) Sometimes incorrectly listed

H. 'Vicar's Mead' makes dense clumps of nearly round leaves.

as *H. gracillima* 'Variegated'. Small, stoloniferous: spread about 38cm (15in), height 15cm (6in). Leaves small, spatulate with no clear midrib, undulate, twisted as if one side has grown faster than the other, the blade running into the petiole without distinction, matt mid-green above, paler satiny green beneath with an irregular creamy-white margin with some streaking back towards the centre. Flowers funnel-shaped, deep lavender striped purple, on straight, bare 30cm (12in) scapes, mid-season to late. Stable sport of the highly unstable *H.* 'Cheesecake'. Makes dense low

clumps of nicely variegated leaves above which the dark flowers are showy. In the Scottish National Collection the leaf blades are twice as wide as they are in the south of England. Light shade to some sun. Readily available.

***H.* 'Verna Jean'** (Lachman 1990) Small: spread about 38cm (15in), height 20cm (8in). Leaves small, lance-shaped to oval, dark green with an irregular, wide cream margin, resembling *H.* 'Diamond Tiara'. Flowers funnel-shaped, pale lavender on straight, leafy 35cm (14in) scapes in early summer. Light to full shade.

H. 'Vicar's Mead' (Read 1995) Very large: spread about 91cm (36in), height 60cm (24in). Leaves medium, very cupped and heavily puckered, round, very dark green above, lighter beneath. Flowers bell-shaped, near-white, on straight, bare 91cm (36in) scapes, mid-season. It makes a congested, impressive clump.

H. 'Waving Winds' (Lachman 1991) Medium: spread about 50cm (20in), height 30cm (12in). Upright, open habit. Leaves medium, some puckering, heart shaped, undulate, pinched at the tip, closely spaced veins, dark green with an irregular, bright yellowy-green margin. Flowers funnel-shaped, flaring, lavender on 91cm (36in) scapes, mid-season to late. Light to full shade.

H. 'Weihenstephan' (Mussel) Hybrid of H. sieboldii 'Alba', with larger white flowers.

H. 'Whirlwind' (Fortunei Group) (Kulpa 1989) Small: spread about 30cm (12in), height 15cm (6in). Leaves medium, oval to heart-shaped or nearly pear-shaped, folded and somewhat twisted, white, yellowish and yellowish-green with irregular dark green margins. The inside colour of the leaf depends on light, temperature and age of plant. Flowers funnel-shaped, lavender, on straight, leafy 50cm (20in) scapes, the leafy bracts variegated like the leaves, mid-season to late. Viridescent. A presumed H. 'Fortunei Hyacinthina' sport. Sports are H. 'Second Wind', with larger, cupped, leathery, dark green leaves, and H. 'Trade Wind', which has streaked leaves. Light to full shade. Much sought after.

H. 'White Christmas' (Krossa 1966) Medium to large: spread about 60cm (24in), height 30cm (12in). Leaves medium to large, early to emerge, oval, undulate and slightly twisted, white, with a variable green margin, the green overlapping the white resulting in some green, grey and celadon streaking back towards the centre, the leaves gradually becoming cream after mid-summer. Flowers funnel-shaped, lavender, on straight, leafy, 70cm (28in) scapes, mid-season. Often mistaken for H. 'Undulata', it is, however, thought to be a H. 'Fortunei' selection. Very slow to establish and loved by slugs, but well worth taking special care to keep the striking foliage undamaged. H. 'Night Before Christmas' is a sport.

H. 'Wide Brim' (Aden 1979) Large: spread about 91cm (36in), height 60cm (24in). Leaves medium, thick, puckered, heart-shaped, the lobes lifted, causing some cupping, pinched at the navel, satiny above, glaucous beneath, rich mid-green with a wide, irregular cream margin, the cream overlapping the green resulting in some celadon grey streaking back towards the midrib. Flowers funnel-shaped, palest lavender to nearly white on straight, bare 80cm (32in) scapes, mid-season. One of the finest of all hostas, beautiful in the garden, lovely in pots and tubs and excellent for flower arrangement. Rapid increaser. Received the Award of Garden Merit from the RHS. Light shade. Readily available.

H. 'Wind River Gold' (Jenssen) Medium, somewhat stoloniferous: spread about 60cm (24in), height 30cm (12in). Leaves small, thin, wedge-shaped, coming to a graceful point, blade undulate, margin rippled, chartreuse to bright, brassy yellow, satiny above, shiny beneath, pinched at the navel, the petiole somewhat winged and red-dotted at the base. Flowers funnel-shaped, deep lavender on straight, bare 45cm (18in) scapes, the scapes red-dotted towards the base, mid-season. Vigorous habit. Shade.

H. 'Wogon' (syn. 'Wogon Giboshi') (AHS 1986) Sport of H. sieboldii, differing in having chartreuse to yellow leaves and red-dotted petioles and flower scapes. One of the first with leaves of this colour to reach the West and much used for breeding until ousted by H. 'Kabitan' when that reached the West and proved more successful.

H. 'Wogon's Boy' (Burles) Medium to large: spread about 60cm (24in), height 45cm (18in). Leaves medium to large, near heart-shaped, glaucous yellow slowly turning green (viridescent). Flowers

H. 'White Christmas', loved by slugs but worth every effort.

150

bell-shaped, lavender on straight, bare 30cm (12in) scapes, mid-season. Light to full shade.

H. 'Wrinkles and Crinkles' (Englerth 1985) Very large: spread about 92cm (38in), height 40cm (16in). Leaves very large, heart-shaped, puckered, glaucous blue-green. Flowers funnel-shaped, palest lavender to nearly white on leaning leafy 80cm (32in) scapes, mid-season. Grown for its intensely puckered leaves: similar to *H.* 'Crumples', but blue-green whereas *H.* 'Crumples' is light green.

H. 'Yellow Boa' (O'Harra 1991) Differs from *H.* 'Feather Boa' in having a yellower leaf.

H. 'Yellow River' (E. Smith/Ruh 1993) Very large: spread about 122cm (48in), height 60cm (24in). Leaves very large, thick, wedge-shaped, gracefully pointed, blade undulate, the veins deeply impressed, intense, dark bluish-green, satiny above, brighter, shinier green beneath, with a bold, wide, irregular yellow margin, the yellow overlapping the grey-green resulting in celadon and grey streaking back towards the midrib, the navel somewhat pinched and the variegation running down the wings of the petioles. Flowers funnel-shaped, palest lavender to nearly white on straight, leafy 122cm (48in) scapes, mid-season. *H. montana* form or hybrid, but unlike *H. m.* 'Aureomarginata' it is very late to emerge. Makes a sumptuous hosta. Light to full shade.

H. 'Yellow Splash' (Aden 1976) Medium, stoloniferous: spread about 50cm (20in), height 35cm (14in). Leaves medium, oval to spatulate, mid-green streaked creamy-ivory, especially towards the margins. Flowers funnel-shaped, deep lavender on straight, bare 70cm (28in) scapes. An attractive but unstable streaked hosta inclined to turn into the stable form known as *H.* 'Yellow Splash Rim', which has a cream to

yellow margin, unless divided every year or so. *H.* 'Gay Feather' is a sport. Much used for breeding hostas with streaked variegation. Not suitable for container-growing. Shade. Readily available.

H. yingeri (Jones 1989) Small to medium, semi-erect: spread about 40cm (16in), height 15cm (6in) (much larger in the US). Leaves medium, thick, leathery, polished, margins undulate, oval tapering to a fine point, shiny paler green below, decurrent to the petiole. Small, spider-shaped purple-striped lilac flowers, with unequal sets of stamens on 62cm (25in) slightly leaning, leafy bracts in late summer. *H.* 'Treasure Island' is a selected clone; *H.* 'Harpoon' is a newly introduced hybrid between *H. yingeri* and *H.* 'Swoosh'. Light shade to sun.

H. 'Zager's White Edge' (Fortunei Albomarginata Group) (Simpers 1980) Differs from *H.* 'Fortunei Albomarginata' in its crisp white margin and its silvery-pink emerging foliage. Deserves to be better known. Best in shade.

H. 'Zounds' (Golden Sunburst Group) (Aden 1978) Very large: spread about 91cm (36in), height 40cm (16in). Leaves very large, puckered and somewhat twisted, oval to heart-shaped, the lobes lifted and sometimes overlapping at the navel, satiny above, shiny beneath, chartreuse to intense rich yellow-gold, sometimes with green striations. Flowers funnel-shaped, palest lavender to nearly white, on straight, leafy 60cm (24in) scapes, mid-season. A magnificent yellow-leaved hosta which holds its colour even in the shade. *H. sieboldiana* hybrid. Sports are *H.* 'Dick Ward' and *H.* 'Midwest Magic'. Light to full shade. Readily available.

H. 'Zounds' holds its colour even in the shade.

GLOSSARY

Albescent Becoming white.

Anthesis The period of time between the full opening of a flower and the setting of seed. Loosely used of an entire flower raceme when it is in full bloom.

Apomixy The production of seed without actual fertilization.

Bloom Flower; a white mealy surface on a leaf.

Chimaera Plants or parts of plants that contain cells from two genetically different sources. They may play an important part in variegation in hostas.

Chlorophyll The pigment in plants which makes them green, essential to photosynthesis.

Conspecific Belonging to the same species.

Cultivar A taxonomic group of plants that is clearly distinct, uniform and stable in its characteristics and which, when propagated by appropriate means, retains these characteristics.

Decurrent Running downwards. With hostas, usually applied to the way in which the leaf blade may run down the sides of the petiole.

Fasciated Growing together in a bundle. Applied to hosta scapes which are thicker than normal at the base and widen out into a broad, flattened area at the top.

Genus A taxonomic unit below that of family.

Glaucous A grey-blue waxy bloom on the surface of leaves.

Inflorescence An arrangement of flowers and their accessory parts along a stem; loosely referred to as a flowerhead.

Internode The portion of stem between two nodes.

Juvenile The early, non-adult phase or phases of a plant's life, often expressed in different foliage forms or plant habit. In hostas the juvenile leaves are often narrower than in the adult and the variegated margin will be narrower.

Lutescent Becoming yellow.

Membranaceous Having the substance of a membrane: papery or parchment-like. Applied to thin, rather than thick, leaves.

Morphology The study of the external form of a plant; the shape or form of plants.

Necrosis The death of plant cells or of the whole plant. In hostas the term is usually applied to the browning or scorching of leaf margins.

Node The point on a stem where one or more leaves, shoots, branches or flowers are attached.

Perianth The external structure of a flower composed of the calyx and corolla. In hostas these are not differentiated and form a single tubular flower consisting of three exterior and three interior lobes.

Petiole The stem or stalk of a leaf. In hostas this extends from the ground to the base of the leaf.

Pruinose Covered with a white, powdery substance, giving a frosted or dewy appearance.

Raceme A usually elongate inflorescence composed of short-stalked flowers.

Rhizome The thickened, underground part of the stem; the organ of perennation.

Rugose Wrinkled; dimpled, puckered, seersuckered, ruffled, or crinkled.

Scape The stem which bears the flowers.

Species Unit of taxonomic classification below that of genus.

Stolon A prostrate stem taking root and giving rise to a new plant or plantlets at its tip. In hostas, used of underground stems that produce new plants at their tips.

Stoloniferous Forming stolons. Usually denotes a loosely running habit in hostas.

Taxon A unit of classification, plural taxa. Genus, species, subspecies, form and cultivar are all taxa.

Viridescent Becoming green.

A SELECTION OF THE BEST HOSTAS

Pest-resistant

H. 'Blue Umbrellas'

H. 'Fragrant Gold'

H. 'Green Sheen'

H. hypoleuca

H. 'Invincible'

H. 'Krossa Regal'

H. 'Leather Sheen'

H. sieboldiana & forms

H. 'Silvery Slugproof'

H. 'Sum and Substance'

Sun-tolerant

H. 'August Moon'

H. 'Blue Umbrellas'

H. 'Fortunei Aureomarginata'

H. 'Fragrant Gold'

H. 'Green Sheen'

H. 'Honeybells'

H. 'Invincible'

H. 'On Stage'

H. plantaginea & forms

H. 'Royal Standard'

H. 'Sum and Substance'

Miniature

H. 'Blue Moon'

H. gracillima

H. 'Masquerade'

H. pulchella 'Kifukurin'

H. 'Popo'

H. 'Shining Tot'

H. venusta

Container-growing

H. 'Fortunei Aureomarginata'

H. 'Francee'

H. 'Gold Standard'

H. 'Green Fountain'

H. 'Halcyon'

H. kikutii

H. 'Lancifolia'

H. 'Stiletto'

H. ventricosa

H. 'Wide Brim'

Yellow Leaves

H. 'Birchwood Parky's Gold'

H. 'Daybreak'

H. 'Fragrant Gold'

H. 'Golden Medallion'

H. 'Golden Scepter'

H. 'Golden Prayers'

H. 'Midas Touch'

H. 'Piedmont Gold'

H. 'Sun Power'

H. 'Wind River Gold'

H. 'Zounds'

Large Leaves

H. 'Big Daddy'

H. 'Big Mama'

H. 'Blue Angel'

H. 'Blue Umbrellas'

H. 'Colossal'

H. 'Devon Giant'

H. 'Frances Williams'

H. sieboldiana 'Elegans'

H. 'Snowden'

H. 'Sum and Substance'

Yellow-margined Leaves

H. 'Bill Brincka'

H. 'El Capitan'

H. fluctuans 'Sagae'

H. 'Fortunei Aureomarginata'

H. 'Frances Williams'

H. 'Golden Tiara'

H. montana 'Aureomarginata'

H. 'Opipara'

H. 'Radiant Edger'

H. 'Sultana'

H. 'Wide Brim'

White-margined Leaves

H. 'Allan P. McConnell'

H. 'Carol'

H. 'Crispula'

H. 'Decorata'

H. 'Francee'

H. 'Frosted Jade'

H. 'Ginko Craig'

H. 'Mountain Snow'

H. 'Patriot'

H. 'Zager's White Edge'

Centrally Variegated Leaves

H. 'Gold Standard'

H. 'Great Expectations'

H. 'June'

H. 'Mary Marie Ann'

II. 'Paul's Glory'

H. 'Reversed'

H. 'Sitting Pretty'

H. 'Summer Music'

H. 'Tokudama Aureonebulosa'

H. 'Undulata'

Distinctive Leaves

H. 'Bold Ruffles'

H. 'Crumples'

H. *hypoleuca*

H. *longissima*

H. 'Love Pat'

H. 'Phoenix'

H. *pycnophylla*

H. 'Stiletto'

H. 'Tortifrons'

H. *yingeri*

Splashed Variegation

H. 'Beatrice'

H. 'Flamboyant'

H. 'Iron Gate Supreme'

H. 'Neat Splash'

H. 'Sweet Standard'

H. 'Yellow Splash'

Unusual Variegation

H. 'Embroidery'

H. 'Lakeside Symphony'

H. 'Mary Marie Ann'

H. 'Spilt Milk'

H. 'Striptease'

H. 'Whirlwind'

Green Leaves

H. 'Devon Green'

H. 'Green Acres'

H. *kikutii* & forms

H. 'Lancifolia'

H. 'Leather Sheen'

H. *plantaginea* & forms

H. 'Royal Standard'

H. *rupifraga*

H. 'Sea Drift'

H. 'Sea Lotus Leaf'

Blue Leaves

H. 'Big Daddy'

H. 'Blue Seer'

H. 'Blue Vision'

H. 'Buckshaw Blue'

H. 'Dorset Blue'

H. 'Hadspen Blue'

H. 'Love Pat'

H. 'Moscow Blue'

H. 'Serena'

H. *sieboldiana* 'Elegans'

H. 'Tokudama'

H. 'True Blue'

Attractive Flowers

H. 'Carrie Ann'

H. *clausa* 'Normalis'

H. 'Gold Regal'

H. 'Halcyon'

H. *kikutii* & forms

H. 'Pacific Blue Edger'

H. 'Pearl Lake'

H. *ventricosa*

H. *venusta*

H. 'Weihenstephan'

Fragrant Flowers

H. 'Fragrant Blue'

H. 'Fragrant Bouquet'

H. 'Guacamole'

H. 'Invincible'

H. *plantaginea* & forms

H. 'Royal Standard'

H. 'Sugar and Cream'

H. 'Summer Fragrance'

H. 'Sweet Susan'

Flower Arrangement

H. 'Bold Ruffles'

H. 'Dorset Blue'

H. 'Fortunei Aureomarginata'

H. 'Granary Gold'

H. 'Green Acres'

H. 'Halcyon'

H. 'Invincible'

H. 'Krossa Regal'

H. 'Opipara'

H. 'Richland Gold'

H. 'Sea Drift'

H. 'Sea Lotus Leaf'

H. *sieboldiana* 'Elegans'

H. 'Wide Brim'

APPENDIX

WHERE TO SEE HOSTAS

UNITED KINGDOM

Apple Court, Hordle Lane, Hordle, Lymington, Hampshire, SO41 OHU

Cleave House, Sticklepath, Okehampton, Devon, EX20 2NN *(By appointment only)*

Kittoch Mill, Busby Road, Carmunnock, Glasgow G76 9BJ *(By appointment only)*

Golden Acre Park, Leeds City Council, Bramhope, Leeds, Yorkshire

Hadspen House, Castle Cary, Somerset, BA7 7NG

Nunwick, Simonburn, Hexham, Northumberland NE48 3AF *(By appointment only)*

Savill Garden, Wick Lane, Englefield Green, Surrey TW20 0UU

The Beeches, 42 The Green, Houghton, Carlisle, Cumbria CA3 0LL *(By appointment only)*

The Manor House, Heslington, York YO1 5ER *(By appointment only)*

BELGIUM

Arboretum Kalmthout, Heuvel 2, B2920 Kalmthout

CANADA

Trevor Cole, RR2, Kinburn, Ontario KOA 2HO *(By appointment only)*

Alex Waterhouse-Hayward, 5909 Athlone, Vancouver B.C. VCM 3A3 *(By appointment only)*

FRANCE

Clive and Meg Jones, La Roudie, Anglars-Nozac 46300 *(By appointment only)*

M. Thoby, Pepinière Botanique, Château de Gaujacq, 40330 Amou *(By appointment only)*

Didier Willery, 1 Petites Rues, 62270 Boubers-sur-Canche *(By appointment only)*

GERMANY

Dr Ullrich Fischer, Waterloostrasse 19, D3300 Braunsweig *(By appointment only)*

HOLLAND

Arboretum Trompenburg, Groene Wetering 46, 3062 PC Rotterdam

ITALY

Marc King, Via Santa Caterina 6, 14030 Rocca D'Arazzo *(By appointment only)*

AUSTRALASIA

Tempo Two, Pearcedale, Victoria 3912, Australia

Tikitere Gardens, Rotorua, New Zealand

Titoki Point, R.D.1 Taihape, New Zealand

UNITED STATES OF AMERICA

Ralph (Herb) and Dorothy Benedict, 3558 Alpine Court, Wilson Lake, Hillsdale, Michigan 49242 *(By appointment only)*

William Brincka and Basil Cross, 427 E. Furness Road, Michigan City, Indiana 46360 *(By appointment only)*

Dubuque Arboretum and Botanical Gardens, 3800 Arboretum Drive, Dubuque, Iowa 52001

Robert Harris, 1971 Carrington Court, Stone Mountain, Georgia 30087 *(By appointment only)*

Joe and Olive Langdon, 4832 Mill Springs Circle, Mt. Brook, Alabama 35223 *(By appointment only)*

Longwood Gardens, Idea Garden, Kennett Square, Pennsylvania 19348

Michigan State University Garden, Hidden Lake Gardens, 6280 West Munger Rd (M-50), Tipton, Michigan 49287

Minnesota Landscape Arboretum, Hosta Glade, 3675 Arboretum Drive, Chanhassen, Minnesota 55317

Russell O'Harra, 516 43rd Street, Des Moines, Iowa 50312 *(By appointment only)*

Pine Tree State Arboretum, 153 Hospital Street, Augusta, Maine 04330

Warren and Ali Pollock, 202 Hackney Circle, Surrey Park, Wilmington, Delaware 19803 *(By appointment only)*

Peter and Jean Ruh, Homestead Division of Sunnybrook Farms, 9426 Mayfield Road, Chesterland, Ohio 44026 *(By appointment only)*

W. George Schmid, Hosta Hill, 4417 Goodfellows Court, Tucker, Georgia 30084 *(By appointment only)*

Judy Springer, 9216 Sterling Montague, Great Falls, Virginia 22066 *(By appointment only)*

Alex and Gene Summers, Honeysong Farm, Bridgeville, Delaware 19933 *(By appointment only)*

Swarthmore College, Hosta Garden & Terry Shane Teaching Garden, 500 College Avenue, Swarthmore, Pennsylvania 19081

Van and Shirley Wade, 3 Gatton Rocks Road, Beltville, Ohio 4483 *(By appointment only)*

Richard and Jane Ward, 2374 Fishinger Road, Columbus, Ohio 43221 *(By appointment only)*

James and Jill Wilkins, 2585 Spring Arbor Road, Jackson, Michigan 49203 *(By appointment only)*

155

WHERE TO BUY HOSTAS

UNITED KINGDOM

Ann and Roger Bowden, Cleave House, Sticklepath, Okehampton, Devon EX20 2NN

Apple Court, Hordle Lane, Hordle, Lymington, Hampshire SO41 0HU

Goldbrook Plants, Hoxne, Eye, Nr Diss, Suffolk IP21 5AN

Mickfield Market Garden, The Poplars, Mickfield, Stowmarket, Suffolk IP14 5LH

Park Green Nursery, Wetheringsett, Nr Stowmarket, Suffolk IP14 5OH

AUSTRALASIA

Hosta Heaven, P.O. Box 3058, Moorabbin, East Victoria 3189, Australia

Lambley Nursery, Burnside, Lesters Road, Ascot, Victoria 3364, Australia

Tempo Two, P.O. Box 60A, Pearcedale, Victoria 3912, Australia

Tikitere Gardens, P.O. Box 819, Rotorua, New Zealand

Titoki Point, R.D.1 Taihape, New Zealand

Woodbank Nursery, Huon Highway, Longley, Tasmania

BELGIUM

Ignace van Doorslaer, Kapellen Dries 52, B9090 Melle Gontrode

CANADA

Marvelous Gardens, 8929 1st Street, Surrey, B.C. V4N 3N5

Stirling Gardens, RR1, Morpeth, Ontario NOP 1XO

FRANCE

Bulbes d'Opale, Cidex 528, 384 Boerenweg Ouest, 59285 Buysscheure

Les Jardins de Cotelle, 76370 Derchigny Graincourt

Pepinière Botanique, Château de Gaujacq, 40330 Amou

Planbessin, Castillon, 14490 Balleroy

GERMANY

Dr Ullrich Fischer, Waterloostrasse 19, D3300 Braunsweig

Friesland Staudengarten, Husumer Weg 16, D26441 Jever/Rahrdum

Staudengartner Klose, Rosenstrasse 10, 3503, Lohfelden 1

HOLLAND

Coen Jansen, Vaste Planten, Koningsvaren 35, 7721 HM Dalfsen

De Bloemenhoek, Utrechtseweg 275, 3732 HA De Eilt

JAPAN

Gotemba Nursery, 59 Nagatsuka, Gotemba-shi, Shizuoka 412.

Kamo Nurseries, Harasato, Kakegawa, Shizuoka 436-01.

UNITED STATES OF AMERICA

Adrian's Flowers of Fashion Nursery (Bill Zumbar), 855 Parkway Blvd., Alliance, Ohio 44601

Andre Viette Farm & Nursery, Route 1, P.O. Box 16, Fishersville, Virginia 22939

Banyai Hostas, 11 Gates Circle, Hockessin, Delaware 19707

Coastal Gardens & Nursery, 4611 Socastee Blvd., Myrtle Beach, S. Carolina 29575

Carroll Gardens, 444 East Main Street, P.O. Box 310, Westminster, Maryland 21158

Hatfield Gardens, 22799 Ringgold Southern Road, Stoutsville, Ohio 43154

Homestead Division of Sunnybrook Farms, 9448 Mayfield Road, Chesterland, Ohio 44025

Klehm Nursery, 4210 North Duncan Road, Champaign, Illinois 61821

Kuk's Forest Nursery, 10174 Barr Road, Brecksville, Ohio 44141-3302

Plant Delights Nursery, 9241 Sauls Road, Raleigh, NC 27603

Robyn's Nest, 7802 NE 63rd Street, Vancouver, Washington 98662

Savory Gardens, 5300 Whiting Avenue, Edina, Minnesota 55439

Silvermist, 1986 Harrisville Road, Stoneboro, Pennsylvania 16153

Schmid Gardens, 847 Westwood Blvd., Jackson, Michigan 49203

Soules Garden, 5809 Rahke Road, Indianapolis, Indiana 46217

Wade & Gatton, 3 Gatton Rocks Road, Beltville, Ohio 4483

Walden-West Hosta, 5744 Crooked Finger Road, Scotts Mills, Oregon 97375

READING ABOUT HOSTAS

Aden, P. (ed.). *The Hosta Book*. Batsford, London & Timber Press, Portland, Oregon, 1988 & 1992.

Bond, S. *Hostas*. Ward Lock, London, 1992.

Grenfell, D. *Hosta: The Flowering Foliage Plant* Batsford, London & Timber Press, Portland, Oregon, 1990.

Grenfell, D. *Hostas*. The Hardy Plant Society, Worcestershire, 1993.

Köhlein, F. *Hosta (Funkien)*. Ulmer, Stuttgart, 1993.

Watanabe, K. *The Observation and Cultivation of Hosta*. New Science Company, Tokyo, 1985.

Schmid, W.G. *The Genus Hosta*. Batsford, London & Timber Press, Portland, Oregon, 1992.

Bulletin of the American Hosta Society & *The Hosta Journal* of the American Hosta Society.

Bulletin of the British Hosta & Hemerocallis Society Cultivated Plant Code, Quarterjack Press, Wimborne, Dorset, 1995.

SOCIETIES

British Hosta & Hemerocallis Society, Hon. Membership Secretary, Mrs Linda Hinton, Toft Monks, The Hithe, Rodborough Common, Stroud, Gloucestershire GL5 5BN.

Netherlands Hosta Society, c/o Arie Van Vliet, Zuidkade, 97, 2771 DS Boskoop

The American Hosta Society, Membership Secretary, Mrs Robyn Duback, 7802 N.E. 63rd Street, Vancouver, Washington 98662

ACKNOWLEDGEMENTS

There are many people who have helped to bring *The Gardener's Guide To Growing Hostas* to fruition and the book will not be finished until I have thanked those who have given so generously of their expertise and time.

First and foremost, Warren Pollock for all the help he has given me with this book since its inception, for reading the manuscript and for his input on hosta-growing in the United States. My grateful thanks to both Warren and Ali Pollock for their generous hospitality and for so smoothly arranging our visit to the 1995 American Hosta Society's National Convention, for arranging our visits to American gardens and nurseries, and for supplying some of the photographs.

All the writers whose individual contributions have enriched the book: Graham Stuart Thomas, Piers Trehane, Richard Ford, Warren Pollock, Bill Burto, Ullrich Fischer and Gordon Collier.

Ann and Roger Bowden for generously allowing me to use their superbly grown hostas and their delightful garden for much of the photography; and for supplying me with information on many of the newer cultivars and checking the A–Z list of hostas.

Ian Chrystal for his time spent in giving me the benefit of his experience of breeding hostas, and for sharing his knowledge of both streaked hostas and the smaller hostas in which he has a great interest.

Ignace van Doorslaer for his many gifts of hostas over the years, for arranging my introduction to the van Hoey Smiths of Trompenburg Arboretum and for organizing my recent visit to Kalmthout Arboretum.

Gert Fortgens for showing me the Dutch National Hosta Collection at Trompenburg Arboretum.

Piers Trehane, not only for his valuable chapter on hosta nomenclature but also for his helpful suggestions as to the manner in which I have expressed hosta names, and for proofreading the A–Z list of hostas.

Alex Summers for giving me a personally conducted tour of his renowned hosta collection during the American Hosta Society's Convention visit in June 1995.

Didier Willery for giving me much useful information on his Collection Agrée of Hostas.

Arie Van Vliet for sharing his immense knowledge of hostas and showing me his comprehensive collection of hostas old and new, many never grown in British gardens.

Harry van Trier, curator of Kalmthout Arboretum, for showing me some of the mature clumps of *Hosta* which have been growing at Kalmthout for 100 years.

Dan Heims of Terra-Nova Nurseries for his information on some of the newer hostas which he supplies by micropropagation.

Tony and Michelle Avent, Plant Delights Nursery, for sending me many newly introduced American hostas, including many of their own raising, for us to trial.

Pat Jordan for guiding me round her Scottish National Collection of Hosta.

All the members of the American Hosta Society, too numerous to mention individually, whom we met during the Annual Convention at Falls Church, Virginia, in June 1995, for so kindly sharing information and anecdotes with me about hosta-growing in the United States.

Jenny Brasier, not only for her exquisite drawings but for many constructive suggestions.

Gerry and Neil Campbell-Sharp for making themselves available throughout the summer to photograph hostas and for supplying the majority of the photographs.

Dawn and Derek St Romaine for their hospitality and for their brilliant studio photographs of individual leaves.

Vivian Rickman and David Ward, who both, on many occasions, dropped everything to sort out my inefficiencies on the computer.

Anna Mumford, commissioning editor, and Diana Vowles, project editor, for their helpful advice and suggestions.

Lastly, and most importantly, my thanks to Roger for his input, without which this book would not have been written.

INDEX OF PLANT NAMES

Italic page numbers refer to illustrations or their captions.